The Export of Legal Education

Its Promise and Impact in Transition Countries

Edited by

RONALD A. BRAND and D. WES RIST

Center for International Legal Education,
University of Pittsburgh School of Law, USA

Routledge
Taylor & Francis Group

LONDON AND NEW YORK

First published 2009 by Ashgate Publishing

Published 2016 by Routledge
2 Park Square, Milton Park, Abingdon, Oxfordshire OX14 4RN
711 Third Avenue, New York, NY 10017, USA

First issued in paperback 2016

Routledge is an imprint of the Taylor & Francis Group, an informa business

British Library Cataloguing in Publication Data
The export of legal education : its promise and impact in transition countries.
1. Lawyers, Foreign--Developing countries. 2. Returned students--Developing countries. 3. Law--Study and teaching (Higher)--United States. 4. Law--Study and teaching (Higher)--Developing countries--Foreign influences. 5. Law--Political aspects--Developing countries. 6. Law--Mobility.
I. Brand, Ronald A. II. Rist, D. Wes.
340'.0711-dc22

Library of Congress Cataloging-in-Publication Data
The export of legal education : its promise and impact in transition countries / edited by Ronald A. Brand and D. Wes Rist.
p. cm.
Includes bibliographical references and index.
ISBN 978-0-7546-7800-7 (hardback) -- 1. Law-- Study and teaching.
2. Law--Study and teaching--United States. 3. Law reform--Developing countries.
4. Rule of law--Developing countries. I. Brand, Ronald A. II. Rist, D. Wes.

K100.E97 2009
340.071'1--dc22

2009015703

ISBN 13: 978-1-138-26922-4 (pbk)
ISBN 13: 978-0-7546-7800-7 (hbk)

THE EXPORT OF LEGAL EDUCATION

Contents

Notes on Contributors *vii*

1 The Export of Legal Education:
Its Promise and Impact in Transition Countries 1
Ronald A. Brand

2 Making a Difference:
The Role of the LL.M. in Policy Formulation and Reform 13
Wade Channell

3 A Kenyan Experience with LL.M. Education 23
Maurice Oduor

4 The Socratic Method, Clinical Legal Education, and Mediation:
Serving the Promotion of the Rule of Law in Serbia 37
Jelena Arsic

5 Fighting Dragons of the Past:
The Internationalization of Legal Education at Donetsk
National University 45
Daniil E. Fedorchuk

6 The Export of American Legal Education and Its Impact in Serbia 61
Milena Đorđević

7 *Damnum iniuria datum* and the Law of Torts: From Cases to Rules 83
Marco Gardini

8 Teaching in Mexico 95
Luz María Cárdenas Arenas

9 The Big Impact of a Small Program in the Development
of Rule of Law in Kosovo 99
Vjosa Osmani

10	Designing and Implementing a Legal English Course to Develop the Rule of Law in the Context of Transition in Pakistani Society *Naveed Ahmad*	103
11	The Impact of the U.S. Legal System on Peruvian Administrative Law *Adolfo Céspedes Zavaleta*	123
12	Working with Precedents to Develop the Rule of Brazilian Commercial Law in a Global Scenario *Daniela Ballão Ernlund*	131
13	Western Education and Eastern Development: Ensuring Effective Development Assistance in East Asia Through Capacity Building *Jose Luis C. Syquia*	141
14	Comparative Analysis in the Area of Development of Informational and Communicational Technologies: Contemporary U.S. and Uzbek Legislation *Timur Arifdjanov*	183

Index *201*

Notes on Contributors

Ahmaḍ, Naveed (Pakistan), Assistant Professor, Bahauddin Zakariya University Department of Education; Ph.D. in legal English 2006 (Bahauddin Zakariya University); Fulbright Research Fellowship 2004 (University of Pittsburgh School of Law); M.A. in English 1988 (Bahauddin Zakariya University).

Arenas, Luz María Cárdenas (Mexico), Lecturer, Universidad Panamericana; Associate, S & G, S.C.; LL.M. 2001 (University of Pittsburgh School of Law); LL.B. 1997 (Universidad Panamericana).

Arifdjanov, Timur (Uzbekistan), Legal Counsel, Pertsch and Partner, GmbH; Sub-regional Coordinator for Internet Monitoring (Civil Initiative on Internet Policy); LL.M. 2000 *magna cum laude* (University of Pittsburgh School of Law); LL.B. 1995 (University of World Economy and Diplomacy).

Arsic, Jelena (Serbia), Visiting Lecturer, Postgraduate Studies in Mediation (University of Belgrade); Assistant Lecturer (Union University School of Law); Staff Attorney (ABA-CEELI/ABA Rule of Law Initiative); LL.M. 2005 (University of Pittsburgh School of Law); J.D. 2004 (University of Belgrade).

Brand, Ronald A. (USA), Professor and Director, Center for International Legal Education, University of Pittsburgh School of Law.

Channell, Wade (USA), Senior International Trade Adviser, U.S. Agency for International Development.

Đorđević, Milena (Serbia), Lecturer in International Commercial Law, University of Belgrade Faculty of Law; LL.M. 2002 (*Magna Cum Laude*, University of Pittsburgh School of Law); LL.B. 2000 (University of Belgrade Faculty of Law).

Ernlund, Daniela Ballão (Brazil), LL.M. 1997 (University of Pittsburgh School of Law); LL.B. 1995 (Faculdade de Direito de Curitiba).

Fedorchuk, Daniil E. (Ukraine), Lawyer, Beiten Burkhardt, Kyiv, Ukraine; former Senior Lecturer, Donetsk National University; LL.M. 2001 (University of Pittsburgh School of Law); Specialist in Law, 1999.

Gardini, Marco (Italy), Researcher in Roman Law (University of Parma, Italy); LL.M. 1997 *magna cum laude* (University of Pittsburgh School of Law); LL.B. 1994 (University of Parma).

Oduor, Maurice (Kenya), Lecturer (Moi University, School of Law); Advocate of the High Court of Kenya; LL.M. 2004 (University of Pittsburgh School of Law); Certificate, Negotiating International Financial Transactions (United Nations International Center for Training and Research); LL.B Hons. 2001 (Moi University).

Osmani, Vjosa (Kosovo), Assistant Professor of International Law (University of Prishtina); Legal Adviser to the President of Kosovo; LL.M. 2005 (University of Pittsburgh School of Law); LL.B. 2004 (University of Prishtina, Faculty of Law).

Syquia, Jose Luis C. (Philippines), Associate Professorial Lecturer (University of Santo Tomas); Adjunct Professor (Asian Institute of Management), Partner, Syquia Pascual-Lopez & Santos Law Offices; LL.M. 1998 *cum laude* (University of Pittsburgh School of Law); LL.B. 1997 (University of Santo Tomas); B.A. in philosophy 1992 (University of Santo Tomas).

Zavaleta, Adolfo Céspedes (Perú), B.A. in philosophy 1999 (Universidad de Piura); LL.M. 2001 (University of Pittsburgh School of Law).

Chapter 1
The Export of Legal Education: Its Promise and Impact in Transition Countries

Ronald A. Brand[1]

I. Introduction

Legal education has seldom been studied as an export. One is hard pressed to find statistics on education exports in general, let alone on legal education in particular.[2] Even in the ever-growing data on services trade, there is little attention paid to the broader impact of the transmission of education across borders.[3] Despite the fact that the education of foreign students clearly fits within Mode II of services trade under the General Agreement on Trade in Services (delivery of services to a consumer from one Member State within the territory of another Member State),[4] few efforts have been made to catalogue the extent and impact of this component of services trade.

The tie between legal systems and legal education systems is undeniable. Most often this is thought of in terms of a country's legal system determining the structure and approach of the legal education that will train the lawyers of that country—civil law systems generally employ a "scientific" lecture model of instruction focused on learning statutory rules, while common law systems tend

---

1 Professor and Director, Center for International Legal Education, University of Pittsburgh School of Law.

2 Examples of such statistics which do exist focus on the economic impact of education exports. *See, e.g.*, *Export Education in New Zealand: A Strategic Approach to Developing the Sector—An Overview*, *available at* http://www.educationcounts.govt.nz/publications/international/export_education_in_new_zealand_a_strategic_approach_to_developing_the_sector_-_an_overview (28 June 2006) ("estimates are that the export education industry contributed $700 million to the [New Zealand] economy in 2000 and has the potential to realise $1 billion per annum within two years"); *The Value of International Education in Australia*, *available at* http://www.idp.com/research/statistics/education_export_statistics.aspx ("In 2007/08, international education contributed $13.7 billion to the Australian economy"); *America's Hot New Export: Higher Education*, *available at* http://chronicle.com/weekly/v52/i24/24a04401.htm.

3 Education is not listed as an export category in standard U.S. export statistics. *See, e.g.*, U.S. Census Bureau, Foreign Trade Statistics, December 2008, *available at* http://www.census.gov/foreign-trade/Press-Release/2008pr/12/.

4 General Agreement on Trade in Services, Art. I(2)(b).

to employ more active learning methodologies focused on analysis of judicial decisions. Just as important, however, may be the impact a legal education system has on its country's legal system. Intuitively at least, it would seem that the manner in which lawyers are trained is likely to have an impact on the way in which they practice their profession, both in private and governmental roles.

When students cross borders to become consumers of legal education, a new dimension is added. If a lawyer from one legal system studies in a different legal system, he or she takes home something more than a simple transplant understanding of law and legal education. The "export" in this arrangement is knowledge and understanding of host country systems that can generate further influence on the student's home country legal system and legal education system.

Education affects a country's level of democracy,[5] and legal education, in particular, should affect the rule of law component of a democratic society.[6] Social, economic, and political opportunity in any culture is determined at least in part by legal rights and the ability to realize them. Thus unless a state presents an environment in which the rule of law is part of the social, economic, and political culture, opportunity is necessarily restricted and may exist only through what would in more developed countries be considered to be improper channels for influencing decisions.[7]

The chapters that follow are part of an effort to explore the extent to which the export of legal education from the United States has an impact on both legal education and legal developments in other states. They tell the stories of persons who have received legal education in the United States and returned to their home countries. In the process, they confirm intuitive and empirical evidence of the impact of such education, and provide a foundation from which to continue a discussion of the export of U.S. legal education.

---

5 *See, e.g.*, Robert J. Barro, *The Determinants of Democracy*, 107 J. Pol. Econ. S158 (1997); Seymour M. Lipset, *Some Social Requisites of Democracy: Economic Development and Economic Legitimacy*, 53 Am. Pol. Sci. Rev. 69 (1959).

6 *See, e.g.*, Antonio Spilimbergo, Democracy and Foreign Education, IMF Working Paper AP/07/51 (Mar. 2007) (finding "a very strong correlation between the lagged average indices of democracy in host countries and the current level of democracy in the origin country" as a result of foreign education).

7 *See, e.g.*, Thomas Carothers, *The Rule of Law Revival*, *in* Promoting the Rule of Law Abroad: In Search of Knowledge 3, 5–6 (Thomas Carothers ed., 2006). ("For states grappling with democratic consolidation, fortifying usually weak rule of law appears to be a way of pushing patronage-ridden government institutions to better performance, reining in elected but still only haphazardly law-abiding politicians, and curbing the continued violation of human rights that has characterized many new democracies. For backsliding systems, strengthening the rule of law seems an appealing bulwark against creeping authoritarianism and the ever-present threat of sabotage of constitutional order.")

II. The Impact of the Export of Education

A 2007 Working Paper of the International Monetary Fund concluded that, when students study outside their home countries, there is "a very strong correlation between the lagged average indices of democracy in host countries and the current level of democracy in the origin country."[8] The same study noted that in 2007, 46 heads of government were products of U.S. higher education, and that, in 1990, out of 115 world leaders, 66 studied abroad at a certain point; the percentage of foreign-education leaders' increases to more than two-thirds if one is considering only developing nations. These numbers show clearly that foreign-educated individuals do play an overwhelming role in their own home countries.[9]

In a 2005 article in *The American Lawyer* titled, "They Rule the World," Michael D. Goldhaber considered the importance of an LL.M. degree from a U.S. law school to government and business relations throughout the world. Mikhail Saakashvili is an example of that impact.[10] Saakashvili returned to the former Soviet Republic of Georgia after obtaining his LL.M. degree at Columbia Law School to lead a democratic revolt and be elected president of a new state. Once in office, he appointed other U.S. LL.M. graduates to be his foreign minister and his deputy justice minister. Says Goldhaber in his article:

> Lawyers like these are unstoppable when armed with another degree. Former LL.M.'s Giuliano Amato of Italy and Mary Robinson of Ireland rose to become heads of state. A third of the judges on the International Court of Justice hold graduate degrees from U.S. law schools. And in Taiwan, which rivals Georgia for LL.M. power, U.S. alumni include the vice president, the mayor of Taipei, and at least two grand justices.[11]

According to Gocha Lordkipanidze, a foreign policy adviser to the Georgian prime minister and Harvard LL.M. graduate, a U.S. LL.M. education "definitely has an impact on our careers and our lives. It's ingrained in every piece of paper I'm writing or action I'm taking for the government of Georgia. After Harvard, I'm neither European nor American, but at peace with both ways of thinking."[12]

The anecdotal approach of the *American Lawyer* article indicates the importance of a U.S. legal education to its recipient, while the IMF Working Paper noted above indicates that education in a democratic country has a much broader impact on the home country of the returning scholar. These are parts of what should be a much larger discussion of the export of U.S. legal education.

---

8 *Id.* at 20.

9 *Id.* at 21.

10 Michael D. Goldhaber, *They Rule the World*, The American Lawyer, Sept. 14, 2005.

11 *Id.*

12 *Id.*

Few if any other exports can have similar impact. While exports through a GATS Mode II provision of services are in general difficult to compare with the export of goods or even of services such as those of the banking and insurance industries, that should not prevent consideration of their effect, particularly when that effect can be so important to the goals of our nation. For those of us involved in legal education who have observed the export of legal education both in the provision of legal education services in the United States and in its impact abroad, it is difficult not to conclude that one of the United States' most important exports is education, and that, within that more general category, the most important export is legal education.

III. Beyond Anecdotal Evidence: The Importance of More Detailed Stories

At the University of Pittsburgh School of Law's Center for International Legal Education (CILE), we consistently hear from our LL.M. graduates about the influence of their U.S. legal education, both on their own lives and on the legal and educational communities to which they return. This book is the result of an effort to gain more specific information about this influence by presenting the stories of some of those consumers in this export process. When we consider the impact of education taken home, however, it becomes clear that the storytellers are more than just consumers of educational services, they are also very much involved in the dissemination of the results of their education in their home countries. As law professors, government officials, institution builders, and private lawyers, they can have important impact not only on individual circumstances, but also on the structure, application, and effect of national and international legal systems.

A 2004 OECD Policy Brief on the *Internationalisation of Higher Education* noted four "different, but not mutually exclusive, approaches to cross-border higher education."[13] They are:

1. the mutual understanding approach, focused on encouraging the mobility of both domestic and foreign students;
2. the skilled migration approach, emphasizing the recruitment of skilled foreign students to remain in the host country after completing their education;
3. the revenue-generating approach, focused on the presence of foreign students to add to the income of the educational institution; and
4. the capacity-building approach, encouraging cross-border education as a tool in assisting the student's home country upon return after the completion of the educational stay.

13 OECD Policy Brief, *Internationalisation of Higher Education* 4 (2004).

This book is focused almost entirely on the fourth of these policy rationales for cross-border education. In the stories that follow, the reader will become familiar with how LL.M. graduates used their U.S. legal education to improve law school curricula at home, become better teachers, encourage the rule of law and ethical conduct of lawyers, design and implement new legislation, encourage language skills for the use of law on a multinational level, and assist in the administration of international development programs. All of these involve capacity building for nations and regions in transition.

The 2007 IMF Working Paper on *Democracy and Foreign Education* went beyond consideration of the rationale for individual offerings of cross-border education to consideration of the available hypotheses for how foreign-educated individuals bring about changes in levels of democracy in their home countries.[14] The hypotheses considered in the IMF Working Paper included the following:

1. "foreign-educated technocrats are such a scarce resource in many countries that they can impose their own preferences in favor of democratic regimes";[15]
2. "foreign-educated leaders seem to be extremely motivated to introduce democracy and to keep up with the more developed countries where they studied";[16]
3. "foreign-educated individuals make it more difficult for the dictatorial regimes to maintain repression by spreading new ideas at home";[17]
4. "foreign-educated individuals can make repressive activities more costly for a dictatorial regime since they have easier access to external media";[18] and
5. "education abroad may inculcate a sense of common identity with the international democratic community."[19]

Each of these hypotheses can be applied as well to explain how U.S.-educated law professors and lawyers in transition countries serve the advancement of the rule of law. These lawyers return to their home countries as scarce resources to be relied upon for advice and expertise in the development and application of the law, as well as in leading the reform of legal education.

The stories of the LL.M. graduates found in this book provide dramatic indication of the level of motivation exhibited by many returning legal scholars. They also provide clear evidence of a presence that would make divergence from the rule of law more difficult, both by spreading new ideas and by monitoring

---

14 Spilimbergo, *supra* note 6, at 22.

15 *Id.*

16 *Id.*

17 *Id.*

18 *Id.*

19 *Id.*

institutional conduct. Few sectors of society can serve to make repressive activities that are inconsistent with the rule of law more costly than lawyers trained in the traditions of the U.S. legal system. Finally, the following chapters demonstrate a clear sense of common identity, not only with U.S. legal institutions and legal education systems, but also with those from other transition countries around the world with whom graduates studied while in the United States.

IV. Lessons for the Future

It may be that all education affects social, economic, and political opportunity, but U.S. legal education of foreign lawyers who return to important positions in their home countries has a special impact. Social, economic, and political opportunity is in most instances connected to legal rights and the ability of individuals to realize those rights. The realization of those rights will not occur without a system that respects the rule of law, and cannot occur without lawyers capable of providing assistance to individuals and law professors to train those lawyers to function at the highest level. While U.S.-trained lawyers have had a notable impact on the governments and people they have returned to serve in their home countries, a more pervasive impact may well occur through the efforts of those who return to teach the future lawyers of those countries. These new professors will reach hundreds of law students per year in each law school, and will, over time, have a significant influence on the understanding of rule of law and the role of law in the development of their nations.[20]

With the exception of Chapter 2, the chapters that follow catalogue the personal stories of LL.M. graduates who returned to their home countries to make a difference. All of them are graduates of the University of Pittsburgh School of Law, but that is not the important factor in their stories. The important factor is the way in which each of them describes the combination of the influence of the LL.M. education process on himself or herself, and the way in which that influence on an individual has led to broader impact in the home countries of these graduates. While those of us who participate in the education of these individuals have held intuitive beliefs about the benefits of the LL.M. experience, and about the impact of graduates on their home countries, their stories provide clear confirmation of those beliefs, as well as explicit demonstration of how that impact has occurred.

---

20 Thomas Carothers has stated that, "[a]lthough its wonderworking abilities have been exaggerated, the desirability of the rule of law is clear. The question is where to start." Carothers, *supra* note 7, at 7. The proposition here is that the place to start is where the teachers learn, not by telling them how to do it, but by letting them experience legal education in a system that exhibits principal (if not always consistent) adherence to the rule of law, and then returning to their home countries to apply the lessons learned as they find it most valuable to do so.

The stories here elaborate upon this anecdotal information and these intuitive beliefs. They also confirm the limited empirical research on the effect of foreign education on democracy, supporting the capacity building approach to international education. These stories demonstrate that U.S. legal education can have an impact on democracy and rule of law in transition countries. In doing so, they demonstrate very clearly the value of the export of U.S. legal education. They also provide a framework for considering just how this precious export might be improved and enhanced in the future.

The following is a brief summary of the chapters that follow, indicating how they provide a package of stories that, taken together, sets a solid foundation for further consideration of the export of U.S. legal education. They begin with Wade Channell's eloquent presentation of the need for U.S.-trained local lawyers to aid U.S. development efforts. They then move to stories that relate the impact of an LL.M. education on the curricula and teaching methodologies at law schools in a number of countries. From legal education, they turn to impact on national administrative law systems, national and regional development efforts, and the specific area of information and communication technologies in Uzbekistan. Throughout, they demonstrate how individual graduates can make substantial contributions to the development of the rule of law.

Chapter 2: Making a Difference: The Role of the LL.M. in Policy Formulation and Reform, Wade Channell

Channell does an elegant job of setting the stage for the chapters that follow, explaining from the point of view of a development professional just why the LL.M. degree is so important to the consumers of the work of those who have that degree. He paints the picture of impact returning LL.M. scholars can and do have, demonstrating both the need for and the substantial benefit from the application of the education gained in the LL.M. experience. While his story is that of the development professional, and many of the stories that follow are those of new academics in transition lands, they fit well together. Channel's chapter is a must-read for anyone interested in the good U.S. development efforts can have around the world.

Chapter 3: A Kenyan Experience with LL.M. Education, Maurice Oduor

Odour provides a review of the efforts of one law faculty in Kenya, a transition country that has the advantage of several returning scholars trained in the same U.S. LL.M. program, but suffers from the universal problem of limited resources. Like the other stories in this section, his demonstrates the high level of commitment and excitement found in many returning LL.M. graduates; attributes that contribute to overcoming at least some problems of insufficient resources.

Chapter 4: The Socratic Method, Clinical Legal Education, and Mediation: Serving the Promotion of the Rule of Law in Serbia, Jelena Arsic

Arsic describes the transfer of Socratic classroom methods and clinical legal study from the United States to Serbia. Like others here, she demonstrates the successful application of principles and methods from two legal education systems, using her education in the U.S. approach to improve upon legal education in Serbia. Moreover, she focuses specifically on the introduction of concepts and skills from U.S.-style mediation into the legal system of her home country.

Chapter 5: Fighting Dragons of the Past: The Internationalization of Legal Education at Donetsk National University, Daniil E. Fedorchuk

Fedorchuk describes the difficulties of bringing curriculum changes and new teaching methodologies to post-Soviet culture of eastern Ukraine. He illustrates the problems that exist when the lure of the private sector leaves academic life with few tangible rewards, while at the same time acknowledging the clear intangible benefits of making a difference in students' lives.

Chapter 6: The Export of American Legal Education and Its Impact in Serbia, Milena Đorđević

Đorđević provides a clear description of how two legal education cultures can be combined to incorporate the best of both systems. In describing that process at the University of Belgrade, she details how a young group of western-educated faculty members has made a real difference in curriculum, teaching methodology, and impact beyond the university.

Chapter 7: *Damnum iniuria datum* and the Law of Torts: From Cases to Rules, Marco Gardini

Gardini uses very specific examples of his experience teaching in Italy to challenge not only traditional comparisons of common law and civil law, but also of civil law and Roman law. Noting the traditional view that Roman law study involves a type of case-based approach, he compares the teaching of Roman law and common law, providing particular examples from his own experience introducing U.S. type instruction in his own Roman Law course. He even takes on the conclusions of Professor Pierre Legrand, providing a rather elegant discussion of maps and journeys after suggesting that some scholars have fallen into an "attractive illusion" that results in using rules in an inappropriate manner.

Chapter 8: Teaching in Mexico, Luz María Cárdenas Arenas

Cárdenas Arenas provides an instructive summary of how one LL.M. graduate has incorporated teaching techniques common in U.S. law school classrooms into courses in both a business school and a law school in Mexico. She demonstrates the ability to select useful pedagogical tools from different systems in order to increase the impact of the instructional process for the students involved.

Chapter 9: The Big Impact of a Small Program in the Development of Rule of Law in Kosovo, Vjosa Osmani

Osmani provides a very personal account of how her U.S. legal education has affected her work in Kosovo, both as a teacher at the University of Prishtina and as Legal Adviser to the president of Kosovo. In her warm words may be found the thread of individual impact the social and educational impact of an LL.M. program can have on an individual returning from study in the United States.

Chapter 10: Designing and Implementing a Legal English Course to Develop the Rule of Law in the Context of Transition in Pakistani Society, Naveed Ahmad

Ahmad provides the view of a Fulbright language scholar, not an LL.M. student. His story details the importance of the English language, and English legal terminology in particular, in a country with multiple languages but with English as the language of the law. Like other stories here, he takes on the importance of teaching the law both as a language of its own and in the language students will need in applying their education to productive careers. He demonstrates careful research and attention to detail in the design of a course tailored to work in his native Pakistan.

Chapter 11: The Impact of the U.S. Legal System on Peruvian Administrative Law, Adolfo Céspedes Zavaleta

Céspedes gives us the views of someone who has returned both to teach and to work as a government official in Perú. Like others in this collection, he finds the transfer of active teaching styles from his U.S. legal education to be valuable in the classroom in a civil law system. What he adds, in particular, is a clear example of how the results of deductive logic and the case method have also enhanced his work as an administrative lawyer in the Peruvian government.

Chapter 12: Working with Precedents to Develop the Rule of Brazilian Commercial Law in a Global Scenario, Daniela Ballão Ernlund

Ernlund establishes how her U.S. legal education has made a difference in teaching students in Brazil. Tracing commercial law from Roman roots to current-day civil law systems, she provides particular focus on two Brazilian cases that demonstrate common law development of legal rules in a civil law system. From this she extrapolates the need to improve legal education in Brazil so that students will be ready to understand and participate in such developments.

Chapter 13: Western Education and Eastern Development: Ensuring Effective Development Assistance in East Asia through Capacity Building, Jose Luis C. Syquia

Syquia uses examples from his home country of the Philippines, and from other Asian countries in which he has worked, to demonstrate the connection between classroom and practice in the development agenda. Focusing on the topic of corruption in the development process, his story personalizes and brings to life the type of impact on the development agenda that Channell discusses more globally in Chapter 2. In the process of telling this story, he usefully projects the Socratic method beyond academia to its impact on "real-world" events and examples, providing not only evidence that the LL.M. education prepares its recipient for making a practical difference, but a clear tie between legal education and legal system developments; a tie that both pervades the stories in this book and demonstrates the exponential value of the export of LL.M. education.

Chapter 14: Comparative Analysis in the Area of Development of Informational and Communicational Technologies: Contemporary U.S. and Uzbek Legislation, Timur Arifdjanov

Arifdjanov provides a detailed explanation of one area of the law (information and communication technologies) and how examples and experiences from the United States have been used to affect the development of laws relevant to that area in Uzbekistan. While his is less a personal story than a review of the need for application of newly-discovered skills and understanding of the law, it nicely rounds out the set of stories in this book, providing one more view of the impact a returning LL.M. scholar may have the development of rule of law in his or her homeland.

V. A Final Note: The Resource, the Problem, and the Opportunity

If the stories in this book confirm the belief that U.S. legal education can and does have a positive impact in other countries, then legal educators must address the question of whether we are providing that education in a manner that best serves the process that creates that impact. We must ask whether we are making the best use of an important resource. A resource that can have dramatic effect on the development and application of the rule of law throughout the world must be carefully considered and properly administered.

As a starting point, LL.M. programs at U.S. law schools must be something more than sources of revenue that improve budgets and help skew rankings for J.D. programs. They must be designed with an eye to the greater impact they can have. The many pressures on LL.M. programs (budgetary, curricular, and otherwise) too often may bring with them a lack of understanding of the impact of the export of legal education. Moreover, that impact cannot be fully realized if the relationship with the student ends at graduation. The stories below demonstrate the need for relationships that continue between the graduate and the legal education program.

Like other problems, the problem of failure to realize the impact of legal education exports brings with it opportunities. Here it is the opportunity to have an even more dramatic impact on legal systems around the globe. This will not occur simply by sending more LL.M. graduates back to their home countries, though that is a start. The real opportunity lies in legal education for foreign lawyers that is designed with the potential impact in mind and thus structured to serve the purpose of greater impact. This must be carefully addressed so as not to turn the process into a propaganda regime. Students must be free to choose their courses and they must be open to deciding for themselves what elements of the system they study are most beneficially applied upon their return home. The stories that follow demonstrate how individual graduates can and have made those decisions in the application of their U.S. legal education upon their return home. Our hope is that they may serve as a starting point for a broader discussion of how the process can be improved.

Chapter 2

Making a Difference: The Role of the LL.M. in Policy Formulation and Reform

Wade Channell[1]

The field of international legal reform has experienced a period of sustained growth since the fall of the Iron Curtain. Beginning in the early 1990s, international experts from developed Western economies descended on virtually every newly independent state to offer advice on adjusting the legal system to solidify democratic trends and enhance economic growth. Today, experts from Germany, France, England, the United States, Norway, and even Italy compete and collaborate to refashion the legal frameworks of former command economies in Europe and Eurasia, as well as developing countries from Africa, Asia, and Latin America. Legal reform has become an industry, with hundreds of specialists addressing hundreds of laws.

For those who work in the field of international legal and regulatory reform, one of the most valuable partners imaginable is the local legal professional who has studied or worked abroad. Such counterparts improve the efficiency and effectiveness of the reform process by infusing it with a greater understanding of the policy implications under consideration and enhancing acceptance of change based on local values and priorities. In short, the cross-cultural legal professional serves as an irreplaceable bridge between what is and what can be. This reality is founded on a greater reality: law is not simply a system of rules and regulations; it is a policy tool for changing or maintaining certain aspects of socio-economic behavior. As such, policies—and the legislative acts that flow from policies—embody the norms and values of the cultures in which they are adopted, and cannot be properly understood outside of that context. Consequently, local legal professionals with cross-cultural understanding and local sensitivities play a crucial role in reforming local policies in accordance with international standards.

I. Effective Policy Reform and the LL.M.

Competent international policy reform professionals rely heavily on local counterparts to understand, fashion, and implement reforms. (This is true even

---

1 Senior International Trade Adviser, U.S. Agency for International Development.

for those who impose paternalistic approaches, as further discussed below.) Local legal professionals who hold foreign Masters of Law (LL.M.) degrees are one of the most valuable resources available, along with those who have worked abroad (with or without advanced degrees). They can be, if they so choose, agents of remarkable influence.

The value of those who hold LL.M.s arises from their comparative analytical capacity, which is rooted in local realities yet informed by knowledge of other possibilities. They can be the first line of defense against the "hasty transplant syndrome," in which well-intentioned foreign experts seek to reproduce legal practices from their home countries that do not take root in local legal culture. They can guide and inform policy initiatives directly, by artfully crafting new solutions based on local reality and foreign possibility, or indirectly, by influencing those responsible for the reforms. Whatever the method, LL.M.s are important agents in the process of improving public policy.

II. Agents of Understanding

It is frequently noted that people do not understand their own language completely until they study another one. Those who take on a second language (and even more so a third or fourth), quickly find themselves learning their own grammar, syntax, and linguistic assumptions better as they are forced to compare and comprehend a new perspective. The improvement encompasses more than just words or rules; it leads to new ways of thinking, improved communication and better understanding. LL.M.s are inherently multilingual for several reasons. First, most who study abroad must actually learn a second language. Second, the language of law is itself a second language, not spoken by the majority of the local population in any country. It entails terms of art, professional idioms, and communication standards that are not commonly shared by speakers of the mother tongue, so much so that lawyers must often learn how to express legal concepts in "plain language."

The LL.M. has a third level of language: comparative law. Anyone who has worked with an interpreter on legal issues understands that the interpreter must speak "law" as well as the other languages being used. It is not enough to simply translate the word "obligations"—which can have many meanings—when the word needed is "torts." By crossing the cultural divide inherent in comparative legal studies, the LL.M. learns both words and concepts. The concepts challenge and increase understanding of the native system. As a result, the average LL.M. is likely to understand his or her own legal system better than colleagues at home who have never undergone comparative analysis. At the same time, the LL.M. picks up understanding of a foreign system, and in so doing becomes a bridge of understanding between the systems studied.

It is no accident that foreign investors look for local lawyers who understand the investors' home system. They know that the shared understanding will reduce or eliminate mistakes and confusion arising from translation. LL.M.s are the lawyers of choice for multinational corporations, foreign law firms, and foreign investors. They bridge both the language and the legal systems for their clients.

For reformers, this enhanced level of understanding has important implications. Good law must be rooted in the culture and values of the people affected by it; good concepts alone are not sufficient. Consequently, international reformers seek to work with those who have a comprehensive understanding of local reality. The power dynamics of vested interests, historical tensions, and even ethnic rivalries can have a critical impact on the effectiveness of legal reforms. Only the long-term local resident will understand those and be able to guide the reform process more effectively. Local understanding provides the basis for translating foreign concepts that can be aligned with local values and local concerns. There are countless stories of American lawyers working with Asian counterparts who have failed to grasp that American individualism (which emphasizes individual rights and group obligations) is often at odds with Asian communalism (which emphasizes individual obligations and group rights). Rights-based reforms can create concerns for Asians about the impact on the group and particularly the family. If these concerns cannot be met in terms of communalist values, the reforms will fail, even though they may be the best solution for the common good. The cross-cultural LL.M. can negotiate these pitfalls.

Regulatory reform, which has become increasingly popular as a result of the World Bank's *Doing Business* reports, also illuminates the need for cross-cultural understanding. The goal of *Doing Business* reforms is to reduce burdens that unnecessarily impede business. Such reforms are based on a concept of limited government and are not highly popular among regimes that believe in pervasive government involvement in business and the economy. To succeed, reformers must understand and be able to justify changes in the level of government intervention.

Simeon Djankov, leader of the *Doing Business* work, has noted that all business registrations in Guyana must be approved by the president. This law arose from colonial experience in which the colonial governor controlled the small economy and had exclusive authority to authorize or deny various colonial endeavors. The country changed, but the law did not. As local counterparts came to understand the anachronistic foundations of the current regime, they were better equipped to reform it. Conversely, Saudi Arabia has the world's highest fee for business registration, for the simple reason that they do not wish to permit just anyone to start a business. Saudi Arabia has yet to reform this law and is unlikely to until local policy makers adopt a different approach to economic freedom. Local understanding permits better design and greater effectiveness of reforms.

Comparative understanding provides options and directions for change. In the former Yugoslavia, court systems were designed to serve the interests of the executive in support of a state-directed economy. Upon independence, the newly formed republics inherited a judicial system that functioned very poorly in settling commercial disputes. Delays of more than seven years are not uncommon in obtaining a judgment, which is in turn unenforceable for another two or more years.

Early reform assistance, primarily from the United States, tended to focus on reducing delays through better case management. Recently, Macedonia and Bosnia and Herzegovina recognized that the fundamental problem was design, not case management, and redesigned their courts to achieve a new goal: resolving commercial disputes. The understanding needed to bring about effective redesign of the courts came in great part from LL.M.s involved in the numerous court projects. Understanding both local reality and comparative possibility provides the foundation for change.

III. Agents of Change

LL.M.s are uniquely placed to bring about change in their countries. This is not simply a theoretical proposition based on the value of their cross-cultural understanding and experience. The proposition is grounded in reality: LL.M.s hold vital positions in government and business around the world, and include numerous ministers of justice and foreign affairs, high court judges, parliamentarians, executives of companies, partners of leading law firms, and even a prime minister or two. This impact is in part due to the type of motivated people who seek the degree, people with a tendency toward leadership roles. It is also due to the increased understanding achieved through the LL.M. program, which empowers graduates to become leaders and embrace change.

The perspective gained from the LL.M. experience provides a starting point for change. All legal systems need to be upgraded, refined, and reformed from time to time. The intensity and direction of the reforms depend on the goals of those seeking them and the condition of the country in question. Economically wealthy countries tend toward gradual change, often through minor refinements to existing systems. Transition and developing countries frequently consider (or reject) more fundamental changes in hopes of attaining greater economic prosperity by emulating and adopting legal infrastructures that have led to success elsewhere. Unfortunately, former colonial powers sometimes seek to limit the changes under consideration to those which complement the system of the colonial power. Portugal and France have traditionally sought to keep their former African colonies tied to them through similar legal systems. While not officially "colonialists," U.S. specialists sometimes offer only U.S. solutions, despite the tensions of applying common law solutions to civil law problems. A better approach is needed.

Many countries today have both the need and opportunity to make fundamental changes to their legal systems. For some, such as Guinea-Bissau, the existing formal system is so superficial as to permit the choice of starting afresh. Others have reasonable well-functioning German or French foundations that need to be updated and corrected. Croatia, for example, has a legal system established under the Austro-Hungarian empire (long defunct), amended partly in line with German advances, and then redirected for the 50 years of the Yugoslav era before market-oriented changes were reconsidered. Among domestic legal thinkers, there is a tendency to seek German solutions, yet a failure to understand that Germany made dramatic changes in the 1950s while Croatia moved in a completely different direction, so that the historical legacy need no longer be the starting point. A number of attempts to copy Germany have failed or faltered because the German solutions do not fit the pseudo-German root system.

LL.M.s in Croatia often look to other models, including British, French, U.S., and Norwegian, for various needed reforms. The preponderance of preference for Germanic solutions, however, continues to carry the day. Meanwhile, other former Yugoslav republics are either catching up or moving ahead of Croatia as their reformers adopt a more pragmatic approach, imported in part through the experience of their growing LL.M. population. Macedonia has revised its corporate governance regime in accordance with European standards through projects led by Dutch and Canadian specialists in concert with Macedonian experts under U.S. funding. Serbia has adopted a collateral registry system based on the model law of the European Bank for Reconstruction and Development. Bosnia and Herzegovina invented a new judicial approach that joins vital concepts of both civil and common law. In all of these countries, other than Croatia, legal reform projects rely heavily on legal professionals who have received LL.M. degrees since independence and who use comparative analysis to find local solutions.

One of the most effective reform specialists working today holds a law degree from the Middle East and an LL.M. from Canada. An expert in secured transactions and bankruptcy, he uses his comparative knowledge to work with local counterparts to build pledge registry systems that suit their needs. The Albanian system they engineered respects Albanian sensitivities while increasing access to credit. The Bosnian system embraced internet technology to provide one of the most advanced and cheapest systems in the world. He has helped Georgia to consider the addition of mortgages to the movable pledge system, a practical and theoretical possibility that traditionalists reject unnecessarily. This ability to consider possibilities from a wide variety of sources and marry them to local values has provided a number of countries with advanced systems not available from their own tradition or the traditions of the legacy countries they normally look to.

International legal reform efforts tend to focus on comprehensive changes, from new bankruptcy systems and securities regulations to fundamental reform of judicial processes. These are important in the short term for countries in transition, but the massive efforts involved are not necessarily producing capacity for incremental changes over time. As one country after another "graduates" from such assistance, responsibility for future policy reforms falls exclusively to local legal professionals. Moreover, the flood of new legislation will take decades to understand, apply and implement, well after the foreign technical advisors are gone.

While professional reformers have given much attention to amending black letter law, less has been given to the process of legislation and policy formulation. The better systems of policy formulation produce laws through consensus of those affected by crafting agreement between disparate interests to obtain a generally acceptable approach. Whether they define consumer rights, judicial process, or securities regulation, such consensus-based laws tend to be implemented and absorbed more readily, because they respond to the recognized needs of the relevant population. Systems that forego consensus appear to be more efficient than those that employ the often messy and time-consuming process of consensus building. They instead tend toward fiat, in which a dominant elite imposes rules without the negotiated consent of the bulk of the governed population. The legislative drafting process permits little input from affected parties, and the process of adoption allows for little if any public comment or debate. Such laws can be conceived, drafted and adopted within a few months, but often meet prolonged and successful resistance at the implementation stage.

The majority of legal reform specialists working in other countries come from systems of consensus-based policy development and therefore can be expected to approach their work accordingly. Unfortunately, this is often not the case. Paternalism, time and budget constraints, and misguided notions of efficiency all too frequently lead to assistance projects that ignore the socio-economic underpinnings of successful policy development. The presumed efficiency of quick results soon falls victim to implementation ineffectiveness, as those whose interests were ignored in the policy process assert themselves through resistance. The difference between implementation and enforcement is consensus. Where parties agree on the ends and means of a law or contract, they will voluntarily implement that agreement. When there is no such meeting of the minds, one party must seek to compel the other to comply, possibly through state-sanctioned force. A process that ignores the need for consensus must rely on a strong state that can enforce the laws. It is not enough that the reforms in question may in fact be well drafted and exactly what the country needs: without a sense of ownership, the excluded stakeholders are more likely to resist than embrace change.

Enter the LL.M. professional policy reformers who understand their country's context and culture are needed to establish and guide the long-term vision for change. This challenge can be approached from several angles. First, LL.M.s who work with foreign-funded reform projects can and should steer the reformers into a consensus-building approach. Although often hired simply to comment on a law, the LL.M. can recommend or even insist that a broader audience be engaged to ensure greater buy-in.

Second, LL.M.s can work to change the local model for legal reform. Many countries do not have effective consensus-building processes for introducing reforms or amendments. LL.M.s who understand that the proper measure of success is how long it takes to *implement* a law, not just to *pass* it, are in a privileged position of advocating more effective law-making models. They can identify legal solutions from their broad range of legal expertise, then guide the crafting and drafting of the law through a process that incorporates the opinions and input of a wide variety of relevant stakeholders. During the process they act as conceptual translators who explain the new approach in terms of local values.

By remodeling the policy process, LL.M.s can create a more stable and productive socioeconomic environment.

Third, LL.M.s bring tools that may be new to their domestic legal community. Analytical skills acquired through a foreign education can be taken home and introduced to a wider community. Moreover, the LL.M. can be imported and adapted to improve the capacity of local legal professionals to introduce gradual and minor reforms. For example, many countries do not have a community of practitioners—such as a voluntary bar association—that tracks legal developments and promotes reforms. Instead, one or two professors exercise virtual monopoly control over the revision process, often based solely on theoretical principles disconnected from practical application. By creating specialized groups of practitioners to promote changes in a specific area—for example bank regulation or secured transactions—the cross-cultural professional can identify local problems, marry them to practical solutions, and advocate reform more effectively.

IV. Agents of Hope

One of the most prevalent attitudes among college students in many countries is despair. They came of age in a period of great expectation after the fall of the Berlin Wall, when new economic and political models were expected to lift their countries to new levels of freedom and income. Results have been disappointing. Some countries have moved forward, but others have undergone collapse, war, or other destructive cycles. Many young people—and even their parents—have come to believe that they cannot make a difference, that the system is fixed and balanced against them.

While this may seem like a tall order, or even an irrelevant challenge, LL.M.s can be agents of hope within their societies. Through their own experience, they have come to understand that there are other options, models, and possibilities for their countries. They have experienced the reality that the past need not utterly define the future. They have been changed and thus know that change can happen.

Hope is more than wishful thinking or optimism. Optimism is believing that things will get better; hope is understanding that *we can make things better*. The difference is one of agency and responsibility. Hope founded on a realistic understanding of human nature, social dynamics, and local values provides a foundation for the long term tactical and strategic planning needed to bring about reforms and create systemic capacity for reforms. Setbacks are inevitable, but they are not the end of the story.

Change takes time. Some studies have shown that people can take as long as 30 years to adjust their behavior to new economic conditions. Ingrained habits, attitudes, and ideologies can and do change, but they do so slowly. Rapid change creates instability and reaction, even when it is beneficial. The perspective forged through cross-cultural experience suggests that LL.M.s are well positioned to understand these parameters, and to embrace the long-term disciplines needed to bring about change.

Change has enemies. Vested interests, entrenched ideologies, and poor understanding create barriers to reform. Resistance is normally both active and passive. In Macedonia, two professors who did not understand how bankruptcy works in practice were offended by some of the provisions of the new law. They attempted to pass amendments secretly through political connections. Fortunately, the effort was exposed and stopped before it caused tremendous economic damage to the country. It also highlighted the need for ongoing, systematic engagement with stakeholders to explain and inculcate new thinking and understanding. Because change has enemies, those who wish to bring change need support. The United States has a mythology of the "Lone Ranger"—a single individual who stands against the powers and heroically forces reforms. Unfortunately, Superman and Rambo make for interesting movies, but they are a poor model for reformers. Reform requires a network of like-minded and dedicated individuals who can reinforce each other's work and encourage one another when the going gets hard.

The great Nigerian novelist Chinua Achebe describes this problem forcefully in *No Longer at Ease*. His story involves a young Nigerian who has won a scholarship for academic performance in his village school. In England, he adopts the liberal democratic values of British society, only to find himself alone in his beliefs when he returns home. No longer at ease because he is neither fully Nigerian nor fully British, he ultimately finds himself crushed by a system in which he no longer fits.

Achebe's tale describes only one possibility, and not a necessary one. Reverse culture shock affects even professionals upon return from living overseas, and highlights the need for preserving newly acquired skills, approaches and even world views. This can best be accomplished by joining forces with others who hold similar values. In some countries, there are strong networks of foreign-trained attorneys, or even alumni associations in a few cases. In other countries it may be necessary for returning LL.M.s to start an association or network, or maintain close contact with colleagues from other countries. Such groups may provide professional development opportunities, or simply a place of much needed encouragement.

Change is more than possible, it is inevitable. But change must be nurtured and directed over the long-term. The LL.M. experience provides a solid foundation for pursuing positive change.

V. Final Thoughts on Making a Difference

As already noted, despair is pervasive in many countries. The reasons are understandable, but not justifiable. Much of the despair arises from a mistaken assumption that individuals cannot make a difference. While it is true that one individual is unlikely to bring about immediate, pervasive reform in a country or even an organization, that does not negate the basic reality of the impact. It simply demonstrates that expectations are out of place.

The reality is simple: each of us makes a difference. This is unavoidable. In every human interaction, there is an impact. We encourage or discourage those we work with. We support the status quo through inaction, or we bring about change through action. Every decision to action or inaction reinforces or opposes the dynamics of change in which we find ourselves. We do not have a choice: each of us will influence those around us.

Yet we do have a choice, not in whether to make a difference, but in what kind of difference we make. Ultimately, that is the goal and the hope of the LL.M. program—to equip the participants to make better decisions and have greater impact. That, perhaps, is the principle reason that international policy reform specialists so highly value LL.M.s.

Chapter 3

A Kenyan Experience with LL.M. Education

Maurice Oduor[1]

I. Introduction

This chapter addresses the implications that an American style of legal education may have in the social, economic, and political development of transition countries.[2] The question I address is whether students trained in American law schools, having attended American law classes, and being exposed to the American legal method, are enabled to stimulate any positive changes in their own countries in the various aspects of life in those countries and, not least, in the legal system. The role that the University of Pittsburgh School of Law (Pitt Law) has played in this regard will be of specific concern here. The second issue of concern for this chapter is more localized, addressing the impact of the American pedagogical method on the teaching of law in a non-American legal system. What effect, if any, does the use of the casebook method have on the study and teaching of law in a Kenyan law school? The third limb of concern here is evaluating the outlook for the future. The question here is what can we expect to be the impact of an American legal education on the future legal, social, economic, and political framework of countries in transition whose students have received their training in the United States.

---

1 Lecturer (Moi University, School of Law); advocate of the High Court of Kenya; LL.M. 2004 (University of Pittsburgh School of Law); Certificate, Negotiating International Financial Transactions (United Nations International Center for Training & Research); LL.B Hons. 2001 (Moi University).

2 I use the term "transition countries" to describe those countries, which after experimenting with rigid social, economic and political structures, are now loosening up and adopting more liberal market oriented economic models that are consistent with a liberal democracy. Countries that have established new governments following the end of armed conflict or civil wars are also described as countries in transition. *See, e.g.*, Luu Tien Dung, Judicial Independence in Transitional Countries (UNDP 2003). Kenya would be understood to be a country in transition in the sense that a previously authoritarian regime gave way to one that is based on the principle of multi-party democracy punctuated by periodic elections, freedom, and equality of all. Since the 40-year-old de jure single-party dictatorship of President Moi (and before him, President Kenyatta), Kenyans have held four elections.

II. Background: The Moi University School of Law

The Moi University School of Law ("MUSL"or "the school") was established in 1994, 13 years after formation of Moi University itself.[3] However, at the time of establishing the school (then known as the Faculty of Law), it was understood that as a constituent member of the entire university the school's curriculum must be dovetailed into the overall goals of education set out by the university. In this regard, MUSL had to be committed to the development of a curriculum that fit into the overall University's goal of promoting social transformation in the country. The blueprint informing the establishment of the university called upon institutions of higher learning to promote social justice and expand educational opportunities in Kenya.[4] In this regard, MUSL was established "to provide qualified students with a course of study designed to engage and challenge their intellect while exposing them to experiences designed to develop competent advocates committed to the *social aims of high quality legal representation, national development and public service*."[5]

The designers of our curriculum envisaged that the program they suggested would provide the framework for attaining this objective. It is important to note that the main theme in the school's objective is the promotion of national development and public service.[6] Having regard for this theme, the question then turns on the extent to which the "immersion" of Kenyan students into the American legal culture, encompassing, as it does, the legal education system, contributes to the promotion of national development and ideals of public service in Kenya, so as to dovetail with the goals of legal education as espoused by the school. To achieve the objectives of the curriculum, MUSL combines the practical-oriented clinical method with the traditional classroom instruction method.[7] The curriculum stipulates that the bachelor of laws course of study will provide instruction in

---

3 Moi University was established in 1984 pursuant to the recommendations of the Mackay Report of 1981. *See* C.B. MACKAY, REPORT OF THE PRESIDENTIAL COMMITTEE ON THE ESTABLISHMENT OF A SECOND UNIVERSITY IN KENYA (1981) [hereinafter MACKAY REPORT]. The MACKAY REPORT was a culmination of the committee's painstaking visits to all parts of Kenya, collecting views of the expectations of Kenyans from university education and a synthesis of those views. The School of Law was established in 1994 with the objective of "providing qualified students with a course of study designed to engage them to experiences that would develop competent advocates committed to the social aims of high quality legal representation, national development and public service." *See also* Moi University, School of Law, *at* http://www.mu.ac.ke/academic/schools/law/index.html. *See also* the Moi University Act, (1985) Cap. 210A §§ 3(1) & 4(1) (Kenya).

4 *See* MACKAY REPORT, *supra* note 3; *see also* Moi University Act, *supra* note 2, § 4(1) (spelling out the functions of the University).

5 *Id.* (emphasis added).

6 *See* MACKAY REPORT, *supra* note 3.

7 *See, e.g.*, Tom O. Ojienda and Maurice Oduor, *Reflections on the Implementation of Clinical Legal Education in Moi University, Kenya*, 2 INT'L J. C.L.E. 49 (2001).

fundamental legal doctrine, legal theory, and advocacy skills by way of traditional classroom discussion, simulated lawyering experiences, law related externships and live-client representation. It emphasizes an approach with a strong orientation to social justice and public service. Recognizing the many challenges facing Kenyans, the school sets out to prepare students who have the ability to identify social phenomena and the need for change and generating solutions consistent with those needs and phenomena. Thus, the aim of the school is to inculcate among students the values of social consciousness leading to activism that would contribute towards the attainment of the ideals of social justice.

The school, through its curriculum, also seeks to impart the practical skills of advocacy, by which it means the skills of analogical reasoning, use of precedents, fact finding, research writing, persuasive speaking, and effective listening. The ultimate aim of that approach is to imbue in the students the necessary skill and ability to identify legal problems and legal principles applicable thereto, and to use those principles to resolve the problems and to think critically about legal problems and the legal system. At the school, law has less to do with learning legal rules. It is viewed as a process of human interaction transcending moral, social, economic, and political issues.

III. The Place of Legal Education in a Developing/Transition Country

As the term suggests, countries in transition face an uphill task in ensuring the social, economic and political well-being of their citizens.[8] Their changing economic outlook means that most of their citizens are unable to meet their day-to-day needs. Faced with the choice between paying for food and other basic necessities on the one hand, and paying fees for legal services on the other, it is clear what option these citizens will take.[9] In recognition of the attendant injustices suffered by a greater proportion of the population arising from the inability to access the legal system, lawyers must be willing to extend their professional services to those who, because of lack of resources, are unable to pay for it. Where the government in a developing economy seeks to improve the social, economic, and political systems in relation to its citizens, law schools must endeavor to take

8 A good number of the countries in transition are located in sub-Saharan Africa. It has been said that Africa is the only continent in the world that has recorded negative economic growth in the last 50 or so years. According to van der Veen, while the standards of living the world over experienced unprecedented improvement, sub-Saharan Africans became poorer, and were the victims of misrule, violence, corruption and AIDS. *See* Roel van der Veen, What Went Wrong with Africa: A Contemporary History 13 (2004).

9 *See, e.g.*, David Mugonyi and F. Thoya, *The High Cost of Seeking Justice*, The Daily Nation, Nov. 29, 2006 (reporting that Kenya's Chief Justice had just set new remuneration scales for lawyers' services and observing that the costs for legal representation had in certain cases increased by up to 50 per cent).

their distinctive place in such overall national programs. Lawyers must therefore fit within the process of development in transition countries; law schools in turn, must reconsider how they "teach students to think about judicial administration, the litigation process, and socialization of legal services."[10]

Developing countries also tend to have nascent democratic institutions, the nourishment of which requires the active input of professionals, including lawyers. Lawyers are particularly well placed to engage with systems of political governance, pushing them to the limits, and, in the process, engendering changes that conform to current international best practices that entail democratic rule, respect for the rule of law, freedom, and equality for all.[11] To be able to attain these objectives, law schools, as the institutions that prepare future lawyers, must be in touch with the present and tailor their curricula in such a way so as to ensure that they remain relevant to current needs of society. Thus lawyers must be equipped with skills that prepare them to be agents of change in society. In this regard, one author has noted that one of the goals of legal education, particularly in respect to

---

10 *See* James C.N. Paul, *The Goals of African Legal Education, in* PROCEEDINGS OF THE CONFERENCE ON LEGAL EDUCATION IN AFRICA 16–24 (Vanderlinden ed., 1968), *excerpted in* WILLIAM BURNETT HARVEY, AN INTRODUCTION TO THE LEGAL SYSTEM IN EAST AFRICA 2–8, 2 (1975).

11 The so-called struggle for the "second liberation" was spearheaded by lawyers through devices such as public interest suits pursued with a view to pressurizing the government either to repeal repressive laws or to pass new ones that would guarantee freedom for the Kenyan citizens. Before the resumption of multi-party democracy, Kenya was arguably ruled by a repressive government that stifled dissent and that was grossly intolerant of divergent political opinions. Perceived critics of the government were arrested and detained. Lawyers were at the forefront in either representing such dissidents in their trials or alternatively filing challenges to the constitutionality of the acts of government officials. The degree of success was varied. *See, e.g.*, David Mukaru Nganga v. Republic (High Court) Miscellaneous Application No.112 of 1990 (the applicant could not get orders to restrain the police from illegally harassing or detaining him, the judge arguing that this was a case for judicial review rather than one involving a violation of constitutional rights). *See also* Koigi Wa Wamwere v. A.G (High Court) Criminal Application No. 180 of 1990; Kenneth Njindo Matiba v. Attorney General (High Court) Miscellaneous Application No. 666 of 1990; Rev. Lawford Ndege Imunde v. A.G. (High Court) Miscellaneous Application No. 180 of 1990; Harun Thungu Wakaba v. Republic (High Court) Miscellaneous Criminal Case No. 34 of 1992; Kathurima M'Inoti, *The Reluctant Guard: The High Court and the Decline of Constitutional Remedies in Kenya*, THE NAIROBI LAW MONTHLY, No. 34 (July 1991); Githu Muigai, *The Judiciary in Kenya and the Search for a Philosophy of Law: The Case of Constitutional Adjudication, in* ICJ-KENYA, 2 CONSTITUTIONAL LAW CASE DIGEST, 159–89 (2005); J.B. Ojwang and James A. Otieno-Odek, *The Judiciary in Sensitive Areas of Public Law: Emerging Approaches to Human Rights Litigation*, 35 NETHERLANDS INT'L L. REV. 29 (1988), *reprinted in* ICJ-KENYA, 1 CONSTITUTIONAL LAW CASE DIGEST (2004); Gibson K. Kuria, *Litigating Kenya's Bill of Rights, in* HUMAN RIGHTS AND DEMOCRACY IN EAST AFRICA: THE CONSTITUTIONAL IMPLICATION OF THE EAST AFRICAN COOPERATION 67–128 (Kivuatha Kibwana ed., 1997).

Africa, is "to prepare graduates equipped intellectually to serve more effectively as agents of change—since the process of development surely entails dislocation, sacrifice and commitment, notably by those few lucky enough to get parchments from universities."[12]

Limitations on resources affect not only the consumers of justice but also prospective future lawyers. Thus, those who wish to pursue law as a career choice may find that they are incapable of doing so because of the sacrifices involved in paying for it.[13] At the same time, the increasing population means that there are more people in need of legal services today than there were yesterday.[14] If the number of lawyers does not rise proportionately with the population, it is clear that demand will outstrip supply within a short time. Yet this is the situation that exists in most developing economies, including Kenya's. As well as engaging in private practice, lawyers are also needed to fill the many positions in public service that require legal expertise, including judges, administrative officials, heads of legal tribunals and commissions, and registrars. Where there are fewer lawyers than are needed, the provision of services by government is likely to be deficient. The goal of legal education in this regard should be to prepare lawyers who will "provide a very large proportion of national leadership at all levels of authority."[15]

12 See Paul, supra note 10, at 3.

13 In Kenya there are only two legally recognized universities for training lawyers; Moi University and the University of Nairobi. There are two categories of students—government sponsored and privately sponsored. The fees for the former are partly paid by the government but they are eligible for government loans granted through the Higher Education Loans Board. In the latter category the students are entirely responsible for their own fees and other amenities and are generally not eligible for government support. Generally it costs around U.S.$3,000 for tuition fees alone per year. While probably modest by international standards, this is an amount that is well beyond the reach of many individuals in Kenya given the economic status of the country.

14 Kenyans numbered around 30 million by the last census conducted in 1999. It is currently estimated that the population has increased by close to three million. The number of lawyers stands at an estimated five thousand, giving a ratio of one lawyer for every seven thousand people. Even assuming that half of the 33 million is made up of non-adults, and considering that each of the persons in the remaining half will not always require the services of a lawyer, it is clear that we still have people who cannot access lawyers simply because there are not enough of them.

15 *See* Albert Harno, Legal Education in the United States 122–25 (1953), *excerpted in* Harvey, *supra* note 10, at 8–10.

IV. The Collaboration Between Moi University School of Law and the University of Pittsburgh School of Law

The collaboration between Moi University School of Law and the University of Pittsburgh School of Law can be traced back to the year 2000,[16] on the occasion of a visit by Professor John Burkoff to the school. This culminated in participation by a Moi faculty member in the Semester at Sea program. This is only a part of a rich history of American influence in the Moi University curriculum. The first dean of the School of Law, Professor Gaskins, was an American who, together with his compatriot, Dr. Bennett, presided over the launch of the school in 1994 and its subsequent development over the following four years. Both were instrumental in the development of the School curriculum and certain of the courses taught have strong American content.[17]

MUSL has also benefitted from the experience of other American scholars over the years, the effect of which has been to widen the scope of learning at the faculty.[18] The two schools have, over the years, cultivated closer collaboration culminating in the Moi-Pittsburgh Training program by which students from the Moi University benefit by attending a fully sponsored Master of Laws program at the University of Pittsburgh School of Law.[19] Working with other collaborating agencies, companies, and individuals, the Center for International Legal Education (CILE) put together a sponsorship through which Moi University students attend University of Pittsburgh School of Law for an intensive one-year LL.M. Program.[20] It is intensive because it is full-time and students are exposed to the rigors of

---

16 Unlike other similar arrangements with other universities across the world, there is no memorandum of understanding between Moi University and the University of Pittsburgh concerning the manner of training of students from the former institution. The process is based entirely on trust and precedent which so far has been excellent in its working.

17 The Legal Research Methods and Writing course encompasses elements that are drawn from a system that is distinctively American. For example some of the skills imparted to students include briefing cases, brief writing, and writing the inter-office memorandum. In Critical Thinking and Writing, students engage in exercises designed to enable them to question legal doctrine and suggest improvements for the future. Skills of appellate advocacy, complex fact organization, and persuasive writing are core in the Advanced Legal Writing and Advocacy course. Moi University School of Law had a pioneering influence in this and many other areas of legal education. For instance, based on the American model, the School pioneered the concept of clinical legal education and student driven legal aid in the country. *See* Ojienda and Oduor, *supra* note 7, at 57.

18 Professor McDearman taught Trial Advocacy between 1999 and 2001.

19 *See, e.g.*, *From the Director*, 6 CILE Notes 1 (Fall 2001).

20 Sponsorship has been secured from the likes of Alcoa Foundation, Frank and Sara West of the Franklin West Apartments among others. *See, e.g.*, *Tenth LLM Class Arrives*, 9 CILE Notes 15 (Fall 2004); *2004 LLM Class Begins in Impressive Fashion*, 8 CILE Notes 18 (Fall 2003); *Law School Recognizes Generosity of Alcoa Foundation and Franklin West Inc.*, 6 CILE Notes (Fall 2001).

American law schools just like and together with American students. After a two-semester academic exposure, students are normally attached either to a company or law firm for an internship lasting slightly over four weeks.[21]

The understanding with Moi University is that following this training, the students will be absorbed at the Moi University School of Law as part of the teaching staff.[22] In this way, Pitt Law actively engages in training future staff members of the Moi University of Law. So far, five Moi University students have benefited from this arrangement and even though the absorption rate has been slow, there are signs that it will improve in the near future.[23]

V. Impact of American Pedagogical Methods on the Teaching of Law in Kenya

The style of training employed in the law school ultimately determines the approach adopted by the student lawyers when they get out into practice. A method of training that sharpens the research ability and the inquisitiveness of the student will spawn practitioners well placed to identify problems in society and apply the appropriate rules for their resolution. Thus, university legal education must be so poised as to equip future lawyers with the experience that will make them effective in their subsequent professional roles.[24]

To succeed in this endeavor, the Moi University School of Law employs various pedagogical methods: lecture, simulation, tutorials, and clinical.[25] The lecture method has for some time been predominantly applied.[26] Students undergo lecture sessions in which notes are either dictated to them interspersed with explanations

---

21 At the end of the academic year, CILE secures placements for internship for the LL.M. students for purposes of giving the students some practical experience following their formal classroom training. Some of the companies and law firms that have offered internships to LL.M. students are: Alcoa, Buchanan Ingersoll, Cohen & Grigsby, Deloitte and Touche, H.J. Heinz, Pennsylvania Attorney General's Office, Westinghouse, U.S. Steel, Malakoff, Doyle & Finberg PC and many more.

22 *See International Partnerships Reach New Heights of Productivity*, 8 CILE Notes 6 (Fall 2003).

23 Victor Mosoti (2001), Evelyn Kamau (2002), Vincent Mutai (2003), Maurice Oduor (2004), Linda Khaemba (2005), and Annah Konuche (2008) have all benefitted from the program. Oduor, Mutai, and Khaemba are currently employed as lecturers at Moi University School of Law. *See International Partnerships Reach New Heights of Productivity*, 8 CILE Notes 6 (Fall 2003).

24 *See, e.g.*, Henry J.A. Lugulu and John Chebii, *Pedagogical Methods in Law: The Moi University Experience*, Law Soc. of Kenya J. (2003).

25 *Id.*

26 *See* Ojienda & Oduor, *supra* note 6, at 54.

or question-and-answer sessions.[27] The lecture method may be supplemented with readings assigned to the students which may or may not be discussed in class. Tutorials have been less employed at the school, owing to large student populations and the accompanying dearth of resources. The lecture method, while having its potential benefits, including cost-effectiveness and ability to deal with latest developments in the area of study, is limited in many other ways.[28] First, it risks being a monologue where students only marginally participate in the progression of events in the class. It depends more on the preparedness and versatility of the teacher in entwining a lecture style with other methodologies to enhance its effectiveness.[29] The other risk is that it may turn into a one-sided dictation session with the attendant propensity for students to memorize notes and not actively question the principles dotting the numerous pages they may have jotted down.[30] The lecture method also assumes regular class attendance—this, of course, is not always the case, notwithstanding measures taken to eliminate cases of truancy.[31] The lecture method also requires access to up-to-date legal sources to ensure that the sessions remain relevant to current challenges.[32]

27 *See*, *e.g.*, Lugulu & Chebii, *supra* note 23, noting in regard to the lecture method that: "[t]he lecture or text method supplements the case method in second, third and fourth years of the curriculum. Lectures are generally seen as a cost effective way of imparting the main ideas in an area to a large number of students. Lectures also enable the lecturer to tell students the latest development in an area and to explain any particularly complex parts of a subject. With good planning, the lecture may facilitate an orderly procedure in teaching, and arrangement of the subject matter in a way that avoids waste of time and energy and a redistribution of emphasis to secure the greatest cooperation from the students and maintain their active interest. With pauses for a question and answer session, a good lecturer can link up an organic relationship that displays constant mutual interaction. Lastly a good lecturer could help in introducing the subject from the known to the unknown, the simple to the complex, and the concrete to the abstract."

28 *See id.* where the authors note the disadvantages of the lecture method as including: "But this method depends on the personality of an individual lecturer and is therefore teacher centred and not student centred. It therefore does not suit different levels of students' intelligence. It is also dominated by one-sided verbalism without providing enough suitable opportunities for self activity by students. There is also the risk that the lecturer may resort to dictating notes and the students to resort to memorizing them. While note taking may help the students to listen actively and reflectively in order to relate what is being taught to the existing knowledge of the subject the risk that the lecture method may make students to be passive is real. Lectures, like the case method, require class attendance. It is therefore assumed that the students will regularly attend them."

29 *Id.*

30 *Id.*

31 At Moi University, if a student fails to attend 20 per cent of scheduled classes, she is deemed to have failed to attend the course and may be barred by the Senate from sitting for the examinations in that course.

32 Lugulu and Chebii, *supra* note 24.

At Moi University, the deficiencies of the lecture method have been recognized. To counter those shortcomings, the school has incorporated the clinical legal education method as a complement to the theory-intensive lecture method. The clinical method is said to be a problem-solving-oriented approach which exposes students to various legal problems they may have encountered or are likely to encounter in the theoretical phase of their study.[33] The clinical method may assume either the simulated or live-client approach or both. In the simulated approach, students get to deal with realistic problems—problems which have occurred before or are likely to happen again in real life. Students consider the problem and suggest solutions. The problem is posed within the context of simulations whose content is associated with recent or current areas of study. In the live-client representation approach, students encounter real problem as presented by "live" clients. Students at this stage apply the skills learned in other units to practical problem solving.

Generally, there are two broad subject areas that utilize this problem-oriented approach: the clinical seminar and the clinical externship. The externship entails attending court hearings, advising unrepresented accused persons on basic procedures of court, and attending and holding legal literacy meetings and seminars. In a clinical externship, students get to work directly with qualified practitioners on matters where legal representation is contemplated. While the first approach gives an opportunity to students to render on-the-spot legal advice, the second approach is relatively permanent in the sense that it allows for the creation and development of a professional relationship between the students as the lawyers (of course under the direct supervision of a qualified legal practitioner, usually a staff member) and the client. In this regard, the school established a legal aid clinic to provide a forum by which students will meet clients and attend to their legal problems and learn while in the process. The goals of the clinical program are four-fold:

1. to provide students with opportunities for applying techniques and information acquired through prior simulated experiences, especially, interviewing, counseling case, planning and litigation;
2. to provide students with opportunities for legal practice;
3. to provide students with opportunities to develop their ability as problem-solvers; and
4. to provide students with opportunities to provide legal assistance either through the school's own projects or in coordination with external projects.

This process has demonstrated that any attempt to introduce a different way of pedagogy in the School of Law is faced with the immediate concern of inadequate resources. The Pitt Law approach to learning and teaching law requires that the university be endowed with sufficient resources to support the intensity with which

33 *See* Ojienda and Oduor, *supra* note 7.

it is delivered.[34] Thus, faculty members must be the "best in the game," the library must be well stocked with both traditional and modern resources, the school must innovate and create programs that attract a greater number of students, and so on.[35]

The Moi University School of Law was established by the university pursuant to its mandate under a statute.[36] This has meant that, until the recent introduction of privately sponsored programs as income-generating options, it has largely depended on the Kenyan government for funding.[37] The dearth of teaching facilities, coupled with a relatively sparse collection of library materials, means that the casebook approach to legal learning cannot be applied in its entirety. For a law teacher with a "first-hand advantage" in the American pedagogical method wishing to foster in his or her students the habit of finding the law in the cases, questioning the rationale behind judges' decisions and establishing the philosophical underpinnings of law, the task becomes arduous if not well nigh impossible.

Yet this cannot be a reason to abandon the project altogether, for it has its own distinct advantages. Thus, even while attempting to achieve the most within the constrained resources available, it has been possible to combine aspects of American pedagogy, specifically those aspects which can be easily applied without significant resource strain, with those aspects of Kenyan teaching methods that will make the educational experience much more than a passive, unidirectional enterprise.

It is possible to prepare course outlines well in advance, put together some reading material from disparate sources well in advance, and require students to be acquainted with those materials prior to class meetings. During class there will be more discussion of these materials and active questioning rather than a passive activity dominated by the teacher's monologue. At first, students confronted with this new approach have appeared lost, not sure whether the teacher was providing any guidance or merely expressing random thoughts on the subject. Thus, it pays to forewarn the students that a new approach has been adopted, one that involves less note-taking but more active engagement of the mind.

It also pays to warn students that participation in the discussion will be significant in the final assessment of their marks for the course. The problem with tallying the extent of one's participation in class discussion in the final grade is that the teacher has limited ways in which to grade students. The university requires that students be assessed through two continuous assessment tests (CATs)

---

34 *See*, *e.g.*, Richard A. Matasar, *The Rise and Fall of American Legal Education*, New York Law School Public Law and Legal Theory Research Paper Series 04/05 #28, *at* http://ssrn.com/abstract=730563 (decrying the increasing costs of legal education in America).

35 *Id.*

36 *See* the Moi University Act, *supra* note 3.

37 *See* Moi University, School of Law, *supra* note 3, *at* http://www.mu.ac.ke/academic/schools/law/index.html.

administered at varied intervals in the course of the semester (constituting 30 per cent of the overall grade) and a written examination at the end of the semester (making up the remaining 70 per cent). No provision is allowed for the teacher's discretion in the manner of assessment. There is thus little room for creativity in grading students, particularly when it relates to active contributions in class.

While failing to attend at least 80 per cent of the classes may be a reason to bar a student from sitting for the university examinations, this is a rule that is rarely enforced, partly because huge numbers of student make it virtually impractical to take roll in every class.[38] This calls for a method of teaching that combines various approaches, each complementing the other to the extent possible. Thus, in addition to lectures where the teacher may or may not give notes, students may be required to read further on their own, provided the teacher ensures that the materials referred to are readily available. While MUSL has attempted to adopt the clinical method, the success can only be described in measured terms. Lack of support from the university has spawned disinterest on the part of faculty members, which in turn has caused the clinical component to grind to a virtual halt. In view of these challenges, it is important that the School embrace new and innovative ways of teaching law which will be effective and at the same time not constrain limited resources that the school currently commands.

VI. What Is the Potential of the Law School's Pedagogic Approach in Development?

I have tried to describe above how the Moi University School of Law's curriculum is premised on the ideal of development and public service. Thus, the skills imparted to the students must be geared toward preparing them for this role in their future professional lives. In a developing economy like Kenya's, the lawyer's contribution to this development is crucial. In keeping with the wider mandate of lawyers to participate toward the development of the law for the benefit of the public,[39] graduates from Moi University School of Law are to be equipped to play this role. The clinical approach employed by the school is crucial in preparing the school's graduates for various public roles that have a bearing on the development of Kenya, whether social, political, or economic.

In Kenya, the question of access to legal services is critical. The grinding poverty level compromises the ability of a majority of Kenyans to engage the legal system with a view to having their rights protected. At a time when legal practice

38 Currently there are about 500 students in first year alone. Owing to these large numbers, the School has had to split them into three groups. Even then, classes tend to be crowded, making the task of teaching a rather unenvious one.

39 *See* Moi University Act, (1962) Cap. 18 § 4 (Kenya) (setting out one of the functions of the Law Society of Kenya as being to assist the government and the public in matters relating to legislation and law).

has assumed an increasingly commercial outlook,[40] many would-be consumers of legal services are clearly left out. Lawyers in a transition economy like Kenya's have been criticized for pricing justice out of reach of many people.[41] In that regard, a program that inculcates in lawyers the ideals of service to the less-advantaged members of the public is very relevant for this country. Such a program is also crucial in enhancing the development of institutions of governance for the public good. The value of public service imbues in future lawyers the urge to engage with public institutions to ensure that they do their work where government fails to do so or do it in a way that properly secures the rights of citizens.

VII. How Does the Moi-Pittsburgh Collaboration Fit in the Above?

The law schools at both Moi University and the University of Pittsburgh share ideals that are critical.[42] First, there is a strong public service element.[43] Second, there is a deliberate attempt at producing graduates who can engage with the system of governance for the benefit of consumers of justice and the public good.[44] There is therefore potential for even greater collaboration leading to greater benefit for both law schools and the wider university community. Through the Moi-Pittsburgh collaboration, six Moi University graduates have been trained at the University of Pittsburgh.[45] They have gone on to serve various institutions, whether in Kenya or internationally, in various capacities. For those who are working in international institutions, their training at Pittsburgh provided them with not only the opportunity

---

40 The commercialization of law practice the world over has been said to take away from the social roles that lawyers ought to play. According to Berle, legal practitioners are inclined to offer their services to those who pay the astronomical fees they charge. In a capitalistic society, where the vast majority of the resources are placed in the hands of the minority powerful, it becomes clear whom the legal system will serve efficiently. *See* Berle, *The Modern Legal Profession, in* 9 Encyclopaedia of The Social Sciences 340–45 (1933).

41 In regard to the rather unflattering role of lawyers, Dias has noted that "there is a growing criticism of the legal profession in developing countries as being a 'disabling profession' and a strong sentiment that human rights are too important to be left to lawyers alone." *See* Clarence J. Dias, *The Rights of the Child: Emerging Human Rights Agenda for Third World NGOs, in* Rights of the Child: Selected Proceedings of a Workshop on the Draft Convention on the Rights of the Child—An African Perspective 9–11 (May 1988).

42 Leadership and public service being at the forefront. *See, e.g.*, *The School of Law's Mission, Priority Goals and Means of Achievement, at* http://www.law.pitt.edu/about/index.php; *see also* the Moi University webpage, *supra* note 3.

43 *Id.*

44 *Id.*

45 *See International Partnerships Reach New Heights of Productivity*, 8 CILE Notes 6 (Fall 2003).

but also with the skills that have enabled them to exert themselves effectively in those endeavors.

Those employed in public service have also had the opportunity to put into practice the skills acquired in the course of their training at Pittsburgh and in Moi. Three graduates have become lecturers at Moi University School of Law. For them, the challenges are manifold, but it is here that it becomes clear that there is great promise for the continued training of Moi graduates at Pittsburgh. As noted earlier, the casebook method of pedagogy is employed at Moi in limited ways. Partly due to a dearth of resources and partly due to an insular conservative tradition of lecturing, our law school has had to rely more and more on law teachers to provide the bulk of materials for student's consumption.

The attendant passiveness of the process cannot be gainsaid. For a lecturer who has been immersed in the Langdelian method, albeit for only a short duration, continued traditionalism is usually hard to justify, emphasizing, as it does, greater industry on the part of the lecturer rather than the students. On the other hand, the lure of the casebook method is hampered by the inability of both MUSL and the students to absorb the extra costs likely to be incurred by a shift into "modernism." Consequently, there arises a need to consider the merits and demerits of both systems with a view to adopting a system that strikes a balance between the two for the ultimate benefit of the students. This calls for partial use of the lecture method and partial use of cases. Thus, the lecturer would assign individual cases to students which would then be discussed in the class on the basis of questions given before hand or raised during the session. The theoretical aspects would then be filled in by way of lectures or other forms of discussion such as tutorials.

Whatever their stations in life, Pittsburgh graduates from Moi University have had significant impact drawing from their training in both institutions for a transition country. Their contributions, both direct and indirect, cannot be overemphasized. It is for this reason that collaboration must continue to exist and must develop in other areas in the future.

VIII. The Export of Legal Education: What Prospects for the Future?

The collaboration between Moi and Pittsburgh universities has as yet many unexplored opportunities and possibilities. As already noted, Kenya is a country in transition socially, economically and politically. In this state, lawyers can and should play a significant role in shaping the institutions that are responsible for the transformation. Notwithstanding the underdevelopment currently afflicting many African states, there is hope for a future in which those states will play a direct influential role in charting out the social, political and economic goals of the world. But even if this is too optimistic a view, there is no denying the need to train lawyers who are relevant to the current situation prevailing in the society in which they live. Opportunities for agents of change (such as the University of Pittsburgh) to be part and parcel of these changes need not be gainsaid. So far, it has been a one-sided affair between Moi University and the University of Pittsburgh. Some semblance of balance may be created by a faculty or student exchange program which will also serve as an avenue for information exchange and sharing. Students and faculty from Pittsburgh can add to and enliven the learning environment in Kenya just as Kenyan ones have been said to do in Pittsburgh. In this regard therefore, there is room for expanding Pittsburgh's Study Abroad Program to include Moi University as well. Such collaboration exists between Moi University and other universities so it will not require the breaking of new ground.

Having regard to the lack of resources that is a perennial problem for universities in Africa, and particularly so in Kenya, this collaboration must occupy a very central role in Moi University School of Law's program. For this to succeed, it must be a long-term venture probably set down in the form of a strategic alliance between both Schools of Law. Such an alliance might be buttressed with a vision that transcends the law schools and adopts an interdisciplinary outlook that contemplates the inclusion of other faculties, departments or schools. Already there are other alliances between the two universities and it should not be difficult to forge a more broad-minded collaboration that sets out a unified vision.

Other unexplored areas include participation in moot court competitions. The Moi University School of Law is a regular participant in the only intra-Africa moots held annually under the aegis of the University of South Africa's Center for Human Rights. The school has returned very impressive results in successive All African Human Rights Moot Court Competitions. The school has also participated in the International Humanitarian Law Moot Court Competition held annually in Arusha, Tanzania, under the auspices of the International Committee of the Red Cross. The University of Pittsburgh School of Law, on the other hand, has a rich mooting history. The Center for International Legal Education (CILE) has been instrumental in inculcating the mooting culture in the School of Law. Examples of such moot competitions would include the Niagara International Law Moot Court Competition, the Philip C. Jessup International Moot Court Competition, and the Willem C. Vis International Commercial Arbitration Moot. Since both law schools have a strong mooting background, this may be harnessed as just one of the facets of collaboration between them.

Pitt Law has been able to establish very successful centers of excellence and other programs. CILE has broken new ground in fostering development in international scholarship. CILE's experience in this regard can offer valuable lessons for Moi University's School of Law in the latter's endeavor to serve as a beacon of legal education and scholarship within the East African region and beyond. There are many other ways for this relationship to be made prosperous and relevant for both universities. The possibilities are inexhaustible, the opportunities enormous. Of course challenges will lurk around the corners, waiting to bump these lofty ideals off course, but all that is required to deal with those is planning and perseverance.

Chapter 4

The Socratic Method, Clinical Legal Education, and Mediation: Serving the Promotion of the Rule of Law in Serbia

Jelena Arsic[1]

> Each time a man stands up for an ideal, or acts to improve the lot of others, or strikes out against injustice, he sends forth a tiny ripple of hope.
>
> Robert F. Kennedy

I. Introduction

The only thing I have wanted to do for as long as I can remember is to teach. My father was a professor for 40 years and by watching him I developed my love for pedagogy. When I became a law student at the University of Belgrade Faculty of Law, I finally found my area of interest in teaching and was ready for all the hard work necessary to become a legal scholar.

When you study law in Serbia, you immediately become aware of at least two problems. The first one relates to methods of teaching used by most Serbian professors, which are mainly theoretical with little or no space for the development of constructive and critical legal thinking and legal practice skills. The other is simply the fact that you live in a country where laws change very frequently. Such a legal system cannot constitute a stable basis for economic and social development. Realizing this, my motivation to become a law professor grew even stronger and I started looking for ways to make my own contribution to improving the legal system in general and legal education specifically.

I graduated from the University of Belgrade, traveled to the United States to gain my Master's in Law (LL.M.), and returned to my home country to start achieving my long-term goals. I wanted to do that by combining my experiences in Serbia with those I gained from the United States.

I now work as an assistant lecturer at the first private law school in Belgrade and as staff attorney with the American Bar Association Rule of Law Project in

1 Visiting Lecturer, Postgraduate Studies in Mediation (University of Belgrade); Assistant Lecturer (Union University School of Law); staff attorney (ABA-CEELI/ABA Rule of Law Initiative); LL.M. 2005, (University of Pittsburgh School of Law); JD 2004 (University of Belgrade).

Serbia, formerly known as ABA/CEELI.[2] This is where I found my opportunity to become more directly involved in the legal reforms in Serbia and to contribute on the development of the rule of law that would benefit society as a whole. Fortunately, the timing was exactly right.

During the last several years, Serbia has been facing comprehensive social and legal reforms. Just a few years ago, Serbia was often described as a country with a socialist political and legal system. Today, however, drastic reforms are occurring in all areas with rapid changes and high expectations. Citizens and legal professionals alike are overwhelmed by the flood of new laws reflecting the new, democratic values of the society. The Serbian legal education system itself is a subject of some the reforms which aim to bring our law schools in line with the European Union standards set by the Bologna Declaration.[3] This effort should provide future lawyers and lawmakers with the necessary foundation in the rule of law.

There are different fields of my work that are influenced by the education I gained in the United States. The most important ones are closely related to my teaching at the law school and the rule of law projects within ABA/CEELI. In the law school, I use interactive methods of teaching in order to enable my students to develop critical thinking skills so that later they can find their own ways through the problems they face as practicing lawyers. Within ABA/CEELI, I have the opportunity to work with judges and bar associations in order to secure the continuing education of legal professionals. In addition, I often have the opportunity to teach at the Faculty of Political Sciences and Center for Social Work. Through all these activities I try to make my own contribution to the promotion of the rule of law in Serbia. In the end, however, my strongest efforts go toward the creation

---

2 American Bar Association/Central European and Euroasian Law Initiative (ABA/CEELI), funded by the US/AID, has been a key supporter in the field of legal reforms in Serbia since 1997. Throughout the years ABA/CEELI has been able to develop close working relationships with Serbian legal professionals. By supporting different rule of law projects and mainly working with judges, prosecutors, magistrates, bar associations and law schools, ABA/CEELI is giving considerable contribution for the development of the rule of law in Serbia. More on the ABA Rule of Law projects in Serbia may be found at http://www.abanet.org/rol.

3 The Bologna Process, based on the Bologna Declaration signed in 1999 by 29 European countries, is currently the most important process of higher education reform in Europe. The main goal is to establish the European Higher Education Area in which there would be no obstacles to the mobility of students, trainees and graduates as well as for teachers, researchers, and higher education administrators. Serbia has officially joined the Bologna Process by signing the Bologna Declaration in September 2003, although the Bologna Process was started in 2000, when activities for the reform of higher education system began. *See The Bologna Declaration: On the European Space for Higher Education—An Explanation, available at* http://ec.europa.eu/education/policies/educ/bologna/bologna.pdf. *See also* The Ministry of Education and Sport, *Higher Education in Serbia and Bologna Process, available at* www.bologna-berlin2003.de/pdf/Serbia.pdf.

of more practical ways of teaching law, as well as for the development of the field of mediation in Serbia.

II. Introducing Serbian Law Students to the Socratic Method

> One of the benefits of using the Socratic method is that it gives the students a chance to experience the attendant joy and excitement of discovering ideas on their own.
>
> Rick Garlikov

Upon my return from the United States, I started working as an assistant lecturer in the field of contracts and torts.[4] My wish was to offer my students a space in which they would consider various legal problems by using their knowledge with rationality and creativity. This, of course, required more interactive teaching methods, which had not been very familiar to me while I was a law student in Serbia. Most of my professors used teaching techniques that emphasized rote memorization, and therefore only small numbers of law students were able to develop critical legal thinking skills while in law school.[5] While I was a student, there were no required readings or assignments, and students would often graduate from the law school without ever being called upon in class or challenged to express their opinion on any legal matter. When I became an LL.M. student, I was introduced to a more effective method of teaching law. I learned that this technique was well known in American law schools as the Socratic method.

When I work with students I use methods that are interactive in nature and represent my own variation of the Socratic method in combination with the traditional *ex cathedra* teaching style often used in Serbian law schools. I assign cases and other readings to my students for every class.[6] These readings are very important since law, like anything else, is more easily learned if the student has some previous understanding of the subject matter. In class, I encourage them to discuss assigned topics and to freely express their opinion about legal issues that we are working on, instead of simply listening to me talk for the entire class. I try to avoid traditional *ex cathedra* lecturing. Only when students are having difficulty with understanding certain legal principles will I give them explanations

---

4 In Serbian law schools, contracts and torts are taught as a single course that is called the Law on Obligations.

5 The Ministry of Education and Sport emphasizes this problem, stating that the Serbian higher education system is characterized by "outdated and highly repetitive curricula, outdated teaching methodology together with the outdated and internationally not relevant literature." *See* Ministry of Education and Sport, *supra* note 3.

6 My students receive a course syllabus in our first class and they are familiar with the required readings in advance.

they need. Other than that, most of the class time is reserved for our dialogue. I simply prefer "teaching by asking" to "teaching by telling."[7]

While doing this, I have to be patient and supportive, as students in Serbia are not used to being questioned often in their classes or challenged to express what they think. Knowing that, I always tell them that even though I have graduated from law school, I am still learning every day. I remind them that there are no right or wrong questions or answers. This leads to a greater willingness on the part of students to express their opinion.

When there are cases assigned, we discuss these cases together, trying to connect legal theory with life. The Serbian legal system is a part of the European continental civil law tradition, and therefore opinions of courts expressed in their decisions do not represent sources of law, nor do they have the value of legal precedent like cases in the United States. However, by reading the court decisions, students become familiar with the reasoning of judges in implementing legal rules onto sometimes complex concrete life situations. This is very helpful, since students are then able to more easily remember often abstract legal rules and legal theory. In addition, I find that students very much enjoy reading about real-life events and their possible legal consequences. They begin to realize how important it is to become a good lawyer and to gain significant knowledge on the rule of law.

All of these experiences and lessons I almost missed as a student and I am happy to now see my students enjoying classes, eager to express their thoughts and ideas. They realize, as I did before them, how important it is not only to have an excellent theoretical background, but also to develop skills to foresee specific legal problems and to find suitable answers to these problems. When choosing a teaching method, an educator must keep in mind the point of teaching and of any teaching method in order to make a good choice. Generally, just giving students more information than they can absorb or assimilate does not help them learn what you want them to know.[8] Law students have to be supported in exploring hypothetical or real-life cases, in expressing their own views, and in developing critical legal thinking skills. Only law students trained in such a way will be able to become confident and independent in everything that they do as young law graduates and, ultimately, as they contribute to the development and protection of the rule of law in their country.

---

7 See Rick Garlikov, *The Socratic Method: Teaching by Asking Instead of by Telling*, *available at* http://www.garlikov.com/Soc_Meth.html.

8 Rick Garlikov, *Teaching Effectively: Helping Students Absorb or Assimilate Material*, *available at* http://www.garlikov.com/teaching/absorb.html.

III. Developing Clinical Legal Education in Serbia

> You are about to begin an educational adventure unlike anything you have previously encountered in the law school. In your clinic work you are about to try the identity of lawyer.
>
> David F. Chavkin

Related to my work in the law school is my occupation with improving clinical legal education in Serbia. Until now, the Serbian law schools have had the kind of basic clinical education where students provide free legal aid services to indigent citizens. These services were limited to providing simple legal opinions and drafting legal documents for clients, but student involvement in the clinic did not include any kind of legal representation in courts.

While I was an LL.M. student in Pittsburgh, I realized that as a law student there is so much more that one can do within the clinic, which is why I became involved in the University of Pittsburgh School of Law Family Law Clinic. I had the opportunity to provide a wide range of legal services, from drafting legal documents to representing clients before the Allegheny County Court of Common Pleas. The Pitt Family Law Clinic was like a small law firm and, as such, a real challenge for any law student. What I learned there was probably the most valuable knowledge that a law student can receive. Keeping that in mind, I am now looking forward to establishing the first legal clinic in my law school comparable to the Family Law Clinic at Pitt Law. In this clinic, students will have the opportunity to work with real people and to learn from experience. They will have the opportunity to apply legal rules in real cases and to become aware of their own responsibility towards clients, courts, and the legal profession. And I have no doubt that students will enjoy working in that clinic while learning and developing their legal practice skills and helping indigent citizens with their legal problems. In fact, I truly believe that after being given an opportunity to experience clinical legal education students will graduate from the law school with greater knowledge and satisfaction.

The rule of law is applied in specific real-life situations and not in a vacuum. Therefore, legal education should match reality and offer students both theoretical knowledge and practical legal skills.[9] Every part of society would benefit from this style of legal education. Students will receive comprehensive legal knowledge. Everything they have learned in class will become real. Through clinical activities students will increase their lawyering skills and develop professional values. They will gain confidence in their own ability to be practicing lawyers, and will be better prepared to participate effectively and responsibly in the legal profession.

---

9 In its report, the Serbian Ministry of Education and Sport also recognizes that among the weaknesses of the existing system of education is "highly structured monodisciplinary programs that cannot answer the market needs. Focus is placed on theory with practical skills and knowledge being neglected." *See* Ministry of Education and Sport, *supra* note 3.

As clinical legal education expands, the benefits to the rest of society will increase. The citizens that cannot currently afford legal professionals will benefit because they now have trained students to represent them. The legal profession will benefit since the education of future advocates will have improved and society will benefit because equal access to justice guarantees a more stable and healthy society.[10]

IV. Mediation

> Discourage litigation. Persuade your neighbors to compromise whenever you can. Point out to them how the nominal winner is often a real loser—in fees, expenses and waste of time. As a peacemaker the lawyer has a superior opportunity of being a good man. There will still be business enough.
>
> Abraham Lincoln

The last, but certainly not the least important, aspect of my work relates to mediation. The courses I chose as an LL.M. student were oriented towards alternative dispute resolution (ADR), because I was mainly interested in improving my then basic knowledge of mediation. This was a great opportunity to learn about mediation in the country where modern mediation was born. I researched a lot, tried to read as much as I could, and had the opportunity to work with and learn from Pittsburgh mediators and judges, including an internship at the Allegheny Court of Common Pleas.

I came back to Serbia soon after the first Law on Mediation was enacted. This law provides for both court-annexed and private mediation that can be used in a wide range of disputes.[11] The National Judicial Reform Strategy proposed by the Ministry of Justice of Serbia and adopted by the Serbian National Assembly states that "systematic and well-publicized alternative dispute resolution programs will ensure new, more efficient and less expensive avenues for dispute resolution and considerably reduce the burden on courts and judges, which will, in return increase the efficiency of the judicial system."[12] However, the main challenge that mediation faces in Serbia is true acceptance by the judicial and other branches of government, by attorneys, and by the public. Therefore, I knew that the education of judges and attorneys on the benefits of mediation would be a significant step in promoting mediation, since judges and lawyers are in contact on a regular basis with potential mediation clients.

---

10 Drago Radulovic et al., A Spectrum of Views on Legal Clinics 31 (2004).

11 *See* The Law on Mediation, Official Gazette of the Republic of Serbia, no. 18/2005.

12 *See* The Decision on Adopting the National Judicial Reform Strategy, Official Gazette of the Republic of Serbia, no. 44/2006.

For that reason, I have mostly worked with judges and attorneys on different mediation-related projects. I run mediation seminars where I speak on the theory and practice of mediation and the American experience in this field. When I talk to judges, I always emphasize the role of the presiding judge in the process of referring cases to mediation. I try to educate them on the appropriate practices and techniques to encourage settlements. I try to support their willingness to do so by including mediation role-plays in the seminar and quite often the participants tell me that this part of the seminar is the most effective.[13] In my mediation seminars for attorneys, in addition to topics covered with judges, I also talk about the role of an attorney in the mediation process, as this role is quite specific and unique compared to the one that attorneys have in the traditional court setting.

To date, I have had the opportunity to conduct these kinds of seminars throughout Serbia, and I am pleased to confirm that most Serbian judges and attorneys welcome mediation as a new dispute resolution mechanism in the Serbian legal system. In fact, many of them are interested in being trained as mediators. And I can only consider this kind of interest as a positive one.

Finally, I often lecture in the centers for social work where I train professionals with different backgrounds, such as psychologists, lawyers, and social workers, to become family mediators. This is what I enjoy the most out of all my mediation teaching, because I find these people very enthusiastic and ready to learn as much as is needed so that they can provide a full range of quality services to the citizens who approach them asking for help. I talk to them about my experiences in the United States, I share my mediation books and other materials, and I am very glad to hear from them that they are improving in their mediation practice and that the number of cases they have solved through mediation is increasing.

V. Conclusion

The experience I gained as an LL.M. student was valuable and still is for me in so many ways. It confirmed my beliefs that there are better, more effective ways of teaching law. It helped me to improve my knowledge about mediation and enabled me to share what I have learned with our judges, attorneys and my students. With any kind of education, no matter if you teach students or train legal professionals, the point is to lead or take them from the knowledge and skills they already have to the greater and higher levels of knowledge and skills you want them to have, and do it in a way that inspires and enables them to continue to learn and become better at what they do.

I learned a lot from my American professors and the practitioners I had the opportunity to meet. At some times, their methods seemed fairly difficult to me, but this only inspired me to learn more and therefore became a challenge instead

13 My interactive teaching methods work well even when I communicate with legal professionals.

of an obstacle. All these good pieces of my overall law student experience, I offer now to my own students. I truly hope that when they graduate from law school, this will enable them to approach the law as intellectuals and be ready for all the professional challenges they will have as future rule of law leaders.

As far as the legal professionals are concerned, I hope that their new-found knowledge of mediation will enable them to become even better judges and attorneys; to become true peacemakers. One of the judges who attended my seminar said: “These skills of a mediator should be something that we know by heart so that we can become not only better in what we do as judges but also as human beings.” And I agree. The rule of law is not based on abstract values. It comes from a human need to secure humanity in relationships between people. In my opinion, each member of society is given an opportunity to contribute to the development of the rule of law in his or her own way. What I do in my everyday work is what I consider my contribution to, and one which I hope will serve, the welfare of the society to which I belong.

Chapter 5
Fighting Dragons of the Past: The Internationalization of Legal Education at Donetsk National University

Daniil E. Fedorchuk[1]

I. Introduction

After graduating from the Economics and Law Faculty (ELF) at Donetsk National University in 1999 with a Specialist in Law degree,[2] I joined the faculty and the next year was selected to pursue an LL.M. degree at the University of Pittsburgh School of Law with the support of an Edmund F. Muskie Fellowship. I graduated from Pitt Law in 2001 and returned to Ukraine to resume my teaching responsibilities at the Economics and Law Faculty in Donetsk. I joined the Department of Civil Law and Procedure and, as a faculty member with a western LL.M. degree, was immediately promoted to the position of senior lecturer,[3] entitled under Ukrainian academic rules to deliver lectures and develop and teach my own specialized elective courses.

---

1 Lawyer, Beiten Burkhardt, Kyiv, Ukraine; former Senior Lecturer, Donetsk National University; LL.M. 2001 (University of Pittsburgh School of Law); Specialist in Law, 1999.

2 As a legacy of the Soviet past, Ukraine still maintains its original system of academic degrees which is different from that adopted in most Western countries. The *Specialist in Law* degree is roughly similar to the J.D. degree from a U.S. law school. However, unlike the U.S. degree, in Ukraine law is studied at the undergraduate level, so an absolute majority of full-time students enter a law faculty immediately upon graduation from secondary school, being only 17–18 years old. Legal education in Ukraine takes five years, during which students receive a classical higher education aimed primarily at establishing a strong academic foundation, with a number of non-legal subjects being taught during the first two years of study (such as logic, Latin, a foreign language, pedagogy and psychology, philosophy, Ukrainian business language, history of Ukraine, world history, physical training, etc.). As part of the process of accession to the Bologna process, Ukraine has undertaken gradually to bring its academic degree system in line with general European standards and adopt a three-level scheme (bachelor–master–doctor).

3 Ukraine maintains a rather traditional Soviet system of academic ranks: assistant lecturer, senior lecturer, associate professor (Docent), and professor. The positions of associate professor and professor (tenured professor) can only be held by lecturers who have defended their dissertations and were conferred the Candidate of Legal Sciences (C.L.S.) and Doctor of Legal Sciences (D.L.S.) degrees.

From the very beginning, I was committed to incorporating my experiences gained at Pitt Law into the academic process at my home faculty. I contemplated the introduction of changes in two spheres: first, a change in teaching methodology, and second, a change in the content of courses, primarily through enriching them with ample comparative materials and an overview of international developments. Both of these endeavors proved to be difficult tasks, however, since anyone seeking to teach in Ukraine in line with modern academic standards is virtually doomed to be in constant conflict with hidden "dragons" of the past, born and brought up by the old Soviet system of legal education, and now apparently inadequate both in terms of quality of skills gained and the level of professional integrity instilled. Despite the fact that these "dragons" have been extensively written about, identified, and fought with, they are still present in the minds of legal educators, who are simply unable to see how the whole process can function otherwise.

II. "Dragons" of Teaching Law in Ukraine

It has been said about the reform of legal education in the post-Soviet countries that,

> [T]he question is whether post-Soviet lawyers, historically subject to outside control and external standards, can establish and maintain their own standards of behavior and professionalism. ... Ultimately, the greatest challenge facing post-Soviet society is the creation of a new, or perhaps a legal consciousness on the part of the entire population, lawyers and laypersons, citizens and leaders. Lawyers and law students now stand at a critical, historic juncture where they have the chance to generate and cultivate a new legal and political culture—one with Russian (or Ukrainian), not alien, roots.[4]

Indeed, junior faculty—especially those with western educational backgrounds—immediately face the difficult challenge of thoroughly reviewing the whole approach to legal education. That approach has long been under the influence of ideological restraints and bounded by the perception of the legal profession as a "necessary bourgeois holdover"[5] doomed by the path of history to gradually disappear as a profession of obvious obsolescence.

The task a returning scholar faced was difficult: certain criteria of a "new age" of the legal profession had to be set, and standards of professional responsibility needed to be fixed and enforced. Anyone trying to shake the foundations of approaches to training lawyers, however, is likely to face varying levels of opposition from the more conservative senior faculty used to traditional forms

4 Lisa A. Granik, *Legal Education in Post-Soviet Russia and Ukraine*, 72 Or. L. Rev. 963, 974 (1993).

5 *Id.* at 963.

of teaching and interaction with students. As one commentator noted about post-Soviet law professors' attitudes toward innovative techniques in teaching, most teachers are not that negative but are strongly attached to the traditional teaching methods. Only a very few are advocates of a more interactive and creative teaching method that would develop the skills involved in "thinking like a lawyer."[6]

A. The System of Obsolescence

Generally, universities still adhere to the old-fashioned format of teaching, with a primary focus not on training and developing critical thinking and personal qualities of students, but rather on preparing an average level specialist provided with a certain minimum command of legal knowledge and skills which are to be later developed in legal practice. Traditionally, Ukrainian universities rely on in-class training[7] while students are also assigned specific work to be done at home. Students have on average about 15–18 classes a week with about seven or eight mandatory courses being taught each semester. Attendance is compulsory and is checked on a regular basis by the dean's office staff. As one U.S. observer noted in 1998, however, "this is a heavy concentration of time, but it is not time particularly well spent."[8] And we should confess that not much has changed since that time.

The academic process under such an approach is based on the transcription and memorization of information given during lectures, to be reproduced at

6 Peter J. Sahlas and Carl Chastenay, *Russian Legal Education: Post-Communist Stagnation or Revival?*, 48 J. Legal Educ. 194, 209 (1998).

7 This narrow, rather technical, practice-oriented approach seems to be a hallmark of any immature legal education system and always precedes value-based training aimed at developing a comprehensive understanding of the concepts of justice and fairness as well as critical thinking. A good example of similar problems existing in legal education of Bangladesh, which is currently undergoing reform, can be found in: Mohammad Monirul, *Reforming Legal Education in Bangladesh*, 55 J. Legal Educ. 560 (2006): "Legal education has a number of theoretical and practical aims, not all of which are pursued simultaneously. If you ask any law student in Bangladesh about the objectives of legal education, s/he will simply answer that legal education should make the students conversant with substantive and procedural law. Should we be confined to so narrow a space or should we look at the issue from a broader point of view?

"Until recently, legal education in Bangladesh was not perceived as an educational and intellectual pursuit but only as a means of imparting certain principles and provisions of law to enable students upon graduation to become juniors to 'senior lawyers.' But law is much more than principles and provisions—it deals with justice, equity, and fairness as well as the values about which societies organize themselves through orderly institutions. Law is also intertwined with economy, development, business, and the emerging global order. We must see that the objectives of legal education from a broader perspective." (*Id.* at 561, footnotes omitted.)

8 Jeremy T. Harrison, *Legal Education in an Eastern European Law School*, 7 Int'l L. & Prac. 263, 265 (1998).

seminars and ultimately at the final exam, traditionally taken in the form of an oral interview.[9] The Socratic method of instruction so common in U.S. law schools[10] is almost completely unknown in Ukraine. The foundations of the Ukrainian system are lectures during which a professor instructs students on essential issues of a course, juxtaposing theory and law (mainly referring to the provisions of codes, statutes, and supplementary legislation) and trying to cover as many facts and explain as many legal rules as possible.[11] During lectures, students write down concise notes of what is being said from the lectern. Their role in the learning process is usually very passive and at best is limited to occasionally interrupting an instructor to ask a question. While most professors readily answer questions from the class, some of them too obviously frown at such students and generally discourage any attempts at feedback from those being instructed.

Lectures are followed by seminars (comparable to tutorials commonly used in British universities[12]) during which an instructor asks questions and students answer them, relying on the text of the lecture notes, and analyzing hypothetical problems by looking at statutory law (usually codes and some supplementary texts). The principal student material for a course therefore is handwritten lecture notes (a "konspekt"), the quality of which heavily depends on speed and legibility of handwriting of every particular student and is usually written by a few students in the academic group while others simply copy the notes afterwards.

The best students under this system have always been considered those who remember the maximum amount of formalized information despite the fact that they might not understand very well how it applies to practical situations.

9 For analysis of the efficiency of an oral examination as used in Russian law faculties, see John M. Burman, *Oral Examinations as a Method of Evaluating Law Students*, 51 J. Legal Educ. 130 (2001).

10 James R.P. Ogloff, David R. Lyon, Kein S. Douglas and V. Gordon Rose, *More than "Learning to Think Like a Lawyer": The Empirical Research on Legal Education*, 34 Creighton L. Rev. 73, 106–07 (2000).

11 Lecturing seems to have universally been a primary teaching technique of the past. As one American author suggests about development of U.S. legal education, "[i]nitially, classroom teaching of the law was accomplished by lecturing the students about existing law. This teaching technique remains part of the law school teaching and learning environment today. Later, various interactive verbal techniques (through which the professor and student engage in a dialogue about the law using established legal reasoning elements and techniques), including principally Socratic questioning and other techniques centering around the case method, were added to (and, in some cases, supplanted) the lecture method, enabling students to develop oral advocacy and communication skills and engage in real-time legal reasoning and analysis in the classroom." (Joan MacLeod Heminway, *Caught in (or on) the Web: A Review of Course Management Systems for Legal Education*, 16 Alb. L.J. Sci. & Tech. 265, 271–72 (2006), footnotes omitted).

12 Although with a noticeable difference: usually British university tutorials involve a group of 7–15 students, while in Ukraine seminar groups often reach as many as 30 students.

With such an approach, the educator's primary responsibilities are preparing the outline of the core materials (essentially, the main rules of relevant statutes) and presenting it in a condensed form during the limited time for the lecture.[13] As laws become more complex and controversial, however, the outline given at the lectures becomes increasingly more concise and students are expected to find the skipped or referenced material by themselves.

The main focus of legal education remains on studying black letter law primarily as it is reflected in codes, statutes, regulations, rules, and procedural instructions, which creates a huge amount of extremely technical information. Very rarely, an instructor may make reference to foreign laws and experiences to compare them to Ukrainian approaches. Only minor, if any, attention is paid to case law (with the exception, probably, of EC law and human rights law courses built primarily on studying case law of the European Court of Justice and the European Court of Human Rights respectively). If case law is mentioned, usually only a short overview is provided without any recourse to the facts and factors which influenced the judgment or comparison to other judgments involving similar circumstances.[14] In fact, such an approach, apart from being very impractical, is no longer based on positive law, because case law now is a proper source of law in Ukraine.[15]

B. "An Inert Bunch"

Under the U.S. system of legal education, the degree in law always follows undergraduate education, an approach that is viewed as a "strong point of the

13 Normally a class lasts for 80 minutes, but it is a well-established tradition among Ukrainian faculty to be seven to ten minutes late for the class (the so-called "smoking grace period," letting students finish a cigarette and return to the classroom). At the same time, under an old customary student rule, if a professor is more than 15 minutes late for a class, students do not have to wait any longer and may leave the room.

14 For the reflections on the unsuccessful efforts of a U.S. visiting lecturer to urge Russian law students to study judicial decisions, see Harrison, *supra* note 8, at 270–71.

15 See, for example, Art. 17 of "On Enforcement of Judgments and Application of Practice of the European Court of Human Rights" February 23, 2006 No. 3477-IV, which expressly obliges Ukrainian courts in disposing of cases to apply the judicial practice of the European Court of Human Rights "as a source of law," regardless of the fact that the applicable judgment may not be available in the Ukrainian or Russian languages understood by a judge. Moreover, Ukrainian courts of higher jurisdiction have gradually assumed more law-creating authority. For example, according to Art. 111 of the Code of Commercial Litigation Procedure, non-uniformity of decisions of the Higher Commercial Court with decisions of the Supreme Court of Ukraine in similar cases is grounds for cassational review by the Supreme Court of Ukraine. Finally, the decisions of the Constitutional Court of Ukraine giving official interpretation of Constitutional or statutory provisions bind not only parties to the specific dispute but also everyone who will invoke the interpreted rule in the future. Thus, such decisions of the Constitutional Court have an obvious norm-creating character.

American educational system,"[16] and that allows students "to develop broad intellectual capacities in general undergraduate coursework and refine that development via 'majors' or 'concentrations'" in ways that many of their non-American counterparts—who must squeeze liberal and professional training into an undergraduate legal education—may not do.[17] In Ukraine, anyone can apply to a law school (a law faculty) immediately after secondary school. This means that the average age of a typical first-year law student is around 17–18. This is probably one of the main reasons why it is not the students themselves but rather the parents who choose a legal career for the student, sometimes taking account of the degree of prestige attached by society to the legal profession, or with the intention of continuing family traditions and having their children follow in their footsteps as lawyers.[18] Unfortunately, quite often the real aspirations of students are disregarded and remain dormant until several years after graduation, when a lawyer ultimately realizes that he or she has chosen the wrong profession.

Ukrainian students participate in an academic process mostly passively. They are not accustomed to active and responsible participation in an interactive process of learning and are scared by the very idea of cooperating with an instructor. Relations between students and teachers (except probably junior faculty) are much more formal than those in typical U.S. law schools.[19] A Ukrainian student's approach to the educational process can be illustrated by two well-known student proverbs: "Have fun and enjoy life between the finals sessions" and "Cram all night long, pass in the morning, and forget by the evening."

Students are normally discouraged from going beyond the outline and finding extra information on the subject because, as a rule, it is not required for passing a final test and teachers themselves are often not aware of such information. No recourse to the main trends in the development of legal institutions is made, simply because no time is allocated for that. Very often a final test boils down to checking how well students remember the material given at lectures, so an

---

16 Kara Abramson, *"Art for a Better Life": A New Image of American Legal Education*, 2006 B.Y.U. Educ. & L.J. 227, 239 (2006).

17 *Id.*

18 As surveys indicate, in the U.S. the reasons for entering law school may be similar but certainly not identical: "Having a father who was a lawyer, and aspiring to become a lawyer, were the two student entry characteristics which directly influenced whether the student went on to become a lawyer, while race, socioeconomic status, high school achievement, and leadership experiences had little or no direct influence." (Ogloff et al., *supra* note 10, at 83.)

19 Some foreign visitors (especially coming from the United States) are surprised by Ukrainian students standing up to greet an instructor entering a classroom. This practice clearly comes from the secondary school where it has been common for decades. At the same time, Ukrainian students, after getting back to their seats, feel it absolutely appropriate to speak, send text messages, play with their phones during the class.

interview is limited to questions based on the lecture notes (the *konspekt*).[20] As a result, some students who never bother to attend a class or take notes during lectures successfully pass exams after photocopying the notes and reading them the night before the exam.[21]

Another major problem mentioned by western scholars teaching at Ukrainian universities is the absence of any reasonable rules of academic integrity.[22] Unlike U.S. law schools, where integrity policies are regarded by and large as an ethical foundation of legal education,[23] in Ukraine, cheating and plagiarism are common among students and are generally tolerated or at least not severely punished by the university administration. The reason for this is not an "inherent rottenness" of Ukrainian students, but rather a matter of culture. Unlike U.S. law students, who are trained in a highly competitive atmosphere and are ranked according to their academic performance,[24] Ukrainian law students come with secondary school background where they have experienced continual confrontation with teaching staff and tend to be convinced that helping one's classmate against the "evil" faculty member is something to be proud of. As a result, they tend to treat giving notes to a classmate at the exam or helping him answer a question as a part of caring for their neighbor. Students are usually not ranked or, if they are, ranking does not have any impact on their future careers. Involvement of a particular student in cheating is considered to be a sign of courage and bravery by the student body. The university administration often turns a blind eye to such behavior, treating it as a minor violation and not worthy of any serious countermeasures.[25]

---

20 The key importance of the lecture notes (the *konspekt*) for gaining a good grade at a final exam is well illustrated by an old Soviet student joke about two men who decided to find the smartest student in the world. They approached the brightest students from the United States, France, and Germany, one by one and asked them how much time they needed to study Chinese from scratch to the level sufficient to pass a university-level exam. Every time the investigators were given roughly similar answers: "A year," or "ten months." When the investigators came to a Soviet university they could not find anyone in the corridors but a student (obviously not a top-notch one) smoking in the restroom. When he was asked the question about a Chinese language exam, he replied: "Do you guys have a course *konspekt*?" "Yes, indeed!" "Well pals, let me finish my cigarette, and then I'll go and take the test."

21 Another Soviet-time student joke: to successfully pass a final exam a student has to know at least three things: the name of the course, the name of the professor and the color of the course materials cover.

22 *See, e.g.*, George A. Critchlow, *Teaching Law in Transylvania: Notes on Romanian Legal Education*, 44 J. Legal Educ. 157, 164–65 (1994); Burman, *supra* note 9, at 134.

23 Graham Zellick, *The Ethical Law School*, 36 Ind. L. Rev. 747, 751 (2003).

24 As commentators suggest, "law school ranking consistently has the greatest influence over the relative ease or difficulty law students will face entering the workplace." (Ogloff et al., *supra* note 10, at 202.)

25 With, however, one notable exception: official document forgery. Several students have been expelled from the Economics and Law Faculty for forging instructors' signatures

C. Course Materials, Resources and Facilities

One of the most troubling legacies of the Soviet era is the poor physical resources and facilities in Ukrainian law faculties. Library resources are usually scarce and mostly limited to outdated books and basic concise course materials. It is rather uncommon for a lecturer to provide students with their own essential reading materials and core selected laws. One of the main reasons for such a miserable state is underfunding. Universities simply lack the funds to regularly acquire even new Ukrainian books, let alone books from foreign sources, which are usually considerably more expensive. As a result, teachers buys books of professional interest using their own money. This creates numerous, small, "private" libraries and collections of books and law journals maintained in professors' offices, with limited or no access by students. Often students and professors have only limited access to the internet and computer-based resources.

D. Teaching as an Intellectual Rush

Salaries paid to Ukrainian faculty are usually not competitive when compared to compensation available in the private sector. At the same time, the workload of an average teacher sometimes grows to be extreme. While full-time law school teachers normally have about seven or eight classes a week (and sometimes as many as 20 classes a week), very often they are supposed to teach several courses at the same time virtually "from scratch," so the whole process of preparation can become a kind of an "intellectual rush." Taking into consideration that proper preparation for one in-class hour usually requires eight to ten hours of home preparation and library research, the workload of a Ukrainian professor appears truly frightening to his foreign counterparts, allowing no time at all for scholarship. As a result, the amount of scholarly work, writing, and research produced by professors is very limited and rather superficial.

III. Changes Undertaken

A. Teaching Methodologies

The introduction of active methods of teaching is designed to shift the main emphasis of legal education from the outdated "instruct and memorize" approach to a training system essentially based upon the active participation of every student. This requires not only changing standards and guidelines, but more fundamentally reforming the very idea of legal education. We needed to put massive pressure on the university administration and to convince students that they should be much

in their academic performance record booklets.

more deeply involved in the process of learning and gaining new knowledge aimed at developing critical thinking skills.

For those of us interested in change, it was clear that we needed not just knowledgeable attorneys skillful in the deft manipulations of the law, but well-educated and socially responsible lawyers ready to play an important role in the community and ready to provide a framework for our civil society. Such efforts were encouraged by the Civic Education Project (now the Higher Education Support Program (HESP)), which provided support of Western-trained alumni who joined universities upon their return to their home countries.

When I returned to Ukraine, I realized that the whole format of teaching had to be reshuffled. I decided it would be more productive to have essential course texts and reading materials published and distributed to students for study before attending a lecture, so that we could change the classroom experience from instructing students to discussing with students the most problematic issues and trying to work out possible solutions. This was an effort to approach the Socratic method of teaching. I tried to devote seminars not to asking questions based on lecture notes, but rather to solving hypothetical problems based on real cases adjudicated by Ukrainian or foreign courts. These problems would not have an easy solution and would require not just the application of black-letter law, but also discussion of theory and interpretation as well as, ideally, involvement of social and economic arguments (policy reasoning).

In terms of relevant sources, I sought to introduce a case study method. I placed much stronger emphasis on analyzing cases from courts of different jurisdictions, including cases of first instance. At the same time, it became apparent that there was a problem of general ignorance among Ukrainian students and faculty of how a case should be read, analyzed, and applied to similar circumstances. We had to organize a workshop for junior faculty on the development of case analysis skills and then repeat it several times for students. The workshop was based on analyzing the high profile Sovtransauto-Holding case decided by the European Court of Human Rights,[26] which had a major impact on the whole Ukrainian legal system.

I would love to assign to students more cases adjudicated by foreign courts as they sometimes provide much more elaborate legal analysis. Such case law, however, is rarely available in a Ukranian translation and the foreign language skills of most students remain rather inadequate.

B. Curriculum Development and Course Design

Integration of a global element into the content of law courses, emphasizing the importance of comparative law and private and public international law, plays

26 Sovtransavto Holding v. Ukraine, no. 48553/99, ECHR 2002-VII.

a major role in the internationalization of legal education.[27] One of the main focuses of the International and European Law Centre (IELC) at Donetsk National University has been providing assistance in comparative and international law research. A number of new courses on comparative subjects have been developed and introduced based primarily on the resources provided by the IELC, which was established in cooperation with the University of Pittsburgh School of Law through U.S. State Department support. These courses include comparative contract law, comparative commercial law, international sale of goods law (CISG law), international arbitration law, and secured transactions, among others. The latter course was developed in a comparative format with assistance from the Curriculum Development Competition administered by the Curriculum Resource Center of the Central European University in Budapest, Hungary.[28]

Normally, every instructor is encouraged to develop his or her own course of specialization consistent with the instructor's academic interests. The number of comparative and/or international law-oriented courses has grown steadily. The best format for these courses may be as electives chosen by students truly interested in learning new material who find it necessary for their future careers. This often results in a group of 10–25 students. However, the faculty administration often makes these courses mandatory, with up to eight academic groups of 25–30, with rather indifferent students in each; an approach that significantly undermines the course's value.

C. Integrity Policies

In December 2006, I conducted an anonymous student survey on cheating practices among law students of the Economics and Law Faculty at Donetsk National University in the form of a multiple choice questionnaire. I surveyed a total of 90 students in their fourth and fifth years of study (Bachelor's and Master's students respectively). All of them were asked a variety of questions with respect to their understanding of the concept of plagiarism,[29] how it affects the academic process, the reasons students might be involved into plagiarism, their personal experience and the main reasons for personal involvement.

The majority of Donetsk University students (72 percent) believed that the goal of higher legal education is training an expert knowledgeable in law and capable of successfully working in practice and effectively resolving client's problems. Only 12 percent chose as a goal, "training of an expert mindful of his

27 Rennard Strickland and Philip H. Knight, *Legal Education in the Twenty-First Century*, 80 Or. L. Rev. 1449, 1454 (2001).

28 http://www.ceu.hu/crc/.

29 In particular, the survey form included such examples as (1) copying a portion of a text from a book into your paper without indicating the true author; (2) copying a large portion of a text (several pages or a chapter) into your paper with indication of the true author; and (3) borrowing information from the internet without indicating its source.

social responsibility and capable of setting an example of integrity and propriety." Moreover, 37 percent believed that borrowing another's ideas without indicating the real authorship is a practice generally incorrect but acceptable due to its wide prevalence; more than a quarter of students (28 percent) viewed it as a totally unacceptable practice constituting an academic offence (plagiarism), while 15 percent of students admitted that it is a usual practice in minimizing a student's workload. For 11 percent this was a normal method for conducting research, and 8 percent "never thought about it."

The majority of students (64 percent) believed that copying a portion of a text from a book into an academic paper or a writing assignment without indicating the true author was plagiarism, while 22 percent disagreed, and 12 percent were "not sure." At the same time, the majority (66 percent) did not view copying a large portion of a text (from several pages to a whole chapter) into their own paper without indicating the true author as plagiarism. Many students (33 percent) did not see any problem with copying and pasting a text from the internet into their papers without indicating a full web link to the internet resource they used. While 59 percent did not believe it was acceptable to borrow (download) a complete paper from the internet, 26 percent thought it was acceptable. Similarly, 59 percent believed it was wrong to order (buy) a complete paper from another person, while 28 percent saw no problem with that practice.

Answers about personal involvement of students in plagiarism appeared somewhat confused. More that half of the students surveyed (52 percent) admitted they had occasionally been involved in plagiarism in situations when they were unable to complete a paper due to extenuating circumstances. Sixteen percent "never plagiarize as a matter of principle," 12 percent got involved in plagiarism because "everyone does it," 10 percent were "not sure," but might commit plagiarism at some point, and 6 percent admitted to regularly plagiarizing and saw no problem in their actions. Surprisingly, not a single student (0 percent) answered that he or she avoided plagiarism out of fear of possible sanctions from the Faculty administration.

Students generally disagreed about the reasons why plagiarism was so prevalent among the Ukrainian student community. Twenty-three percent answered that the main reason is the lack of research skills; 23 percent believed it to be a forced measure to successfully pass courses which are unnecessary (mainly non-law related) and/or boring; 15 percent thought plagiarism is a completely normal phenomenon in any student community; 14 percent believed that plagiarism is wide spread due to indifference of the administration/professors and lack of any serious discipline; 12 percent cited a special "Ukrainian mentality" as a primary reason for plagiarism; and 9 percent complained about the unavailability of resources for student research.

Most students did not believe in the effectiveness of harsh measures to combat plagiarism. Only 9 percent thought the administration should introduce severe punishment for plagiarism as soon as possible, while 22 percent viewed the most appropriate time for the introduction of such measures to be several years in the future. The remainder of the students were very reluctant or had no clear opinion about such measures. Finally, most students, having admitted their occasional involvement in plagiarism, answered that they do so when they obviously lack time for research due to an excessive workload (30 percent), or they do so only with respect to "unimportant," non-law courses (21 percent).

Generally speaking, the survey indicated that only a few students are consciously involved in plagiarism because they blatantly disregard academic rules. The majority indicated that they find themselves forced into plagiarism because of poor research resources and facilities, excessively burdensome and time-consuming assignments, and limited research skills. Of course, work is necessary to insure the development of integrity rules and policies, and to see that they become one of the top University priorities. One of the prospective steps of essential importance is the development of a code of ethical conduct for students. Such a code should serve three general functions: aspirational, educational, and regulatory,[30] and should inspire the student community to cooperate with the administration as well as take their own measures in order to ultimately bring cheating practices to an end.

D. Institutional Changes

Of course, most of the effort behind reform would be in vain if it were not for the institutional changes undertaken at the Economics and Law Faculty (ELC) at Donetsk National University. The principal such development has been the establishment of the International and European Law Centre (IELC). The IELC was founded in January 2003 as part of a long-term academic linkage between the ELC and the University of Pittsburgh School of Law funded through the grant of the U.S. State Department. The IELC was created and currently operates as a structural subdivision of the Economics and Law Faculty (a center). The mission of the IELC is defined as providing support and co-ordination of legal research in the fields of international, European Community, comparative, and human rights law; promoting international exchange and degree programs; assisting in the introduction of state-of-the-art teaching methodologies; and maintaining links with law schools in Ukraine and abroad.

The IELC operates primarily as a resource center offering faculty, post-graduates, and law students wide opportunities in high-quality legal research as well as providing them with technical support and assistance in searching and applying for degree, non-degree, and professional internship programs abroad. Through IELC assistance, a number of ELF alumni received their LL.M degrees at American, British, German, and Dutch law schools. The IELC maintains an outstanding library of law books, periodicals, CD-ROM materials, and videotapes. Library resources were purchased through the partnership program with University

30 Steven K. Berenson, *What Should Law School Student Conduct Codes Do?*, 38 Akron L. Rev. 803, 810–16 (2005).

of Pittsburgh, and funds were allocated by the Civic Education Project and the Curriculum Resource Center, along with donations by the Human Rights Law Centre of the University of Nottingham and the British Council.

Since its foundation, the IELC has organized and conducted a number of research and academic events. These have included seminars on active methods of teaching, the National Student Conference on Civil Law (in cooperation with the Civil Education Project), two summer schools on international business law, an International Symposium on Law Practice Management (jointly with the University of Pittsburgh School of Law), a summer school on information technology law (in cooperation with Queen Mary College, University of London), an Introductory Comparative Law course (in cooperation with the University of Iowa College of Law), and the Fall School on International Business and Comparative Law (through the assistance of the Center for International Legal Studies (in Salzburg, Austria).[31]

ELF students are involved in extra-curricular activities arranged by the IELC, including classes by visiting foreign lecturers, and summer-school classes. These students considerably enhance their chances of successful professional employment or nomination for a scholarship if they choose to continue their education abroad. The IELC coordinates pre-selection and training of students for participation in international moot court competitions; assists legal clinics, NGOs, public institutions, and practitioners; distributes information on international, EC, and foreign law, and supports public presentations.

The IELC serves as a principal ELF tool for establishing and maintaining partnership relations with foreign educational and academic institutions. The academic partnership project between the University of Pittsburgh School of Law and the ELF, which from the ELF part was coordinated by the IELC, was acknowledged in 2004 by the U.S. Embassy as the most successful in Ukraine. Today, the Faculty, largely through IELC efforts, maintains academic links with Pitt Law and the University of Iowa in the U.S., the University of Regensburg in Germany, Amsterdam University in the Netherlands, Central European University in Hungary, Durham and Nottingham universities in Britain, and the University of Athens in Greece.

My particular observation is that since the Centre was established, the quality of student and post-graduate research papers has substantially improved. According to recently approved standards of academic research adopted at the Economics and Law Faculty, a graduation thesis qualifying for the highest grade should include comparative analysis of relevant laws and doctrines from at least five legal systems of the world (with Russia, Germany, France, the United States,

31 Two U.S. practicing attorneys—Mr. Reeder Fox from Duane Morris, LLP, and Mrs. Nancy McCaslin from McCaslin and McCaslin law firm were brought to Donetsk. Mr. Fox gave lectures on "Democracy and Rule of Law in the USA" and "Mediation, Arbitration and Alternative Dispute Resolution"; Mrs. Nancy McCaslin taught courses "Legal Business Terminology" and "International Business Transactions."

and England being the most popular), and the IELC's library is a primary resource for such research.

E. Moot Court Competitions

One of the best and most valuable challenges law students can be exposed to is a moot court competition. The Economics and Law Faculty participated for the first time in an international law moot court competition in 1995 (the Central and East European EC Law Moot Court Competition), and after that has regularly sent teams to a number of international moots. These include the Philip C. Jessup International Law Moot Court Competition, the Benjamin F. Telders International Law Competition, and the Central and East-European EC Law Moot Court Competition. In 2001, with initial funding from Pitt Law, the ELF started participating in the Willem C. Vis International Commercial Arbitration Moot. This experience brought something new and truly international to the lives of those students who participated, and had a fundamental impact on their minds. Many of them became committed to an international legal career, and after graduation joined international law firms based primarily in Kyiv or went abroad to pursue LL.M. degrees.

The initial successes of EFL moot teams[32] gradually faded as the number of competing universities grew. Poor results called for radical measures. In 2002, somebody came up with an idea for organizing a moot court club, a group of students coordinated by a senior student who had participated in international moot competitions. As a result, the ELF teams performance started improving (in spring 2005, one ELF team received an award for best written memorials at the Jessup Competition, while another one was awarded a plaque for the best oral arguments at the Telders Competition). Some problems still remained, the largest being an inadequate initial command of English by Ukranian law students, which is simply impossible to significantly improve within the several months of preparation allocated for a moot competition.[33] Another problem which significantly hampers the mooting skills of students is the lack of legal writing courses resembling those taught in any U.S. law school and considered essential to legal education.[34]

---

32 In 1996, the ELF team won the national round of the Jessup International Moot Competition and competed at the international rounds in Washington D.C. (the USA) while the next year, in 1997, the ELF team ranked first at the national round of the Benjamin Telders Moot Court Competitions and proceeded to the international round held in The Hague (the Netherlands).

33 Oddly enough, the ELF curriculum drawn in compliance with the Ministry of Science and Education model curriculum for law faculties allocates eight semesters for physical training and only three semesters for studying foreign languages.

34 Kristen Konrad Robbins, *Philosophy v. Rhetoric in Legal Education: Understanding the Schism between Doctrinal and Legal Writing Faculty*, 3 J. Ass'n Legal Writing Directors 108, 109 (2006).

As a result of these developments, we decided to nurture a new generation of "mooties" by working with students from their very first year at the Faculty. In fall 2005, for the first time in Ukraine, we introduced a moot court clinic where students are taught the basics of international legal research, English language legal reasoning, case analysis, use of available internet and other resources, writing memoranda, using different standards of citations, academic integrity policies, and oral presentation training before a simulated panel of judges.[35] Possibly due to such measures, in 2006 the ELF team finally, after a ten-year gap, won the national round of the Jessup International Moot Competition and went to Washington D.C. to represent Ukraine at the international round. Every September, a pre-selection round is organized by the IELC to choose the students who will represent Donetsk National University in national and international rounds of moot court competitions. About six to eight students out of 15–25 participants are selected on the basis of their skills (knowledge of the subject, ability to present, responsiveness to judges' questions, and command of English). Those participants who were not selected for the teams are invited to improve their mooting skills by participating in the moot court clinic.

We have also managed to transpose our international experience to the process of preparation for national law competitions. In October 2006, an ELF team won the National Competition in Civil Law and Procedure. I prepared the competitors by using techniques usually engaged in preparation for international moot court competitions, such as case analysis and policy reasoning.[36]

IV. Conclusions

My personal experience of study abroad at the University of Pittsburgh School of Law LL.M. program has proven to be extremely helpful in changing my attitude toward studying law and serving as a model for reforms I have advocated at my home institution. Ultimately, what we struggle for is not a complete demolition of all pre-existing values and traditions, but rather departure from those post-Soviet legacies that have proven obviously outdated and now hamper the development

---

35 Some commentators critique training through moot competitions as being too unrealistic and having nothing in common with a live litigation on behalf of a real client due to overemphasis of oral arguments and advocacy skills over brief-writing (see for example: Alex Kozinski, *In Praise of Moot Court—Not!*, 97 Colum. L. Rev. 178 (1997)). With this criticism in mind, we primarily train team members and clinic participants to write their memoranda, since this skill has proven to be essential for law students looking for an international career.

36 Notably, these techniques appear to have been too innovative for some judges. When providing feedback to participants, one member of the moot board, a law professor from Lviv University, expressed his concern about the Donetsk team relying on the European Court of Human Rights jurisprudence as a proper source of law (despite the fact it already *was* a proper source of law at the time of competition—see *supra*, note 13).

of legal education. Existing impediments can be remedied by increasing the focus on developing critical thinking skills and the ability to learn instead of trying to forcibly stuff the students' minds with abundant information that we believe is necessary for their future career. New-generation lawyers should certainly be highly moral, creative, and independent-thinking persons, understanding their social responsibility and ready to make their own professional choices. The main tool for such experts is a state-of-the-art legal education.

There is still a lot of work to be done. Ukranian universities desperately need new courses and re-training programs on legal ethics, professional responsibility and integrity, comparative analysis, and legal writing. We continue to lose our most promising junior faculty to law practice and experience considerable problems with funding. Law schools remain limited in terms of facilities and library resources. Most of the time, it seems we are working for free. But we retain our enthusiasm and strong commitment to our profession. Despite the existing problems and the drain of qualified personnel, we still do our best to keep up-to-date with the modern trends in higher education and seek to train competitive law students who later become excellent lawyers and bright researchers. Our alumni are successful in law practice and academia, business and NGO activities. The changes are visible and are underway; however, overnight fundamental reforms of a system built over decades and minds molded by a now extinct ideology are simply impossible. These endeavors need further support and call for encouragement and cooperation from the part of the government, society, and other universities, both in Ukraine and abroad.

Chapter 6

The Export of American Legal Education and Its Impact in Serbia

Milena Đorđević[1]

> The business of legal education is not merely to teach law, or to make lawyers, it is "to teach law in the grand manner, and to make great lawyers."[2]

After a decade of declining economic activity, sanctions, and a mismanaged macroeconomic policy; along with technological stagnation, loss of traditional markets, and a complete absence of foreign investment; and in the wake of democratic transformation of the then Federal Republic of Yugoslavia in October, 2000; Serbia embarked upon a complex process to reform its political, economic, and legal systems. In doing so, it sought to establish an open economic system based on a private sector, free markets, transparency, and the rule of law.[3] Significant economic policy changes were launched addressing privatization and foreign trade. Changes within the higher education system, and more specifically in legal education, were a part of the overall reform.

In this chapter I will attempt to shed some light on the recent progress achieved through educational reform in Serbia and how my education in the U.S. had an impact on some of the developments on both the Faculty of Law at the University of Belgrade and the implementation of the rule of law in Serbia. I will first outline the Serbian legal framework. Secondly, I will contrast the major differences between the Serbian and American models of legal education. Thirdly, I will point out the recent changes in the University of Belgrade Faculty of Law curriculum.

---

1 Lecturer in International Commercial Law, University of Belgrade Faculty of Law; LL.M. 2002 (*Magna Cum Laude*, University of Pittsburgh School of Law); LL.B. 2000 (University of Belgrade Faculty of Law).

2 Michael I. Swygert, *Striving to Make Great Lawyers—Citizenship and Moral Responsibility: A Jurisprudence for Law Teaching*, 30 B.C. L. Rev. 803 (1989), quoting Oliver Wendell Holmes, *The Use of Law Schools*, *in* Collected Legal Papers 37, 47–48 (1920).

3 On the difficulties that Serbia faced as of 2000 in establishing the rule of law *see* Vojislav Kostunica, *Most Dangerous Path: Establishing the Rule of Law in Serbia*, Harv. Int'l Rev. Fall, 2003; Boris Begović and Dragor Hiber, *EU Democratic Rule of Law Promotion: The Case of Serbia* (Center on Democracy, Development and the Rule of Law, 2006), *available at* http://cddrl.stanford.edu/publications/eu_democratic_rule_of_law_promotion_the_case_of_serbia/.

Finally, I will demonstrate the impact my own legal education in the U.S. has had on legal developments in Serbia.

I. Serbian Legal Education

The Law on Higher Education (LHE) regulates the system of higher education in Serbia, including conditions and manners of conducting the activity of higher education, financing, and other relevant issues.[4] The LHE grants the right to higher education to all persons who have previously obtained primary and secondary education, notwithstanding their race, skin color, sex, sexual orientation, ethnic or national origin, language, religion, political orientation, status acquired by birth, or property status.[5] While the LHE regulates the general framework for higher education, individual academic faculties are given specific authority to determine the criteria for qualification of candidates for enrollment.

Legal education in Serbia is part of the higher education system. There are currently five state law faculties in Serbia,[6] and a number of private law faculties. The oldest amongst them is the University of Belgrade Faculty of Law, which recently celebrated the 165th anniversary of its founding. All law faculties in Serbia must comply with the general requirements of the LHE, and are subject to inspection and supervision by the National Council for Higher Education. However, subject to the accreditation and quality assurance procedures, they have significant freedom to design the contents of the legal curricula they offer. Still, for some time there has not been much difference between the overall systems of legal education amongst different law faculties in Serbia.[7] All have curricula designed to provide legal training based on positive law, legal history, and legal philosophy.

II. American vs. Serbian Legal Education

A comparison of the American and Serbian systems of legal education reveals numerous differences. These include, inter alia, contrasts in: admissions policy,

4 *Law on Higher Education*, Official Gazette of the Republic of Serbia, No. 76/2005 (LHE).

5 *Id.* Art. 8.

6 Beograd, Nis, Kragujevac, Novi Sad, and Pristina.

7 Modern private law faculties offer more specialized study programs in business law, insurance law, international law, etc. However, this may lead to their graduates being ineligible for the bar exam under the current Law on Bar Exams.

financing, length of studies, curriculum, course materials, exam and grading policy, teaching methods, and professors' profiles.[8]

A. Admissions Policy

Unlike American students, Serbian law students may begin legal studies without undergraduate degrees and most students apply to universities directly after completing high school. In Serbia, law school applicants are evaluated according to the scores achieved on their admissions test and their high school grades. Law schools emphasize the evaluation of a student's knowledge gained during his or her prior education, primarily in history and literature, as well as in general culture. Law school admissions examinations in Serbia do not necessarily measure a student's ability to be analytical and "think like a lawyer." Instead, the focus is on assessing their current knowledge and willingness to learn.

Unlike the educational system in the United States, standardized testing is not a common method of examination in Serbia. Tests like the GMAT, GRE, or LSAT are examples of examination techniques almost never applied within the Serbian educational system. Multiple-choice testing with strict time constraints is not a trait of Serbian legal education. Admissions examinations, which are equivalent to the U.S. LSAT, are multiple question exams focused solely on testing the knowledge obtained and are successfully accomplished primarily through memorizing the necessary materials and not necessarily through the study of practice exams. Arguably, the admissions tests in Serbia are mainly focused on actual knowledge while in the United States prospective law students have to demonstrate the ability to recognize what the examiner is actually asking in order to be able to answer the question. The reasoning behind the different testing methods could be that in the civil law system knowledge of the law is as important in the practice of law as the understanding of the court's rationale when deciding a case is in the common law system. Therefore, standardized tests composed of problem questions test a student's ability to spot issues that repeat themselves throughout practice exams, just as a common law lawyer needs to identify rationales from prior cases and apply them in his or her argument.

---

8 On differences between various national systems of legal education and the American system, see John H. Merriman, *Legal Education There and Here: A Comparison*, 27 Stan. L. Rev. 859 (1975); Walter Gellhorn, *Impressions of Japanese Legal Training*, 58 Colum. L. Rev. 1239 (1958); John Henry Merriman, The Loneliness of the Comparative Lawyer (The Hague, 1990); Gregory S. Crespi, *Comparing United States and New Zealand Legal Education: Are U.S. Law Schools Too Good?*, 30 Vand. J. Transnat'l L. 31, 40–41 (1997); Juergen R. Ostertag, *Legal Education in Germany and the United States—A Structural Comparsion*, 26 Vand. J. Transnat'l L. 301 (1993); Sandra R. Klein, *Legal Education in the United States and England: A Comparative Analysis*, 13 Loy. L.A. Int'l & Comp. L.J. 601 (1991); Alexander J. Black, *Separated by A Common Law: American and Scottish Legal Education*, 4 Ind. Int'l & Comp. L. Rev. 15 (1993); Ross Nankivell, *Legal Education in Australia*, 72 Or. L. Rev. 983 (1993).

The law school application process in the Unites States is multifaceted and designed to select a student body with a commitment to excellence. In addition to the required score on the admissions exam and grades from previous education, prospective law students have to submit their personal statement, letters of recommendation, resumes, and appraisals from previously attended institutions.[9] Prospective American law students must demonstrate their personal interest in the study of law and describe their past achievements in many spheres of life. These descriptions demonstrate that the student is capable of overcoming the challenges that lie ahead in his or her future educational and professional life.

In Serbia, prospective students are not required to submit written illustrations of their prior experiences and abilities. The Serbian admissions system is primarily based on objective criteria rather than a subjective appreciation of the character and determination of each applicant. Arguably, admissions officials in U.S. law schools are looking for candidates with numerous talents, self-discipline, and motivation, while in Serbia, outstanding academic success is not a prerequisite.

It is worth noting that the prestige associated with the universities and law schools in the United States is not present in Serbia. There seems to be a certain level of discretion within the admissions procedure in the United States, where law schools may prioritize applicants from Ivy League schools or private schools, unlike in Serbia where such distinctions are not present. There are many more factors that are taken into consideration when deciding upon the application of a prospective law school student in the United States than in Serbia and it could be argued that, although the selection process is more rigorous, it is at the same time less merit-based.

Unlike their Serbian counterparts, law schools in the U.S. compete to attract outstanding candidates. Law schools are ranked and praised for the opportunities they offer to their students. In Serbia, students are chosen by the universities, but students do not have the opportunity to choose amongst different schools. This lack of choice is another reason why the admissions policy is more lenient in Serbia. There is no incentive for the law school in Belgrade to select a distinguished but smaller student body, improve the quality of teaching, and raise the level of academic competition amongst brilliant students, since Belgrade does not need to compete with other law schools for its students. This, in part, accounts for the policy of the Ministry of Education, which sets the number of entering students each year. In any event, the number of students entering each year is extremely high: about 2000.[10]

---

9 For more on the admissions procedure in the U.S., see Carl E. Schneider, *On American Legal Education*, 2 Asian-Pac. L. & Pol'y J. 18, 77 (2001); Crespi, *supra* note 8; Klein, *supra* note 8, at 601, 602–603.

10 The number of graduates, on the other hand, is much smaller. About 50 percent of all entering students abandon their legal studies along the way. The reasons may be different. As one example, it has been stated that in the years of civil wars raging across

A comparison of the admissions procedures in Serbia and in the U.S. is skewed by the simple fact that law school applicants in the U.S. are graduate students while in Serbia they are high school graduates. Moreover, very often, prospective law school students in the U.S. have prior work experience and are often times in their mid or late twenties. The admissions procedure in Serbia probably has more in common with the admissions procedure for undergraduate students in the U.S. Assessing the capabilities of 18-year-olds is a very different process than comparing applicants with much more life experience. Having said that, a student's personal profile, biographical information, and standardized testing are present in the undergraduate admissions process in the U.S. also, while, as already mentioned, Serbian schools do not consider this information.

As a result, U.S. law schools have a very different student body than do the Serbian law schools in terms of the students' age profile, academic background, and general level of maturity and experience. American law professors encounter more mature individuals who have already obtained their undergraduate degree and know how to learn in a university atmosphere, whereas Serbian professors, especially in the first year, have a heavy burden to teach students that the high school studying experience differs greatly from a university-level experience.

The difference in admissions policy truly reflects John Henry Merriman's opinion that the fundamental distinction between legal education in the United States and the European civil law countries lies in a distinction between democracy and meritocracy.[11] On the one hand, there is a desire to make higher education available to everyone without distinction, while on the other hand there is a desire to make the university a place in which academic merit is recognized and rewarded.

B. Financing

Many U.S. law schools are private rather than publicly-funded institutions, whereas most Serbian law schools are state universities. Law school tuition fees in the United States are much higher than those charged by Serbian law faculties.[12] Additionally, a high percentage of the student body at Serbian law faculties is given the right to free education and are exempted from paying tuition.[13] This contrast between law school tuition fees in the two countries has an impact on both the composition and the attitudes of the law school student body. Most students in the U.S. take out loans or spend their savings on tuition and living

---

the Balkans, many young man chose to enroll at the faculty in order to avoid or at least postpone military service.

11 MERRIMAN, *supra* note 8, at 53.

12 Tuition at the Serbian law faculties, both state and private was no higher than $1,600 per academic year in 2007.

13 At the Belgrade Faculty of Law, 700 out of 1,800 students in the first year are financed from the state budget and do not have to pay for tuition.

expenses required during their studies.[14] The consequence of high U.S. tuition is that U.S. law students have a more serious attitude towards their studies than their Serbian counterparts. Good grades are a prerequisite to getting better and higher paying jobs. Therefore, students who graduate highly indebted have an additional incentive to achieve good results throughout their studies. Another consequence is that the lack of financial responsibility for their studies creates a spirit of uninterest in the topics being covered in Serbian law schools and poses additional challenges to professors trying to educate a large class.

C. Duration

In the United States, the basic law school curriculum is a three-year course of study designed for students who already have an undergraduate degree, whereas in Serbia, the basic law school training is a four-year undergraduate degree. Law school graduates in the U.S. are immediately eligible to take the bar exam, while in Serbia graduates have to spend two years as practicing law clerks before they can sit for the equivalent professional qualifications exam.

D. Structure

To a large extent, legal education in Serbia consists of formal lectures, typically an organized, abstract, one-way presentation by the professor. Lectures last 45 minutes and are fairly structured. Core subjects are taught seven times a week, and sometimes nine. Students are not required to prepare or participate in any discussions. Professors do not take attendance and students are not required to attend the lectures. The number of students assigned to each lecture is so large that there is no feasible way for the professor to take attendance.

In-term control is exercised only through the "exercises," special classes complementing the lectures for the compulsory subjects. Here students are presented with hypothetical fact situations and instructed in methods of delivering legal opinions. The purpose is mainly the application of statutes, doctrines, and cases to these factual situations. During each semester, students must take two or more examinations and one paper on these fact patterns. For each class, students are divided into smaller groups in order to facilitate the discussion between the professor and the students. These classes are designed to supplement lecture material, but often are used by professors as a chance to get to know their students, as this is the only time professors have to evaluate students' knowledge level and interest in the course. Research papers are assigned periodically and are often the only occasion for students to carry out more in-depth research and interact closely with their professors. Research papers are not a compulsory part of the curriculum,

14 The difficulties of financing legal education in the U.S. are elaborated in John R. Kramer, *Will Legal Education Remain Affordable, By Whom, and How?*, 1987 Duke L.J. 240.

however, and normally only enthusiastic students volunteer to take on additional responsibilities.

At the end of each semester students are given the opportunity to take an exam in subjects that were covered in the previous semesters. Recently the structure has changed so that most of the courses are completed within one semester, whereas in the past the majority of the courses would take a full year (two semesters) to complete. This was accomplished by dividing the subjects that were covered simultaneously throughout the year between two semesters and assigning a greater number of lectures for a particular subject per semester.

E. Curriculum

A common characteristic of all state law faculties in Serbia is that they are designed to provide all-around legal education and not technical or professional training.[15] The bedrock of all European legal education is that legal education must provide the widest intellectual and theoretical foundation. Presumably, graduate programs throughout law schools in the U.S. aspire to prepare students for the practice of law, rather than to provide a well-rounded education.[16] Therefore, graduates in the U.S. are regarded as associates when they join law firms while in Serbia and the rest of Europe law graduates begin their careers as trainees. Unlike in the U.S., vocational training in Serbia takes place after the completion of university studies, during training in a law firm or in the courts.

The program of legal studies in Serbia is very strict and oftentimes unnecessarily burdensome. Students have to cover a great number of compulsory subjects and optional courses and have very little freedom to choose their subjects of interest. Compulsory courses take up all four years of studies, with students opting for a particular field of interest in their third year. However, optional courses are added to the courses that are compulsory for all students. Over four years the curriculum covers six compulsory courses, with students selecting four optional courses in the field they wish to specialize in. In contrast, most of the core courses are covered in the first year of U.S. J.D. programs and students can choose courses in the areas that find most interesting in the final two years. Clearly, the American system is more flexible and accommodating to the particular interests of its students.

In Serbia, the majority of the courses are considered core subjects and only a smaller number of courses are for the students to choose. In addition, the subjects covered by each course often explain in great detail marginally important topics.

---

15 In contrast, some of the private law faculties tend to offer more profiled courses such as the ones focused on business law entirely. However, they have encountered significant problems after the passage of the new law on the accreditation process. It may be that some of these faculties will not be fully accredited, limiting their graduates' ability to take the bar exam.

16 More on this aspect practical aspect of U.S. legal education *see* Schneider, *supra* note 9, at 18, 77–79.

Rather than focusing on areas that are theoretically or practically essential to legal training, students have to cover an array of insignificant issues. Finally, the needlessly comprehensive requirements leave no room for expansion of existing core subjects or the addition of new areas that should be part of the curriculum—for example, environmental law, European law, or consumer law.

There were some attempts to reform legal studies at the Belgrade Faculty of Law so as to reduce obligatory subjects and encourage specialization through electives. However, the actual reformation was half-hearted and the grouping of electives resulted in continued utilitarian choices. Overall, the sheer number of compulsory courses and the materials covered by those courses are extensive and all-inclusive. The curriculum in the U.S. differentiates clearly between a smaller number of core courses and a larger number of electives. In Serbia, however, the division is reversed.

Students in Serbia arguably gain a deeper understanding of the law as a social tool, the historical and philosophical background of the social science of law, and its origin and development through the centuries than do their counterparts in the U.S. This is because most of the subjects in the Serbian first year of study are not purely legal-oriented. They provide a broad introduction to the study of law. Legal history, Roman law, an introduction to the law, and legal philosophy are mandatory classes for all students. It is considered crucial for the students to grasp wider aspects of the law, including its role in society, its relation to society, the historical development of the law, and the interplay between law and ethics, among others. In the opinion of one American professor, first-year law students at the University of Belgrade have a more sophisticated understanding of the relationship of the law to society, the historical underpinnings of the law, the impact of the foreign law, and the operation of law in the society, than do American law school graduates.[17]

F. Course Materials

Generally, American professors rely heavily on casebooks in their classes. These books include a number of cases relevant for the topic, and questions to be discussed in class. Students are supposed to identify issues and understand legal holdings from the text of each case. Casebooks do not outline the main principles of the subject and do not provide an overall theoretical background. For these reasons, American students often lack an understanding of the nature of the rationale, the legal development behind it, the weight of the legal doctrine, and the authority of the law from another jurisdiction, etc. In Professor Watson's view, "[i]t is the students themselves who are expected to build up a picture of law from the few generally disconnected scraps available to them and with virtually

17 Alan Watson, The Shame of American Legal Education 175 (Dosije, Belgrade 2005).

no tools. Students are left to guess what the editors' view of the law is rather than getting to what the law is all about."[18]

In Serbia, casebooks are rare. Instead, course books are comprehensive materials which outline basic principles and peculiarities of the law, including legal doctrine, opposing arguments, and comparative law. Casebooks are used only as a supplement to the basic materials and are not the main source of a student's knowledge on the topic. For that reason, students often lack understanding of how to apply the basic principles to different factual patterns even as they are exposed to a heavy burden of understanding different legal doctrines and the positions of different legal jurisdictions.

G. Exam and Grading Policy

Most of the exams at Serbian law faculties are oral. Written exams are rare and exist in the form of elimination rounds prior to oral exams. Exams often consist of three randomly chosen questions from the list of questions that were covered during the semester. Depending on the professor's style of examination, the student may or may not have a chance to show a deeper understanding of the course material. It is necessary to correctly answer all three questions to pass the exam. The grades are not assessed by the level of knowledge of other students but depend on the thoroughness and presentation of each individual student. The confidence demonstrated by the student presenting is almost as important as the substance of the answer. Grades are not scaled and there is no such thing as a "curve." Instead of letter grades, student are graded by numbers from 5–10, where 5 is equivalent to a failing grade and 10 is equivalent to an "A+."

The examination method in the U.S. is very different. Most of the exams are written test exams and usually involve essay-type questions. Exams are anonymous and grading is generally based upon a curve with a forced mean and a predetermined standard deviation.[19] Hence, the American model encourages competition among students and greater objectivity in awarding grades. Since there is no limit to high grades and best grades cannot be "used up," Serbian students are not competing against each other. Therefore, the grading system encourages collaboration and support amongst students. Students are more likely to help each other, advise each other, and share knowledge openly with their colleagues. Although grades are important for a future career, they are not considered crucial for students' future employment prospects. Consequently, students are relieved from the tremendous amount of stress, anxiety, and pressure to get the highest grades on their examinations—feelings that their American counterparts often struggle with.

Exam policies in the two countries differ in another respect. Serbian students are entitled to take exams until they pass, whereas American students are entitled

18 *Id.* at 34.

19 Klein, *supra* note 8, at 601, 621.

to sit for an exam only once per course. There are four exam periods per year in Serbia—January, April, June, and September. Additional exam terms are granted upon students' request in October. As a result, students have less pressure to pass the exams the first time and often repeatedly "try their luck." The number of students that are examined on a particular day is therefore large and waiting for one's turn often takes hours. Keeping in mind that an exam period never lasts less then one week, and some last for as long as four (June and September), the academic year in Serbia is often interrupted with periods of examinations. Students become even less interested in their classes, since they are focused on exams. This also interferes with a professor's duties to lecture, examine, and conduct research all at the same time. Arguably, the lenient approach to the number of times that the student is eligible to sit for an exam is one of the main flaws of the educational system in Serbia. The length of study is often prolonged and students on average take seven years to complete the four-year program.

H. Teaching Methodology

In Serbia, law professors use the systematic presentation of assigned materials for a particular subject. This method was developed in the medieval period and it mainly involves lecturing by the instructor without an open discussion. In contrast, in the U.S., an interactive method of teaching is preferred and Socratic discussions are commonplace.[20] Legal education entails the learning of methods specific to the practice of law, including skills in legal analysis, the ability to distinguish the relevant from the irrelevant, the ability to deal with a large mass of facts, the ability to bring together persuasive arguments on any side of a legal question, and the ability to think constructively about societal and human problems and their solutions. The approach taken to one's problems and their solutions is more important than the content of the solution.[21] It seems that the Serbian model of teaching has neglected these basic premises and has failed to recognize the advantages of the Socratic method, which stimulates the thought process as well as the learning of law. Hence, *ex cathedra* lectures in Serbia are often not intellectually challenging and depend heavily on the oral skills of the professor. If a professor is not capable of keeping students interested and holding their attention, students may easily get bored and lose focus during the presentation.

On the other hand, some American students find the Socratic method a humiliating and stressful experience.[22] Oftentimes this method may slow down

---

20 Schneider, *supra* note 9, at 18, 79; Arthur D. Austin, *Is the Case Method Obsolete*, 6 Wm. & Mary L. Rev. 157 (1965).

21 Marcel Storme, *The Consequences of European Unification for Legal Education in the Member States*, Eur. Rev., Vol. 9, No. 2 (2001), at 137.

22 Quotations from Watson, *supra* note 17, at 16–17. For a critique of the Socratic method, *see* Klein, supra note 8, at 601, 628–631; June Cicero, *Piercing the Socratic Veil: Adding an Active Learning Alternative in Legal Education*, 15 Wm. Mitchell L. Rev. 1011,

the class discussion because the student in the hot seat is not responding to the professor in a way that is most conducive to sharing knowledge. Professor Watson claims that the Socratic method actually means teaching by terror.[23] Instead of being bored during classes like Serbian students, American students may experience other problems such as nervousness or anxiety. Therefore, students may find it difficult to follow the discussion as they wait for the inevitable moment when they will be called on.

Even though the Socratic method in its purest form may not be the best way to convey knowledge, it should be kept in mind that this method has certain advantages. Open discussion gives students an opportunity to learn in a different manner than straight forward lecturing. It forces students to develop other skills such as critical thinking, confidence, mental agility, the ability to "think on your feet," and the ability to deal with high-pressure situations. All these skills are necessary for lawyers, both in America and Serbia.

I. Professors' Profile

American law professors think of themselves, very seriously, as educators. Obviously, every professor everywhere is a teacher. But those who have studied in Europe will agree that continental professors do not concentrate very much on their students. They study, write, and lecture, and thus, they teach. Professors work in a professor-oriented rather than a student-oriented atmosphere, and have few direct obligations to the learners who sit at their feet.[24] As a result of the student–professor ratio, and the traditional university hierarchy, professors usually maintain a distance from their students. Personal attention and availability to students, the hallmark of the American approach, are exceptions within Serbian faculties.

In Serbia, tenure does not depend on the teaching qualities of a professor. Instead, the main focus is on his or her academic and scientific ability. Hence, there is a strong contrast between Serbia and the U.S. in terms of evaluating teaching qualities of a professor. Whereas in the U.S. the tenure of a professor arguably depends on a professor's teaching qualities, similar requirements did not exist in Serbia until recently. Only with the recently enacted LHE has student evaluation of teaching competency become relevant to a professor's academic advancement.

III. Reform of the University of Belgrade Faculty of Law Curriculum

The Belgrade Faculty of Law was established in 1841 as part of the University of Belgrade and is one of the largest law faculties in the region. Since its founding,

1014 (1989); Frank R. Strong, *The Pedagogic Training of a Law Faculty*, 25 J. Legal Educ. 226, 235–36 (1973).

23 Watson, *supra* note 17, at 25.

24 *See* Gellhorn, *supra* note 8, at 1239, 1240.

the Faculty has produced almost 50,000 law graduates, around 1,200 magistri iuris and 830 doctores iuris, as well as hundreds of specialists in various areas.[25] A great many Faculty of Law alumni have become recognized experts and scholars in all branches of law, law professors, and high ranking government officials.[26] All the faculties of law established subsequently in Serbia, Montenegro, and other parts of the former Yugoslavia were created using the University of Belgrade Faculty of Law as a guide.

Starting with the 2003/2004 school year, the Faculty undertook significant efforts to improve academic quality of research and education in accordance with the Bologna Declaration from 1999 and the Follow-up Documents from Prague and Berlin, with the aim of integrating itself into the European Higher Education Area.[27] These efforts resulted in a large-scale reform of the law school curriculum and teaching methods. The process of curriculum reform was initiated in order to secure:

1. attractive and ambitious university education on all levels, making an effort to reduce brain drain;
2. a modernized higher education to cover the need for scientific and professional knowledge;
3. efficient teaching and training of university teachers; and
4. a coherent higher education system all the way from the undergraduate to the doctoral level in accordance with the Bologna Declaration.

This reform of teaching methods has been initiated to provide students with a more practical insight in the legal issues they will encounter in practice once they graduate. The backbone of this reform lies in the belief that the law faculty must not just teach law, it must train lawyers. This has resulted in a higher number of legal clinics and moot court opportunities offered to law students.

A three-cycle system of studies has been introduced. The first lasts four years (providing a Bachelor's degree), the second lasts one year (providing a Master's

---

25 Mirko Vasiljević, 165 Godina, p. 10, *in* Miodrag Jovanović (ed.), Sto šezdeset pet godina Pravnog fakulteta Univerziteta u Beogradu, 1841–2006 (Beograd 2006).

26 The University of Belgrade Faculty of Law has had amongst its faculty members some of the most eminent experts in various legal disciplines, as well in a range of other social sciences (economics, sociology, philosophy, political science, legal history etc.). Amongst them, there have been 19 members of the Academies of Sciences, 15 rectors of the University of Belgrade, six judges of the Constitutional Court of Serbia, and several dozens high government officials—prime ministers, deputy prime ministers and ministers, ambassadors etc.

27 These documents require faculties to develop transparent and coherent curricula, provide the ECTS for the equal assessment of studies, enable mobility among students and professors, provide effective quality assurance, and recognize study achievements made abroad. It is believed that this process will increase the competitiveness of European institutions of higher education in a globalizing world.

degree) and the third lasts three years (providing a doctoral degree). Undergraduate studies include mandatory courses and a selection of one of three major streams of study: judicial-administrative, business law, or legal theory, as well as a number of elective courses from which students can choose according to their personal interests and preferences. The courses available in each year of study are listed in Appendix A, at the end of this chapter

The Master's program encompasses two basic areas of law: the business law program and the administrative-judicial program. The courses available in each year of Master's study are listed in Appendix B, at the end of this chapter. For the Master's degree, mandatory practical training in courts, state administration, or private companies has been introduced, in addition to a 30–50-page paper requirement.

The Faculty has introduced the ECTS system, with new standards for the mandatory literature, rules for evaluating students' pre-exam obligations, a diploma supplement, measures aimed at conforming to the European standards in higher education, a system of teaching evaluation, and additional quality assurance and control. In addition, the Faculty now offers a number of courses in foreign languages (English and French) on all levels of study.

Students who commenced their legal studies in October 2006 did so in accordance with the newly established system in which each course lasts only one semester. Only time will tell the impact of this new system will be and how it will be adjusted to take into account differences among various models of legal education outlined above in section two of this chapter.

IV. The Impact of American Legal Education in Serbia

Based on the experiences of a number of junior faculty members at the University of Belgrade Faculty of Law, the impact of the American legal education system on legal education in Serbia is substantial. Assistant professors who are currently teaching have completed their LL.M. degrees at various law schools in the U.S.: Pittsburgh, Duke, Harvard, Brooklyn Law School and George Washington University. In my personal view, studying at the University of Pittsburgh School of Law gave me a different perspective on my Serbian education and a new guidance in my professional career as a professor at the university. First of all, it enabled me to evaluate all the peculiarities of the Serbian system of legal education, and its qualities and flaws in contrast to the American model. Secondly, it gave me an opportunity to extend my knowledge of the area of law I now teach in Belgrade. Thirdly, and most importantly, it helped me improve the teaching methodology for my classes by exposing me to the Socratic method. Consequently, it has helped me develop a better course for my students. Last but not least, it got me involved in the Willem C. Vis International Commercial Arbitration Moot competition, which I consider to be one of the key aspects of my work at the Belgrade Faculty of Law.

A. Impact on Serbian Students

Serbian students have benefitted from their professors' American education in a number of ways. This has occurred primarily through interaction with their professors who have been exposed to the Socratic method of teaching and are willing to implement what they have been exposed to during their studies in the U.S. New opportunities have also been created for students in Serbia, such as participation in the moot court competitions.

1. Socratic Method In comparison to the European method of teaching, law classes in the U.S. often involve open discussion between professors and students. Arguably, the time in class is best spent in a probing discussion, not in lecturing. By doing so, the professor enables students to engage in presenting and understanding the subject-matter of the course, motivates students, and makes the class more stimulating. The Socratic method encourages classroom discussions and teaches students to think like a problem-solving, analytical, and creative lawyer.[28] The theory behind the Socratic method is simple: students think and learn better when they are required to think through and figure out answers to questions cooperatively than when a teacher tells them the answers. Socratic teaching offers the professor another reward: it is boring to lecture year after year on the same topic. But Socratic discussions can be actively interesting, since the professor never knows just what his students will say and thus where the discussion might lead.

Those who have experienced the Socratic method as students have implemented it at the Belgrade Faculty of Law, adjusting its main principles to their practical needs. In Serbia, the Socratic method is complemented with a short introduction on the main concepts and rules as they developed, then followed by a discussion of a few cases selected to illustrate the rules. The reactions of students have been positive. The new teaching method has been praised in the course evaluation forms and has led to increased lecture attendance.

2. Moot Courts American legal education of Belgrade faculty members has generated yet another benefit for Belgrade students. Law students have been offered a new opportunity to participate in various moot court competitions. In this respect, Belgrade Law Faculty is indebted for the support provided by Pitt Law. Through financing and training provided by our Pittsburgh colleagues, the Belgrade team has been a successful participant in the Vis Moot competition since 2003. Participating in the competitions requires hard work by all involved,

28 For more on the Socratic method *see* Carl E. Schneider, *The Socratic Method and the Goals of Legal Education: With Some Thoughts Inspired by Travel*, Hogaku Kyoshitsu 180 (1995); Mary K. Kearney and Mary B. Beazley, *Teaching Students How to "Think Like Lawyers": Integrating Socratic Method with the Writing Process*, 64 Temp. L. Rev. 885 (1991); Steven A. Childress, *The Baby and the Bathwater: Developing A Positive Socratic Method*, 18 Law Teacher 95 (1984).

both coaches and students, and at the same time provides unique practical and educational training, different from anything else offered at the Faculty. Different skills are developed through mooting: the ability to identify legal issues which arise in a factual situation, the ability to formulate concise submissions in relation to such legal issues, and the ability to present those submissions to a court or tribunal in a convincing manner.

Overall, Serbian legal education does not encourage teamwork. Therefore, mooting is a unique opportunity for students to learn how to work in teams and share responsibilities. At the same time, it incites their initiative and leadership skills. Students also perceive participating in the moot as an excellent opportunity for better access to the job market and postgraduate studies. For example, Vis Moot Court alumni had no obstacles in continuing legal education at universities in the west, such as the Central European University in Budapest, Hungary, the University of Leuven in Belgium, the University of Nottingham in England, the University of Pittsburgh in the U.S., and the University of Amsterdam in the Netherlands, often with full scholarships. Those who focused on the practice of law rather than on the academic work are now employed by the most prestigious corporate law firms and consulting firms in Serbia.

The success of the first moot court team from the Faculty of Law in Belgrade (at the Willem C. Vis Moot) was acknowledged by both the Faculty and the general public, including participation in TV shows, newspaper reports, radio shows, and web reports. The success also opened doors for students to participate in many other competitions. The Belgrade Law Faculty now offers students a chance to take part in various moot courts on topics ranging from international commercial law and arbitration to international public law, humanitarian law, international criminal law, human rights law, and European jurisprudence.

B. Impact on Other Faculty Members

Having recognized the advantages of the Socratic method, many young faculty members have applied it in their classes. There are certain hardships associated with the Socratic method which at first caused a level of skepticism among the teaching staff. For example, the Socratic method is best suited for case discussions, which are not commonplace in the study of law in the civil law system. However, even civil law jurisdictions have cases, and statutes can readily be taught by inventing cases that pose illuminating problems about interpreting a statute. The Socratic method is gradually being introduced by an increasing number of faculty members. Also, teaching materials that reprint judicial opinions, devise hypothetical cases, and set problems for students to resolve and questions to reflect on, are now more frequently published in Serbia and used in classes. Unfortunately, lectures, unlike exercises, often involve over-sized groups of students who are not afforded a chance to participate in the discussions. Hence, it is difficult to apply the Socratic method when teaching such large groups. This is also true for the core courses that are taught to large groups of students in the U.S.

C. Impact on the Curriculum Reform

It goes without saying that an American legal education has enabled its beneficiaries to obtain better positions in the Belgrade Faculty of Law. They now hold positions within the Faculty that grant greater responsibilities, including responsibility for international cooperation. Moreover, U.S. graduates have become an invaluable component of any committee engaged in the reform of legal education at the Faculty since 2003. This has enabled them to advocate for an improved academic environment, and to propose the incorporation of advantageous teaching methods they have experienced while studying in the U.S. These include establishing legal clinics, introducing more optional courses, developing a wide scale of moot courts for students, and organizing job fairs.

These young faculty members have also lobbied for the implementation of new information technology capabilities, such as improving the Faculty website, providing lecture materials and handouts on-line, and modernizing teaching tools and equipment so as to enable PowerPoint presentations in the lecture theatres. E-learning and distance learning systems are currently being developed. In addition, this initiative has resulted in the creation of a souvenir store where, for the first time, students can purchase T-shirts and sweatshirts with the university logo, thus promoting a sense of belonging to and pride in their educational institution.

D. Impact on the Legal Community

The U.S. experiences of junior Belgrade faculty members have enabled a closer cooperation amongst the Serbian private sector, the Bar Association and the students at the Faculty. This began with personal contacts and individual scholarships given to the best students participating in the international competitions, and gradually emerged as the first Job Fair at the Faculty in May 2006. More importantly, the Faculty has established the Career Centre, with a goal to create career opportunities and to assist hundreds of graduates in making career decisions.

E. Impact on the Development of the Rule of Law

On the eve of the October 2000 regime change, Serbia purported to have many institutions of standard market economy and the rule of law. However, the codified law suffered from a multitude of flaws and was often not implemented. The state informally and illegally took over the role of all-powerful arbitrator with decisive influence on all economic flows.[29] Following the October 2000 changes, Serbia has manifested a strong commitment towards developing a civil society based on

29 Boško Mijatović claims that there was a legal lawlessness in Serbia at that time. *See* Boško Mijatović, *General Overview of Transition in Serbia*, 16–17, *in* Boris Begovic et al., Four Years of Transition in Serbia (Center for Liberal Democratic Studies, Belgrade 2005).

the rule of law and transition to a functioning market economy.[30] When, after over ten years of economic mismanagement and regional conflicts, the new democratic government took office in January 2001, its primary objective was to stabilize and transform the economy and to restore Serbia's position in the international community.[31] This objective included integration into the international economy,[32] economic growth and membership in the WTO, and the rapprochement and integration of Serbia into the EU. To that end, the Government set out to reform Serbia's economic policy, laws, and institutions as required for accession to the WTO and integration into the EU. It launched appropriate monetary and tax strategies to achieve macroeconomic stability, streamlined public financing and tax policy in order to increase public revenues and ensure transparency, liberalized price and foreign trade policies, installed a new pension system, reformed its competition policy, accelerated privatization, created favorable conditions for investments, encouraged employment, liberalized capital flows, and arranged debt rescheduling. Experiences gained in the U.S. by legal professionals were utilized to accomplish many of these goals.

In 2000, the Serbian administration was outdated and staffed with people from the old regime who had trouble coping with new tasks and an open market philosophy. The opposition parties had different problems. They were mainly comprised of inexperienced personnel and were unable to fill numerous governmental positions with skilled and qualified individuals. Various international organizations offered their assistance, including USAID, European Agency for Reconstruction, the World Bank, Organisation for Security and Co-operation in Europe, OECD, UNDP, and others. Domestic capacity was lacking, however. Serbia craved young intellectuals with both Serbian and western education. It turned out that U.S. graduates of Serbian origin were a perfect fit for this rather difficult assignment.

In September 2002, I started working as a legal consultant for the USAID-sponsored WTO Accession Project for Serbia and Montenegro. My main duties were to consult with the Serbian government with respect to the World Trade Organization (WTO) accession process. This included preparing complex legal documents relevant to WTO accession, responding to questions coming from

---

30 Serbia and Montenegro had a history of a relatively open society when compared to other Soviet states. As a result, the citizens of Serbia and Montenegro are relatively worldly, educated, and well traveled compared to other post-Soviet states. They also tend to have a more pro-Western orientation. *See* USAID/Serbia and Montenegro Trade Assessment, Final Report (Apr. 22, 2005), at 10.

31 Some of the more significant hurdles that the new government had to overcome were: a sharply reduced output since 1989 (production cut by half and exports by two-thirds), substantially reduced investments, high unemployment rates (estimated at over 30 percent), a high inflation rate (120 percent), a large number of refugees and displaced persons, a doubled number of poor, a strong presence of the gray economy and corruption, and high internal and external debt (about 20 billion euros).

32 In recent years the country has rejoined the International Monetary Fund, the World Bank, and the European Bank for Reconstruction and Development.

WTO members regarding the Serbian foreign trade system, and preparing Serbian trade negotiations strategy. My tasks also included reviewing and commenting on existing legislation relevant to the WTO accession process, reviewing and commenting on amendments drafted by the relevant governmental entities, and, more importantly, participating in the drafting of new legislation and amendments as a member of the legal committee of the Government. The education and training that I gained in the U.S. helped me to understand the goals of the ongoing reform. The insight into the American legal system and economic policies made it easier for me to implement free market principles in commercial and trade legislation.

During my work at the USAID WTO project, many aspects of foreign trade were deregulated, customs duties were significantly reduced, pricing policy was considerably liberalized, the government demonstrated its wish to create a favorable investment environment, and the tax system was substantially reformed. A number of new laws, fully complying with WTO rules, were passed, revised, or amended.[33]

Nevertheless, the economy is still facings major problems, mostly resulting from regional conflicts (especially the one in Kosovo), international isolation, and sanctions.[34] Consequently Serbian exports of goods in 2003 were lower than in 1998. It is estimated that direct damage from the bombing in 1999 reached U.S. $30 billion, which is approximately the value of the country's GDP in 1989.[35]

Serbia's accession to the WTO is an important priority for the Serbian Government. In view of the purpose and importance of this organization for world trade it is clear that the Government is resolved to assume an active role in implementing the WTO's objectives and to offer its contribution to the revival and development of the world economy. However, the strongest impetus for reforms in Serbia is the EU accession process and regional cooperation through free trade agreements. Both are served by efforts to create the South East Europe Free Trade Area. In that respect, I have been called by the EU-sponsored Policy and Legal Advice Center to evaluate the current framework of bilateral free-trade agreements between eight countries of South Europe (Serbia and Montenegro, Albania, Bosnia

33 The most important legislation I was specifically involved in drafting is the Foreign Trade Law (enacted in Nov. 2005) and the set of intellectual property related laws (enacted from Nov. 2005 to May 2006).

34 Other major problem areas include a third of the population living below the regional poverty line, and 10 percent below the national poverty line of U.S. $2.40 per day; average wages amounting to U.S. $250 per month in 2004; external debt currently estimated at around 61 percent of the GDP; employment in the informal economy estimated at over a third of overall employment; and refugees and internally displaced persons numbering 377,731 and 200,000 respectively (578,000 in total), according to the 2001 census.

35 Twenty-four bridges were destroyed, 36 damaged; direct damage to electric power industry was around U.S. $270 million; the damage to the telecommunications systems was estimated at around U.S. $75 million; and damage to remote heating systems was estimated at around U.S. $5.3 million. Total direct damage to commercial facilities was around U.S. $2.9 billion. Total loss of human capital was estimated to U.S. $2.3 billion.

and Herzegovina, Bulgaria, Croatia, Macedonia, Moldova, and Romania)[36] and to propose further changes in order to allow undisturbed flow of trade between these countries, reduction of non-tariff barriers, and the establishment of efficient dispute settlement mechanisms.

In January 2006 I was asked to review the pertinent legislative framework for exports and to help the Serbian Ministry for International Economic Relations, in cooperation with the Policy and Legal Advice Center, to prepare the national strategy for export promotion.[37] The seriousness of the trade deficit meant that our work was of great importance for the Serbian economy. I am still involved in the drafting of the national strategy for export promotion while a number of emergency measures that were recommended by our team are currently being implemented.

The enactment of modern legislation is not sufficient without proper implementation. For this reason I have been asked several times to participate in seminars for the education of judges, attorneys, ministry staff, and others who are entrusted with the implementation of the new legislation. In addition, I have contributed to educating the general public by commenting on these new legal and economic developments in the most prestigious Serbian daily newspaper—*Politika*. It is evident that many of the recent reforms in Serbia could not have been possible had it not been for the young academics with western legal educations. The impact of the American model of legal education in Serbia has indeed been significant. As the country is opening up and becoming a part of the globalized world, educational experiences abroad are implemented more effectively than ever before.

Realization of the need to replicate what can be applied in Serbia is present in all areas of education. Legal education is particular to each nation; however, the method of teaching and the support systems that should be provided for the students are universal across the world. Arguably, neither the American nor the Serbian system of legal education is superior. They both have their strengths and weaknesses. A clear-cut transplant of the American model is not possible, but implementation of its strengths with modifications and improvements in line with Serbian legal culture has proved rewarding. The same applies for the overall reform of the rule of law. Complete unification of legal systems is not possible and diversity of legal cultures has to be maintained, but cross-cultural ideas and

---

36 Currently there are approximately 30 bilateral free-trade agreements signed in the region, whereas another seven are expected to be signed in the near future. Additionally, considerable efforts have been made on creation of a single regional free-trade system, which would significantly increase investments and ease the whole process.

37 World Bank, Serbia and Montenegro, Republic of Serbia, An Agenda for Economic Growth and Employment, Dec. 6, 2004. The causes of the high trade deficit should be sought in the present structure of the economy and the previously pursued economic policy. Despite the good intentions and some positive results (macroeconomic stability, curbed inflation), the reform policy has not yet sufficiently contributed to an increase in production, change of its structure and a substantial export growth.

philosophies can be applied concurrently. The implementation of contemporary American principles of education, free market economics, and democracy within the Serbian legal system has produced great results and I believe there are still more to come.

Appendix A: Bachelor's-level Law Courses at the University of Belgrade

First-year courses: Introduction to the Law and Legal Philosophy, Roman Law, Comparative Legal History, Foreign Language, Constitutional Law, National Legal History, Sociology, and Computer Skills relevant to the practice of law.

Second-year courses: Introduction to Civil Law and Property Law, Family Law, Political Economy, Criminal Law, Inheritance Law, and an optional course from one of the streams of study: Criminology (judicial-administrative stream), Economic Law (business law stream), or Political System (legal theory stream).

Third-year courses: Administrative Law, Criminal Procedure, Company Law, Contract Law, International Public Law, Law of European Integrations; an optional course from one of the streams of study: Criminalistics (judicial-administrative stream), Securities Law (business law stream), or Canon Law (legal theory stream); and one elective from the list of courses including: Rhetoric, Court Psychology, Autonomous Law, Parliamentary Law, Gender Studies, Media Law, and Diplomatic Law.

Fourth-year courses: Trade Law, Labor Law, Tax Law, Civil Procedure, Intellectual Property Law; two optional courses from one of the streams of study: Legal Medicine and Organized Crimes (judicial-administrative stream), Transport Law and White Collar Crime (business law stream), or Political and Legal Theories and Legal Philosophy (legal theory stream); and one elective from the list of courses including: Environmental Law, Moot Court, International Relations, International Humanitarian Law, International Labor Law, and Writing Legal Eocuments.

Appendix B: Master's-level Law Courses at the University of Belgrade

The business law Master's program includes the following courses: International Private Law, International Commercial Law, Arbitration Law, Foreign Legal Terminology, Economic Policy, Insurance Law, and two electives from the list of courses including: Legal Clinics, Telecommunications Law, Competition Law, Banking Law, Energy Law, Economic Analysis of Law, Accounting for Lawyers, Business Ethics, Internet Law, Bankruptcy Law, Legal Philosophy, and Legal Methodology.

The administrative-judicial Master's program includes the following courses: International Private Law, International Criminal Law, Administrative Procedure, Foreign Legal Terminology, Human rights, Public Finance and Budget Law, and two electives from the list of courses including: Juvenile Criminal Law, Legal Clinics, Law of Notaries, Medical Law, Legal Ethics, Legal Methodology, and Legal Philosophy.

Chapter 7

Damnum iniuria datum and the Law of Torts: From Cases to Rules

Marco Gardini[1]

I. Introduction

As a researcher in the field of Roman law, my main object of study is represented by Justinian's Digest.[1] The LL.M. experience has strongly contributed to a widening of my knowledge of the legal field by granting me experiences that were lacking in the formation of my legal education. That experience has contributed significantly to my development of a more thoughtful comprehension of the law contained in the Digest and in the Italian Civil Code.

The favored approach to law adopted by Roman lawyers is the "rule" and not the "case," as is normal in common law systems. To Roman jurists, however, the meaning of the rule was not that of a tool for enforcing a specific result as it is understood in the continental tradition of civil law, but was rather a means of pointing out a path to be followed while looking for justice. Roman law cared more for the setting than the solution of disputes. To Roman jurists, the case at hand ended when the standard to be respected was brought up. From then on, it was only a matter of careful arbitration, a place where the law had little to say. I believe that focusing attention on a quest for what is right, instead of focusing on the simple enforcement of a pre-established result, distinguishes the Roman law approach from that of civilian jurisprudence and furthermore represents a contact point with the common law experience.

II. A Seminar at the University of Trento

In order to set my observations on solid ground, let me use an example and describe what happened when I was asked to prepare a seminar that had to be held in a classroom setting dedicated to the study of a Roman tort called "*damnum iniuria datum*."[2] The seminar had to have a practical approach. It was supposed

---

1 Researcher of Roman Law (University of Parma, Italy); LL.M. 1997 *magna cum laude* (University of Pittsburgh School of Law); LL.B. 1994 (University of Parma).

2 *Damnum iniuria datum* ensues from a *plebiscite* of uncertain age (most commonly dated in the third century B.C.) that mainly tackled the issue of quantifying the amount of

to be a training session, so that the students could have a direct experience with issues of tortuous liability. The different approach was intended to differentiate the seminar from a course taught in the traditional way (that mainly consisted in the reading of and comment on the Title on *lex Aquilia*).[3]

The task was not as simple as it may seem. I had in mind a clear idea of what I wanted to do. I had experienced it many years ago, during my LL.M. education at the University of Pittsburgh School of Law, where all of my lessons were based on real problems that were discussed in collaboration with the students. As I put myself to work on preparing the lessons, however, I realized that the legal material available on the topic did not constitute a sufficient basis on which one could organize a genuine debate on pragmatic issues. The qualification of Roman law as "case based" is, nevertheless, commonly maintained. This led me to question why I was unable to obtain the necessary subject material to use in a more discussion-oriented environment.

III. The Available Sources of Roman Law: Some Examples

Ancient Roman lawyers in their writings often make reference to fact patterns (those that prompted the need for a legal opinion or those that are reported as an essential background to some piece of the explanation) and to potential legal arguments. However, it is very rare to find something that resembles a "real" case. Let me present five examples of the legal writings on *damnum iniuria datum*.

1. We must here not take "*iniuria*" as meaning some sort of offense, as it indicates in the action for affront, but as indicating something done not accordingly to what is put forward by the law, or as indicating something done against the law, that is, when someone kills with fault. Sometimes the action under the *lex Aquilia* and the action for affront concur, and in such a case there will be two assessed heads of damages, one for wrongful harm and one for affront. Therefore, we interpret *iniuria* for

damages that were to be awarded to one suffering harm as a consequence of the killing of a slave or of a domestic animal or as a consequence of the destruction of a thing. The punishable conduct was the killing, the burning, the shattering, or the breaking (*occidere, urere, frangere, rumpere*). For example, the first chapter of the law provides as follows: "If anyone kills unjustly (*iniuria*) a slave or female slave belonging to someone else or a four-footed beast of the class of cattle, let him be condemned to pay the owner the highest market value that the property had attained in the preceding year."

3 The Digest is subdivided in books (50), titles, fragments, and paragraphs (the specific material regarding the *lex Aquilia* is contained in the fragments of the second title of the ninth book: D.9.2).

present purposes, as including damage caused in a blameworthy fashion, even by one who did not intend to do harm.[4]

Ulpian is trying to clarify the meaning of the adverb "*iniuria*" (roughly translated as "unjustly") with which the text of the law connotes the action of the wrongdoer. With a text like this, it would be possible to indulge in a discussion with the students focused on the interpretation of three potentially different delicate nuances of the concept of *iniuria* (*non iure* = "not in accordance with a prescription," *contra ius* = "against the law," *culpa* = "blameworthy"). This is what is normally done during traditional Roman law classes, but that is exactly the kind of work that I was not supposed to do in my seminar.

2. The question is asked whether there is an action under the *lex Aquilia* if a mentally impaired person causes damage. Pegasus says there is not; for he asks how there can be any accountable fault in him who is out of his mind; and he is undoubtedly right. Therefore, the Aquilian action will fail in such a case, just as it fails if an animal has caused damage or if a tile has fallen; and the same must be said if an infant has caused damage, though Labeo says that a child could be liable under the *lex Aquilia* in just the same way as he could be liable for theft. I think this is correct, provided the child was capable of *iniuria*.

Here, the narration contains references to factual circumstances. The jurist is asked whether or not there is a cause of action under the *lex Aquilia*, and the problem of subjective liability is investigated through a potential analogy between mentally impaired persons, animals, and tiles blown off by the wind. The analysis culminates with the rule that even a child can be considered liable provided that he is capable of *iniuria*. This rule, however, depends on the elusive notion of *iniuria*.[5]

---

4 In this excerpt, like in all others, I follow, with some variation, the translation edited by Alan Watson, *The Digest of Justinian* (University of Pennsylvania Press, 1998). Ulp. 18 *ad ed.* D.9.2.5.1:

Iniuriam autem hic accipere nos oportet non quemadmodum circa iniuriarum actionem contumeliam quandam, sed quod non iure factum est, hoc est contra ius, id est si culpa quis occiderit: et ideo interdum utraque actio concurrit et legis Aquiliae et iniuriarum, sed duae erunt aestimationes, alia damni, alia contumeliae. igitur iniuriam hic damnum accipiemus culpa datum etiam ab eo, qui nocere noluit.

5 Ulp. 18 ad ed. D.9.2.5.2: *Et ideo quaerimus, si furiosus damnum dederit, an legis Aquiliae actio sit? et Pegasus negavit: quae enim in eo culpa sit, cum suae mentis non sit? et hoc est verissimum. cessabit igitur Aquiliae actio, quemadmodum, si quadrupes damnum dederit, Aquilia cessat, aut si tegula ceciderit. sed et si infans damnum dederit, idem erit dicendum. quodsi impubes id fecerit, Labeo ait, quia furti tenetur, teneri et Aquilia eum: et hoc puto verum, si sit iam iniuriae capax.*

3. If a teacher kills or wounds a slave during a lesson, is he liable under the *lex Aquilia* for having done unlawful damage? Julian writes that a man who had put out a pupil's eye in the course of instruction was held liable under the *lex Aquilia*. There is all the more reason, therefore, for saying the same if he kills him. Julian also puts this case: A shoemaker, he says, struck with a last at the head of a boy (a freeborn youngster) who was learning under him, because he had done badly what he had been teaching him, with the result that the boy's eye was knocked out. On such facts, says Julian, the action for affront does not lie because he struck him not with intent to make an affront, but in order to correct and teach him; he wonders whether there is an action for breach of the contract for his services as a teacher, since a teacher only has the right to administer reasonable chastisement, but I have no doubt that action can be brought against him under the *lex Aquilia*.[6]

In the paragraph that follows this one, the jurist Paul adds the point that "in fact, excessive brutality on the part of the teacher is blame-worthy."[7] Here, Ulpian examines the issue of the potential "not unjust" nature of the harm in a manner that is quite tangible; he recalls a case described by Julian where a shoemaker strikes a young apprentice in the neck. The global analysis is a mix of facts and hypotheticals, but the arguments presented by the opposing parties and, most of all, the exact set of facts that prompted the dispute of the shoemaker solved by Julian, are not available. What had the pupil done to anger the master? What exactly did the master do? Did he intend to strike the pupil or did he just react in anger, throwing the last without paying attention to whom was nearby? We cannot ask these questions because Julian's case is described by Ulpian only to support the opinion that the presence of a specific defense (the right to castigate) nonetheless leaves room for a cause of action.

4. Mela writes that some people were playing with a ball. One of them hit it vehemently and it knocked the hands of a barber with the result that the throat of a slave whom the barber was shaving was cut by the jerking of the razor. Whoever is at fault (*culpa*) has to answer under the *lex Aquilia* action. Proculus says the *culpa* is the barber's, and surely, if he was doing

6 Ulp. 18 *ad ed.* D.9.2.5.3:

Si magister in disciplina vulneraverit servum vel occiderit, an aquilia teneatur, quasi damnum iniuria dederit? et Iulianus scribit aquilia teneri eum, qui eluscaverat discipulum in disciplina: multo magis igitur in occiso idem erit dicendum. proponitur autem apud eum species talis: sutor, inquit, puero discenti ingenuo filio familias, parum bene facienti quod demonstraverit, forma calcei cervicem percussit, ut oculus puero perfunderetur. dicit igitur Iulianus iniuriarum quidem actionem non competere, quia non faciendae iniuriae causa percusserit, sed monendi et docendi causa: an ex locato, dubitat, quia levis dumtaxat castigatio concessa est docenti: sed lege aquilia posse agi non dubito.

7 Paul. 22 *ad ed.* D.9.2.6 pr.: *Praeceptoris enim nimia saevitia culpae adsignatur.*

shaving in a place were people customarily played games or where there was much going to and fro, the blame will be imputed to him; but it is no bad point in reply that if someone entrusts himself to a barber who has his chair in a dangerous place he has only himself to blame for his own misfortune.[8]

1. The analysis of Ulpian this time offers an example of two potential opposing arguments: the owner of the slave blames the barber for the choice of the workplace; the barber replies that the slave was well aware of the danger. These opposing arguments are, as I said, hypothetical. Was it the slave who asked the barber to shave him there because he wanted to look at the game? Was the game conducted in a place customarily used to play with a ball? Could the player who kicked the ball be blamed as well for having used an improper kick? A thorough discussion on all the implications of the dispute is once more precluded.

2. Finally, in order to fully appreciate the rule-oriented nature of the cases contained in the Digest, consider the following example, one of the most notorious:

5. "Some mules were pulling two loaded carts up the Capitoline hill. The front cart had tipped up, so the drivers were trying to lift the back to make it easier for the mules to pull it up the hill, but suddenly it started to roll backward. The muleteers, seeing that they would be caught between the two carts, leaped out of its path, and it rolled back and struck the rear cart, which careened down the hill and ran over someone's slave-boy. The owner of the boy asked me whom he should sue. I replied that it all depends on the facts of the case. If the drivers who were holding up the front cart had got out of its way of their own accord and that had been the reason why the mules could not take the weight of the cart and had been pulled back by it, in my opinion no action could be brought against the owner of the mules. The boy's owner should rather sue the men who had been holding up the cart; for a damage is imputable even when someone voluntarily lets go of something that, as a consequence, hurts someone. For example, if a man failed to restrain an ass that he was driving, he would be liable for any damage that he caused, just as if he threw a missile or anything else from his hand. But if the accident that we are considering had occurred because the mules had shied at something and the drivers had left the cart for fear of

8 Ulp. 18 *ad ed.* D.9.2.11 pr.: *Item Mela scribit, si, cum pila quidam luderent, vehementius quis pila percussa in tonsoris manus eam deiecerit et sic servi, quem tonsor habebat, gula sit praecisa adiecto cultello: in quocumque eorum culpa sit, eum lege Aquilia teneri. Proculus in tonsore esse culpam: et sane si ibi tondebat, ubi ex consuetudine ludebatur vel ubi transitus frequens erat, est quod ei imputetur: quamvis nec illud male dicatur, si in loco periculoso sellam habenti tonsori se quis commiserit, ipsum de se queri debere.*

being crushed, no action would lie against them; but in such a case, action should be brought against the owner of the mules. On the other hand, if neither the mules nor the drivers were at fault, as, for example, if the mules just could not take the weight or if in trying to do so they had slipped and fallen and the cart had then rolled down the hill because the men could not hold it when it tipped up, there would be no liability on the owner or on the drivers. It is quite clear, furthermore, that however the accident happened, no action could be brought against the owner of the mules pulling the cart behind; for they fell back down the hill not through any fault of theirs, but because they were struck by the cart in front."[9]

1.The granularity of the description is finer than in the previous examples. Alfenus has to give an answer to this question: Whom should the owner of the boy sue? The central issue here is causation. The narration, still, does not tell us many essential details and Alfenus does not seem to care; in fact, the answer is given through hypothesis. The first step taken by Alfenus is really remarkable and should be regarded as a keystone of legal methodology: "it all depends on the facts of the case." In the above excerpt the facts, however, serve only as examples to better illustrate the alternatives that branch out of a long chain of events complicated by the issue of indirect causation.

9 Alf. 2 *dig.* D.9.2.52.2: *In clivo capitolino duo plostra onusta mulae ducebant: prioris plostri muliones conversum plostrum sublevabant, quo facile mulae ducerent: inter superius plostrum cessim ire coepit et cum muliones, qui inter duo plostra fuerunt, e medio exissent, posterius plostrum a priore percussum retro redierat et puerum cuiusdam obtriverat: dominus pueri consulebat, cum quo se agere oporteret. respondi in causa ius esse positum: nam 'eam' si muliones, qui superius plostrum sustinuissent, sua sponte se subduxissent et ideo factum esset, ut mulae plostrum retinere non possint atque onere ipso retraherentur, cum domino mularum nullam esse actionem, cum hominibus, qui conversum plostrum sustinuissent, lege Aquilia agi posse: nam nihilo minus eum damnum dare, qui quod sustineret mitteret sua voluntate, ut id aliquem feriret: veluti si quis asellum cum agitasset non retinuisset, aeque si quis ex manu telum aut aliud quid immisisset, damnum iniuria daret. sed si mulae, quia aliquid reformidassent et muliones timore permoti, ne opprimerentur, plostrum reliquissent, cum hominibus actionem nullam esse, cum domino mularum esse. quod si neque mulae neque homines in causa essent, sed mulae retinere onus nequissent aut cum coniterentur lapsae concidissent et ideo plostrum cessim redisset atque hi quo conversum fuisset onus sustinere nequissent, neque cum domino mularum neque cum hominibus esse actionem. illud quidem certe, quoquo modo res se haberet, cum domino posteriorum mularum agi non posse, quoniam non sua sponte, sed percussae retro redissent.*

IV. The Teaching Experiment: From Common Law Cases to Roman Law Rules

My firm intention, as mentioned above, was to model the seminar along the same lines of teaching I had experienced in Pittsburgh. The brief descriptions were not enough. I therefore decided to begin with a discussion on common law tort cases. I chose a set of classic cases, some of the most traditional cases studied by first-year common law students. Let me just remark on how "revolutionary" the opening of *Palsgraf*[10] sounds to the ears of a student who is used to reading the "customary Italian case law" where the factual circumstances consist of a few neutralized details. I left the more theoretical analysis to the very end of the class and that was when I made reference to Roman law, connecting the factual problems experienced in the common law tort cases with the solutions offered by Roman lawyers. The students showed interest and seemed to have reached a deeper understanding of the complexity concealed underneath the apparent linearity of the Roman rules regarding *iniuria*, fault, intent, etc.

The reasons for the success of the "transplant" of cases from a certain place and time to another place and a very removed time are in part due to the special characteristics of the law of torts, a legal field in which the dynamics are less susceptible to being disciplined in detail: it is an area were logical argumentation takes precedence over legislative authority and, therefore, it is an area particularly disposed to accepting the transfer of experiences.

V. A Debate on Methodology

Even those professors who do not think that law has more of the character of a practice than an intellectual activity must concede that judicial disputes are at the core of everyday legal activity. The challenge, then, is how to train students. Confronted with this problem, different legal education traditions have resorted to different solutions and each solution is obviously coherent with the way in which the everyday activity of law is conducted.

Earlier, I said that I integrated Roman law sources with common law cases. An implicit question that I did not answer at the time was whether it was possible to use Italian contemporary cases. I am afraid it would have been more difficult. Most Italian databases contain "abstracts"; only the most relevant "holdings" are offered to the user. In addition, the few databases that contain "full text" judgments do not offer a thorough description of the facts and of the opposing arguments. Moreover, a tradition of selected, commented, and complete civil law cases has yet to be established.

If I compare the two most important didactic experiences I participated in personally, I draw the following conclusions. All of the courses I took during the

10 *Palsgraf v. Long Island R.R. Co.*, 248 N.Y. 339, 162 N.E. 99 (1928).

LL.M. program at Pitt Law shared three fundamental characteristics. First, the main didactic tool in every course consisted of a casebook. Second, the lessons were based on real cases. That is, actual disputes were the fact patterns and the opposing arguments were described in detail. Finally, the lessons were conducted in the form of a dialogue with the students, so that when and if a specific conclusion was reached ("the rule"), it came out at the end of the class and was not simply given to students without their involvement and effort. In Italy, the current didactic methodology takes the opposite approach. In contrast to the casebook, the main didactic tool in Italian classes consists of a "book of instructions" (the "manual"). The manual and the lessons start and finish with concepts and general rules. Italian lawyers, therefore, too often take their first steps in the law with the incorrect belief that the law is mainly comprised of abstract concepts. And finally, the lessons are based on a lecture format. The professor describes to the students a network of concepts and the students (try to) listen.

The result of this is that the civil law student encounters many difficulties in looking beyond the rules in order to face the "law as it is."[11] It is true that he or she develops a good familiarity with legal thinking but, on the other hand, the student is rarely allowed to obtain a firm "grip" on the problem. Most of the time the rules become a sort of shield that veils the problematic background.

Recent academic innovations, however, have promoted a rethinking of the consolidated Italian didactic methodology. After having obtained the traditional five-year degree, students can now enroll in "schools of specialization" established by most universities. These schools are designed to propel the student towards the real legal life that is waiting "out there." This aim has encouraged the more vigilant professors to search for a new didactic methodology. The students are the first to ask for something different. They do not want erudite lessons any more. They have a contingent aim of passing an examination and want to learn how to organize a brief and how to find a solution to a specific legal problem. Unfortunately, the progress we make in this new approach is slow and many students protest that the "schools of specialization" tend to replicate the model of the five-year degree.

VI. Civil Law and Common Law

The observation made above regarding the better position of the common law didactic methodology in conveying the law in reality to students inevitably brings me to reflect, once more, on the differences between the two legal traditions of common law and civil law. As previously mentioned, it is easy to assume that the didactic methodology adopted at law schools in the United States reflects a different way of "living" the law in the first place. As always happens whenever someone attempts to elaborate upon a complex experience, the risk of producing sterile considerations that repeat what has long and more properly been said is very

11 *Ex iure quod est.* Paul. 16 *ad Plaut.* D.50.17.1.

high. Here the risk is even greater because of the innumerable efforts displayed by comparative lawyers in defining the essence or, at least, the characteristics of the two traditions.

In order to reduce that risk, let me make reference here only to the content of a lecture given by Professor Pierre Legrand, invited by Professor Vivian Curran, during my LL.M. studies at Pitt Law in 1996–1997. Among the many contributions I read and heard on the topic, I still bear in mind the assertions of Professor Legrand which, back then, sounded almost provocative. He contended that common lawyers differ from civil lawyers in the way in which they "experience the world" and, as a result, their traditions are doomed to remain separate. I rediscovered this thesis in an article that dates back to the year I was in Pittsburgh: "European Legal Systems are Not Converging."[12] I have found this article to be precious for the purposes of this paper: it both brings back memories from my LL.M. experience and gives some sharp insights regarding the reasons for the influence of that program on my didactic activity here in Italy. The article makes observations that strongly confirm my impressions regarding the Roman law sources, the Italian case law and, finally, the Italian didactic methodology.

Among the many aspects upon which Legrand postulates irreducible differences between civil law and common law, special attention is given to the role of rules (opposed to the role of facts) in continental Europe. Legrand directs his attention to rules because he wants to refute a thesis. This thesis is that a European convergence is taking place because European countries are in the process of having common sources of law, and that they are creating a reservoir of common rules and concepts. Legrand proposes that rules and concepts, which he qualifies as "propositional knowledge," do not reveal much of a legal system.[13] In fact, he argues that "whether they be legislative or judicial in origin, rules are pernicious to the extent that they present but a surface image of a legal system" because "they limit the observer to a 'thin description.'"[14] Furthermore, he summarizes his thoughts by saying "[m]y contention is, therefore, that law simply cannot be captured by a set of neatly organized rules, that 'the law' and 'the rules' do not coexist, and there is much 'law' to be found beyond the rules."[15]

After saying this, Legrand tries to illustrate reasons why the common law *mentalité* is irreducibly different from that of the civil law:

1. "The common law has not left the inductive stage of methodological development";
2. "One cannot axiomatise English legal thought";

---

12 Pierre Legrand, *"European Legal Systems are Not Converging,"* 45 Int'l & Comp. L.Q. 52 (1996).

13 *Id.* at 53.

14 *Id.* at 56.

15 *Id.* at 60.

3. "The common law mind … is repelled by brevity";[16]
4. "In England, law is seen as a technique of dispute resolution";
5. "English lawyers and writers have tended to think of it as almost a virtue to be illogical … 'being logical' is an eccentric continental practice";[17]
6. "The alphabet is virtually the only instrument of intellectual order of which the common law makes use";[18]
7. "The rules of judge-made law are never authentically promulgated as rules, but are left to be inferred from cases";[19]
8. "The 'rules' are, therefore, no more than renditions by later judges of patterns which they perceive as having emerged from discrete and particularistic judicial interventions."[20]

The impact of this tradition on education is synthetically described in the following two propositions:

> The empirical approach privileged by the common law inevitably favors an idiosyncratic frame of thinking focusing on experience, casuistry and description, which reflects itself into, and conditions, legal education;
>
> The English lawyer is taught to remember factual situations: for '[e]very decision must be read in light of the facts on which it is based.'[21]

The civil law, by contract, is portrayed as "a system of *institutiones*[22] capable of transcending disputes by moving away from factual immediacies," because "the instinct of the civilian is to systematize."[23]

16 *Id.* at 65, citing A.W.B. Simpson, *The Common Law and Legal Theory*, *in* Legal Theory and Legal History: Essays on the Common Law 381 (1987).

17 *Id.* at 66, citing Neil MacCormick, Legal reasoning and Legal Theory 40 (1978).

18 *Id.* at 67, citing Bernard Rudden, *Torticles*, 6/7 Tulane Civ. L. Forum 105, 110 (1991–92).

19 *Id.* at 68, citing Oliver Wendell Holmes, *Codes, and the Arrangement of the Law*, 44 Harv. L. Rev. 725, 728 (1931) (reprint from the 1870 publication).

20 *Id.* at 68, citing Frederick Schauer, Playing by the Rules 175 (1991).

21 *Id.* at 70, citing *Masterson v. Holden*, [1986] 3 All E.R. 39, 43 (Glidewell, L.J.).

22 Reference is here symbolically made to the prototypical systematic law book, the Institutes of Gaius (*Gai institutiones*), a rule-based "manual" written by the Roman jurist *Gaius* who lived in the second century A.D. In this manual the law is treated systematically and is divided into three parts: *personae* (law regarding persons), *res* (law regarding things, succession and obligations), *actiones* (law regarding the forms of actions).

23 Legrand, *supra* note 12, at 67, citing Thomas Mackay Cooper, *The Common and the Civil Law—A Scot's View*, 63 Harv. L. Rev. 468, 470 (1950).

VII. From Cases to Rules

If, after more than ten years, I still consider these arguments, it is probably because they did capture something that is really important. This something can be described as "a taste for the particular ... for reality ... apart from all abstract ideas,"[24] that should be regarded as the essential characteristic of the common law as opposed to that of the civil law, where the instinct is to transcend the disputes. But where does Roman law stand? Its lesson is different and has its most crystalline display in an excerpt of Paulus: "a rule is something which briefly describes how a thing is; the law cannot be derived from a rule, but a rule must arise from the law as it is (*ex iure quod est*); by means of a rule, therefore, a brief description is handed down."[25] What is the meaning of the message that Paulus is trying to convey? According the Paulus, the rule is a proposition which summarizes the outcome of a judgment; the rule only briefly describes (*enarrat*).[26] Legrand may be right when he contends that rules are pernicious, but that is true only if we use them in an inappropriate manner; that is, when we fall into the attractive illusion[27] that it is possible to build the law by means of rules to be enforced, without having to fully discuss the case. If the rules are taken as a direction for judging a dispute, and not as a prescription of an outcome to be imposed, they represent only the map that is to be used for making a journey. The map can never replace the actual journey, but is nonetheless precious and not pernicious. Should we recommend getting rid of the maps for the fear that many will be tempted to replace the actual journey with looking at the maps?

The real issue, therefore, is how we give to the rules their proper value. If they are but a brief description, they have the value of presumption, in that they only point out a preferred solution, which may always be overcome should contrary elements worthy of being taken into account emerge from the dispute at hand. The rule, therefore, suggests the first solution and the case suggests the potential developments. The rules should never be taken as prescriptions of conduct to be inexorably imposed on the vicissitudes of life.

The rules contained in the Digest (though I believe that the same can be said for the rules contained in the Italian Civil Code) should be regarded as the product of a whole legal experience and not just as simple narrations. The key to their

---

24 *Id.* at 80–81, citing Fritz Pringsheim, *The Inner Relationship Between English and Roman Law*, 5 CAMB. L.J. 347, 348 (1935).

25 Paul. 16 *ad Plaut.* D.50.17.1: *Rugula est, quae rem quae est breviter enarrat. Non ex regula ius sumatur, sed ex iure quod est regula fiat. Per reguam igitur brevis narratio traditur ...*

26 The meaning of this excerpt comes near to being captured quite accurately by the quotation of F. Schauer, *supra* note 20.

27 The peak of that illusion is probably to be found in article 4 of the Code Napoleon, where the activity of the judge is described as the "voice of the law," which is supposed to be contained in the Code in a form ready to be enforced.

value and appropriate use lays in the ability to pierce the veil of their apparent self-sufficiency in order to be able to recover their roots in the concreteness of life (real facts, real problems). Since my return from my LL.M. experience, whenever I am confronted with an excerpt contained in the Digest or with a rule expressed in an article of the Italian Civil Code, I immediately look for the problems that may be disguised under their apparent perspicuity. By doing so, it is possible to better discover their limits and potential developments.

VIII. Conclusion

I can at least reverse one assertion of Professor Legrand's ("an English lawyer can never step into the shoes of a German or Dutch or Spanish lawyer: all he can do is imaginatively step into his shoes"[28]), by saying that during my LL.M. studies I had the opportunity to step a little bit into the shoes of a common lawyer; in fact, I had the opportunity to experience (not just to "learn") a different way of studying the law that, in turn, put me in a position to look at Roman and civil law sources through a new perspective.

In the end, I agree with Professor Legrand's position that, at least in the Italian didactic approach, the feeling for the importance of facts has progressively dwindled and has reached its lowest point. Something is changing, but it is still difficult to predict whether the change will result in the complete reversal of the tradition or in the wise recuperation of the same.

28 Legrand, *supra* note 12, at 76.

Chapter 8
Teaching in Mexico

Luz María Cárdenas Arenas[1]

I have had the opportunity to teach law classes for more than five years to different generations of students of the Law School, Business and Marketing School, and Business and Finance School of the Universidad Panamericana in Guadalajara, Mexico. Each class has had its own characteristics, but I have learned more than I could possibly imagine from each experience. Being a professor in front of a group of students forces one to update one's knowledge in the subject area and to continually be ready to solve the problems and questions students might have. One can never know what they will ask you and what level of knowledge will be required to answer any specific question.

As part of my academic formation, I had the opportunity to obtain an LL.M. from the University of Pittsburgh School of Law, and that has allowed me, besides acquiring teaching methodology in different areas of the law, to have the opportunity to gain a global and more complete vision of the practice of my profession, including my particular specialization in intellectual property law at the international level. It also has allowed me to develop the way I teach my students. I have had the opportunity to experience two completely different legal systems and to take from them the best methods in order to offer my students an improved pedagogy. The result is classes with a higher academic level, including issues of theory and practical, where the students pay attention, participate, and even have fun.

This chapter will be divided in two parts: my experience teaching law in business schools and my experience teaching law in law schools. The reason for this division is that the techniques used for each situation are different, as the profile and characteristics of the students being taught are quite unique.

I. Teaching Law in Business Schools

In Mexico, law students are not the only ones required to study law. Business schools include the study of legal subjects such as constitutional law, labor law, commercial law, intellectual property law, banking law, foreign investment law, consumer law, and civil law (including family law and civil contracts). The reason

---

1 Lecturer, Universidad Panamericana; Associate, S & G, S.C.; LL.M. 2001 (University of Pittsburgh School of Law); LL.B. 1997 (Universidad Panamericana).

for this is that the students are better prepared to become professionals if, at the time they are seeking employment, they have basic knowledge in areas that are indirectly related to the practice of their profession.

For example, a finance director of a company, besides his purely business-related functions, needs to know his rights and obligations under the Mexican Constitution. He also needs to know the main clauses a credit contract must have at the time his company forms a contract with a bank, or the benefits of hiring a person paid by commission, or how to open an independent commission merchant. In all these cases, this finance director will most likely consult a lawyer who will explain to him his rights, obligations, benefits, and risks in each case. However, he will perform better as a professional if he understands what law will be applicable in each case, and whether as a general matter the advice from legal counsel is correct.

In the case of students studying business administration and marketing, their careers are often related to copyright and intellectual property law, which is why providing basic knowledge of these topics gives them a real competitive advantage in the marketplace, preparing them to offer more comprehensive services when dealing with these areas of the law.

Teaching students with a business focus can be a personal and professional challenge because—as a lawyer—one can have a completely different mental structure. Classes on legal subjects for business professionals have to be complete, practical, dynamic, and focused directly on the students' planned profession. They should include theory and fundamental topics, but should not be as complex as they would be if being taught to law students. Most of the business students enter a course asking themselves why they are required to study and pass the subject in order to graduate. They believe the course will be completely theoretical and that it has no connection to their profession. In most cases, the students are not wrong, as many law professors in the business school teach the classes on a completely theoretical level.

In contrast to those professors—and because I had the experience of being taught by professors at the University of Pittsburgh School of Law, where the classes are practical and based on real cases, and where the theoretical principles are learned and extracted from the resolutions of those cases—I have introduced in my classes a completely new teaching dynamic. This dynamic includes a brief theoretical reference to law concepts that the students should know and understand for each topic. Those concepts are exemplified with a practical case focusing on their profession or covering with an issue they will have to deal with and resolve in their future profession. In classes, we introduce a topic and later on we propound a problem, the resolution of which is based in the theoretical concepts they should understand.

At Panamerican University, we evaluate students four times per semester. Three of the evaluations are monthly and together account for 50 percent of the grade. The other 50 percent come from a comprehensive examination at the end of the semester. From my point of view, this number of evaluations is acceptable as the schedule requires the students to study throughout the semester and not just for their next class, hopefully avoiding a heavy load of studying at the end of the semester. Evaluations of my students are divided into two parts: the first is completely theoretical, while the second requires students to solve legal problems presented from a businessperson's point of view.

Using this teaching methodology in the business schools has given me significant professional satisfaction as the students seem truly to enjoy and value the knowledge they acquire. In fact, at the end of the course, many express a desire to explore the possibility of majoring in law, while others marvel that they will remember a law class as one of the best in their education.

II. Teaching Law in Law Schools

I have also taught corporate law—an area I truly enjoy—at the Universidad Panamericana Law School. There, the subject of corporate law includes the topics of intellectual property, copyright, foreign investment, and consumer protection. Most of the professors in the Law School use a teaching system based on the exposition of theoretical concepts. Occasionally, students bring questions from a real case. Most students, however, complain that these classes make even interesting topics boring and say that they find it hard to concentrate. Many students, after joining the workforce, discover that the classes failed adequately to prepare them for the task of applying the theoretical knowledge they gained in their classes to practical situations.

Most of the Law School teachers do not require students to study before each class. Thus, most students arrive at the classroom not even knowing the topic for discussion that day. Consequently, student performance and knowledge are low, as are classroom interaction and discussion. My personal experience as a student in Mexico gave me the feeling that law schools are missing more practical professors, and that more should be demanded of students in the classroom, not just during the evaluation period.

Following my opportunity to pursue my LL.M. at the University of Pittsburgh, I decided to return to my home city and seek to change some of the structure and the dynamic of teaching in modern law schools, taking practical concepts I had enjoyed during my time at Pitt Law and applying them to theoretical concepts used in the legal education system in Mexico.

The method I use in my Law School courses begins with the distribution of a written syllabus to the students in the class. Students are then asked to study prior to each class the topic that the professor will discuss that day. At the beginning of class, at least five students are orally evaluated on both the topic studied in the previous class and the topic to be studied during the current class. At least once per month, I evaluate the students with a surprise test that will be part of their monthly grade. This encourages students to study every day and raises the level of learning and understanding of each topic presented throughout the course.

Each class begins with the theory of the law, as I believe it is very important that each student knows and understands the concepts that will form the basis of their profession. At the end of this theoretical exposition, there is an illustration with a real or hypothetical case, which has to be solved at the moment by one or more students. This method allows each student to have both the theoretical basis needed to understand the law and the practical tools necessary to perform successfully in their professional life and be competitive with other lawyers.

My in-class evaluations measure two different abilities for each student. The first part tests the theoretical knowledge of the student and permits no outside assistance from any source, such as books, codes, or computers. This ensures that key theoretical elements are clearly understood by the students. The second part of the exam is the resolution of real or hypothetical cases where the students may use any tool except for interaction with each other. This second part sometimes involves more than one topic and helps students to shape the mental structure lawyers need in the exercise of their profession.

The application of this system has resulted in higher grades, students that enjoy being in class and participating, and students that become lawyers well-trained in the area of law studied in class. I enjoy this new system of teaching and the results it has on my students' performance. I remain convinced that a careful balance of teaching systems from the U.S. and Mexico makes for a good class. I have seen the results in myself and in my students' performance.

Chapter 9

The Big Impact of a Small Program in the Development of Rule of Law in Kosovo

Vjosa Osmani[1]

My first encounter with University of Pittsburgh School of Law (Pitt Law) professors was in September 2002. I was still a first-year law student in Kosovo, but I had taken a couple of courses with international professors, which is why I was invited, along with another student, to join a dinner held for University of Prishtina and Pitt Law representatives. The discussion was about the possibility of establishing a partnership between the two Universities. One of the elements of this partnership would be the funding by Pitt of a team from the Prishtina Faculty of Law to participate in the Willem C. Vis International Commercial Arbitration Moot. The University chose me as one of the students to go to that competition. At that time, I did not know what I was getting myself into. I must admit that during the six months of preparations for that competition, many times I regretted accepting a role on the team because of all the hard work it required. But it cannot compare with the number of times I have thanked God and Pitt Law for giving me an opportunity that has opened so many doors for me. This was just the beginning of not only a professional but also a personal partnership with the University of Pittsburgh. Over the years, my constant work with Pitt professionals, professors, and students created strong bonds and friendships that I knew would last long after my involvement in the actual partnership between the two universities was over.

For three years during my studies in Prishtina, I also acted as a coordinator of many projects with Pittsburgh. The University of Prishtina had partnerships with many universities around the world. However, the particularity of this partnership with Pittsburgh was that its projects were mainly focused on addressing the problems, needs and difficulties that students (rather than professors) were facing. It was one of the few programs that included the organization and funding of summer schools, courses, competitions, visits, conferences, seminars, and other activities for Prishtina students. But, the most important aspect of this whole partnership was by far its LL.M. program.

Just like many other Kosovar students, I had dreamt many times of studying in the United States. I always thought, and still think, that one of the best investments

1 Assistant Professor of International Law (University of Prishtina); Legal Adviser to the President of Kosovo; LL.M. 2005 (University of Pittsburgh School of Law); LL.B. 2004 (University of Prishtina, Faculty of Law).

a country can make in its youth is in their education. And, in that sense, legal education is by far the most important. I finished my studies in Prishtina with top grades in all exams and immediately after I graduated (and even before that) I had a couple of offers from foreign Universities to pursue my Master's degree in their respective countries. One of them was the University of Pittsburgh. I was offered a full scholarship, including tuition, travel, and living expenses. I did not have to think long before I made my choice. Pitt had proven to me and the University of Prishtina that the educational opportunities they offer are exceptional, their legal professionals are among the best in the United States and worldwide, and their methods of teaching are something that can be taken as a role model for every other country. In addition, the area of law I was planning to specialize in, international commercial law, was taught at Pitt Law by some of the most prominent experts in the field, Professors Ronald Brand and Harry Flechtner. However, once I got to Pitt and the whole LL.M. adventure started, I understood that it offers much more than that.

While pursuing my LL.M. studies, for the first time I learned that teaching students how to think like a lawyer is much more efficient than making them learn theories and definitions by heart, an approach that unfortunately is still applied in Kosovo in many cases. I learned that working closely with each and every student—which is what Pitt Law professors did with us since we were a small group—can help you learn from your students almost as much as they learn from you. Besides promoting and encouraging the students' group and individual work, the experience also helps students to understand the truth of living. This is especially true when you work with people from different legal backgrounds and cultures. It can help you overcome any misconception or stereotype you might have had about any group or people. The program is fully designed to prepare you to go back to your home country and to put in practice all the things learned during that time.

When I came back to Kosovo, I was fully committed to joining the people who work for positive developments in Kosovo. I immediately got a job with the Council of Europe Office in Kosovo (CoE), which is an organization making an outstanding contribution to the rule of law process in Kosovo, and my work was mostly focused on legal and human rights matters. The legislative drafting process is currently very intensive in Kosovo, and I represented the CoE in many legislative drafting working groups. Considering that these working groups included people from different legal systems and countries, clashes were sometimes inevitable. The groups were mainly headed by U.S. experts, but included a handful of European and Kosovo experts that had worked for many years in civil law systems. The obvious differences between the common law principles which dominate the U.S. system and the experience of the European and Kosovo experts in the civil law system created potential obstacles. I was lucky enough to have studied and worked in both systems and therefore I had the opportunity to understand and grasp the ideas and proposals of all stakeholders. This also gave me the chance to help the group clarify many things and overcome many obstacles, thus making the whole process move quickly and smoothly.

One critical area of legislation for Kosovo, for which my work with was heavily influenced by my experiences with the University of Pittsburgh, is the law concerning the sale of goods. Kosovo, because of its status of as a former administrative subordination under the United Nations, was party to the U.N. Convention on Contracts for the International Sale of Goods (CISG) with regard to international sales. Moreover, this law has been introduced, perhaps unwisely, for domestic sales as well, and interpretation of this law by Kosovar courts has been unsatisfactory.

After the war ended, legal gaps were evident in all areas of Kosovo law, thus, one of the standards Kosovo had to reach before talks for its final status could begin included having a sound legal framework for a sustainable, competitive market economy, compliant with European standards.[2] When setting these standards, the UN Security Council also reiterated the primacy of the Regulations promulgated by UNMIK and subsidiary instruments as the law applicable in Kosovo.[3]

As far as contract law is concerned, until 1999, the Law on Obligation Relations covered all issues concerning contractual relationships, including provisions on sales. In the attempt to fulfill one of the standards, which was creating a market-based economy, one of the very first Regulations UNMIK adopted was Regulation 2000/68 on contracts for the sale of goods. By means of this Regulation, the sales provisions in the Law on Obligations were repealed and were no longer applicable. The interesting fact, however, is that the Regulation takes as a model, or better to say it is mostly a copy-paste of the text, of the UN Convention on Contracts for the International Sale of Goods rather than being adjusted to the needs of Kosovo.

With regards to Kosovo courts, many judges confirm that the CISG was applied by them in cases involving a foreign party. The problem is finding those cases. Since there was never a system for publishing cases, they were never accessible to the public. Moreover, in 1989, all Kosovo Albanian judges were dismissed from their jobs and they got their jobs back only in 1999 when the war was over. When they went back to their courts however, the whole inventory of files had either been burned down or taken away by the Serb police when they left Kosovo.

Now, with the CISG being applied in domestic cases, judges and practitioners are facing many other problems while trying to ensure the proper application of this Regulation. One of these problems is the inaccurate translation of Regulation 2000/68 into local languages. Many judges have indicated that in most cases it is unclear what the Regulation is saying, thus instead of applying it, they turn to the old Law on Obligations, which was applicable before 1999. In addition, since the majority of judges cannot speak English, it is impossible for them to follow international precedents. Even for the ones who speak the language, international

---

2 Standards for Kosovo, presented in Pristina on December 2003, *available at* www.unmikonline.org.

3 *Id.*

case law is hard to find because they do not have access to the internet, which would enable them to use the relevant CISG websites. Moreover, they are not accustomed to the concept of international precedents and sometimes consider this a breach of the sovereignty of lawmaking in their jurisdiction. These are issues for which I developed a deep understanding in Pittsburgh, and have tried to address since my return to Kosovo. It is only with the kind of education that I received that I may explore the issues with an eye to improving the system in my home country.

Apart from my work with the CoE, upon my return to Kosovo, I immediately got involved in work with the University of Prishtina, Faculty of Law. I taught part-time courses in International Humanitarian Law and International Commercial Law and also trained the students for moot courts in both these areas of law. The Socratic method and other approaches of teaching that I learned at Pitt Law have been an enormous help for me while working with the students. It is so obvious that these methods can be successful and at the same time can earn you the respect of your students, because they feel that this respect is mutual and that you care about their professional advancement.

Today, I am involved in the most important process in our history—the process of building the state of Kosovo. I left the CoE after accepting an offer to work as Legal Adviser to the President of Kosovo. While the experience I gain is immense and unparalleled, it is also a job full of daily challenges. Nevertheless, my Pitt Law experiences have taught me how to face this type of challenge bravely. I have learned so much there not only about the law, but also about culture and life, and at the same time I boosted my self-confidence, took advantage of my future, and above all, I made friends for life. Certainly, when I applied to Pitt, I knew just a small part of its importance and how it would feel. This program showed me what I can do as a professional and as a human being. Apart from the outstanding educational experience, it is also about growing up, opening your eyes, and preparing you to come back to your home country fully equipped to work hard towards strengthening the rule of law in the best ways possible.

I would like to conclude with an experience from a business event that took place in Kosovo. I was sitting at a table with representatives of some of the biggest companies in Kosovo. They started a discussion about their import–export activities and the business relationship with the United States. They were mentioning the wide range of goods exported from the United States. At the end, without hesitation, I told them that they had missed one: the export of legal education. This is the most important investment the United States has made in Kosovo, this newly emerging state that hopes and believes that this support and investment will yield positive results in the future.

Chapter 10

Designing and Implementing a Legal English Course to Develop the Rule of Law in the Context of Transition in Pakistani Society

Naveed Ahmad[1]

This chapter differs from others in this volume. I was not an LL.M. student at the University of Pittsburgh School of Law, but rather a Fulbright Scholar with the objective of studying the legal English program (then titled "English for Lawyers") at the School of Law and replicating it as appropriate in academic institutions in Pakistan. In the discussion which follows, I describe my experience in six parts. Part I provides an introduction to the study, my statement of the problem which is the focus of the study, discussion of my objective, and information about the research that informed my study. Part II is a review of literature in the field of the language of law, keeping in view its features related to the development of a legal English course. Part III describes the research methodology I chose for the study, and Part IV reports my findings. Part V takes into account three things: the rationale for recommending a course, the recommended course outline, and my guidelines for implementation. Finally, Part VI evaluates the implementation in the light of the goal of implementation and enforcement of the rule of law.

I. Introduction to the Research

A. Introduction

Pakistan is a common law country. In 1947, colonialism ended with the division of India into two independent states called India and Pakistan. Pakistan is a multilingual country having two official languages: Urdu and English. Other major languages are Punjabi, Sindhi, Saraiki, Pushtoo, Balochi, and Potohari. In addition, other

---

1 Assistant Professor, Bahauddin Zakariya University Department of Education; Ph.D. in legal English 2006 (Bahauddin Zakariya University); Fulbright Research Fellowship 2004 (University of Pittsburgh School of Law); M.A. in English 1988 (Bahauddin Zakariya University).

languages and dialects are spoken in different regions of the country. The British introduced English in India, and this language still occupies a special position in Pakistan as it is widely used for running the affairs of the government. English plays a significant role in legal settings as well: keeping in view the common law tradition, judges in Pakistan write their judgments in English. Pakistan also has a Federal Shariah Court (FSC) that monitors the application of Islamic law. The judges of the FSC, like the judges of other courts, usually write their judgments in English. The language of statutory law is also English, making English the clear language of law in Pakistan.

Nonetheless, there are two languages of instruction for legal education in Pakistan: English and Urdu. Despite the fact that the language of law is English, the majority of students study law in Urdu. Thus, most law students and recent law graduates do not have the required academic and professional competence in English. To earn their degrees, students study law for a period of three years after the completion of their undergraduate studies. In Pakistani institutions of legal education, the majority of students study law for the LL.B. degree that enables them to practice law after going through the bar exam. Some legal institutions, however, also offer diploma courses in specialized fields of law. Very few institutions offer research degrees such as a M.Phil. or Ph.D. in law. Institutions of legal education in Pakistan are typically known as law colleges. In the public sector, each law college is a part of a university, whereas a private law college must be affiliated with a university that is recognized by the Higher Education Commission of Pakistan (HEC). The HEC monitors universities in Pakistan in terms of quality assurance and funding from the federal government.

B. Statement of the Problem

Development of the rule of law in states at risk, like Pakistan, is significantly important as the rule of law is a basic precondition for political, social, and economic development. In the context of the war against terrorism, Pakistan has a dire need to transform its society. Establishment of the rule of law is one of the key issues in this context. Most law students and recent law graduates do not have adequate competence in legal English. This results in a variety of problems, including a lack of proper understanding of the law, delays in justice, and non-availability of proper expertise at grassroots' levels. Such problems create hindrances to establishing the rule of law.

To address this issue, Pakistan's legal education system needs improvement in curriculum development. Law students need to be fully groomed in the basic skills of reading, writing, speaking, and listening in English, in addition to acquiring proficiency in supplementary skills like giving presentations, taking part in legal discussions, and using appropriate language in the courtroom.

C. The Objective

The objective of this study is to recommend an English course for law students in Pakistan in response to their linguistic inadequacy in academic and occupational settings. To improve the standard of legal education in Pakistan, legal educational institutions can implement the proposed course by making it a part of their curriculum. Improvement in the standard of legal education will help in the development of rule of law.

D. Present Research

The present research is a thorough investigation aimed at measuring the existing linguistic adequacy of law students in Pakistan with reference to the specific roles they are required to perform in their academic and occupational legal settings so that their problem areas could be systematically identified and subsequently reported for recommending a course in legal English. My research was carried out at the University of Pittsburgh's Center for International Legal Education (CILE) as I stayed there as a Fulbright Scholar during the academic year 2003–2004. Working under the close supervision of Professors Ronald Brand and Ann Sinsheimer at CILE, I received insights from the U.S. legal system, reviewed literature in the field of language of law with regard to curriculum development, constructed research tools and analyzed the data, and finally reported the recommendations.

II. Literature Review

In this part, I will review literature related to the language of the law with a specific focus on features that are useful in developing a legal English course. This section begins by taking into account the term "language of the law" or "legalese," and then moves toward studies related to the written language of law. This is followed by a review of literature with regard to the spoken language of law.

A. Introduction

Over the past three decades, there has been a dramatic expansion of interest in studying the language of the law. In applied linguistics, the main concern has been to design and teach language support courses for academic and professional legal purposes. The term "language of the law" or "legalese" encompasses a number of usefully distinguishable genres that have communicative purposes they tend to fulfill in different academic, professional, and social contexts.

> The linguistic status of legalese is open to dispute among persons within the field of law and language. It is considered by some … to be a dialect in its own right. It can alternatively be viewed as a register of English, a form of jargon—that

> is, a speech variety restricted to an occupational group, or a form of diglossia, … diglossia being a distinct speech variety restricted to use on formal, public occasions, contrasting with speech varieties used for everyday purposes.[2]

S. Thorne describes a main and two subordinate functions of legal language: the main function is *referential* (to convey information), whereas the subordinate functions are *conative* (persuasive), and *metalinguistic* (discussing language itself).[3]

B. Written Language of the Law

Legal genres are defined as "[t]he highly institutionalized, and sometimes ritualized discourse of the law … organized sequences of elements which each play a role in achieving the purpose of the discourse."[4] Some fundamental written genres in legal English are statutes (legislative writings), cases, law reports, law review journals, and law textbooks. These written genres are examined below.

1. Statutes or Legislative English D. Crystal and D. Davy have stylistically analyzed legislative English at various levels: graphitic and typographical, lexical, syntactic, and phonological, among others.[5] For graphitic and typographical levels, elements such as capitalization, spaces, and numbering have been taken into consideration. Archaism, collocations, and French and Latin influences are discussed for lexical features of legal language, whereas grammatical characteristics and sentence length have been analyzed while highlighting the syntactic properties of language of the law. The phonological level has been discussed in the context of utterances of legal texts written with special graphology of the discipline. The significance of the use of articles and linguistic conservatism are also topics of discussion. Some general characteristics of language of the law are that it is "least communicative," "subject-specific," "all inclusive" and has "sub-varieties."

V.K. Bhatia demonstrates that legislative statements have "conventionalized communicative purpose mutually shared by the practicing members of the specialist community."[6] It has also been indicated that

2 Susan Berk-Seligson, The Bilingual Courtroom: Court Interpretations in the Judicial Process 295 (University of Chicago Press 2002).

3 Sara Thorne, Mastering Advanced English Language (Palgrave Macmillan 1997).

4 John Gibbons, *Language and the Law*, *in* The Handbook of Applied Linguistics 286 (Alan Davies & Catherine Elder eds., Blackwell Publishers 2004).

5 David Crystal and Derek Davy, Investigating English Style (Longman 1969).

6 Vijay K. Bhatia, *Cognitive Structuring in Legislative Provisions in* Language and the Law 153 (John Gibbons ed., Longman 1994).

> the typical use of complex prepositions, binominal and multinominal expressions, nominalizations, the initial case descriptions, a large number and variety of qualificational insertions make syntactic discontinuities somewhat unavoidable in the legislative statements, and to a large extent, account for the discourse patterning that is typically displayed in such provisions.[7]

A great number of other studies and reports have also appeared on the problematic nature of legislative writing in general.

2. Cases Another sub-variety of legal writing is cases. According to Bhatia,[8] because precedent plays an important role in legal arguments, proceedings, and legal decisions, legal judgments and case-descriptions inevitably form a major part of law students' reading lists. Moreover, students are not only supposed to have general comprehension of the case, they are to perform different tasks which are complex in nature. For example, they are to distinguish material facts from immaterial, understand the reasoning, and understand subject specific vocabulary. Badger indicates that the most important task is to find the rule (*ratio decendie*) from a case.[9] Nearly all of the legal cases and judgments available to date, and there are millions of them, consistently display a typical discourse organization, which is unique to this genre.[10]

Because different features of judicial opinions are juxtaposed with statutes, W. Burnham gives a detailed description of the relationship of legislative law with case law (judicial opinions), including a detailed commentary on the process of reasoning in judicial opinions.[11] Two basic types of legal reasoning are used with case law: deductive reasoning and analogical reasoning. Deductive reasoning takes case law "rules" and applies them in a manner similar to statutes. Analogical reasoning directly compares the facts of the prior precedent to the facts of the case to be decided.[12]

3. Law Reviews and Journals The journal article is a common genre used in academic legal settings. Feak divides material published in legal journals into two categories: law reviews and law notes.[13] She focuses her study on an analysis of

---

7 *Id.* at 4.

8 Vijay K. Bhatia, *Textual-mapping in British Legislative Writing*, 6(1) World Englishes 1–10 (1987).

9 Richard Badger, *Legal and General: Towards a Genre Analysis of Newspaper Law Reports* 22(3) English for Specific Purposes 249–63 (2003).

10 Vijay K. Bhatia, Analysing Genre: Language Use in Professional Settings (Addison Wesley Publishing Company 1993).

11 William Burnham, Introduction to the Law and Legal System of the United States (West Group Publishing 2002).

12 *Id.* at 5.

13 Christine B. Feak et al., *A Preliminary Analysis of Law Review Notes*, 19 English for Specific Purposes 197, 220 (2000).

published student-written legal research papers, which can serve as a model for teaching seminar paper writing. Law reviews, one kind of legal journal, are an interesting forum for academic legal scholarship. A typical review will contain several articles authored by scholars and or practitioners, reviews of books, and a small number of single-authored, student-written articles known as law review notes (henceforth notes). Notes clearly have a lower status than do law review articles written by scholars and practitioners as evidenced by the fact that:

1. they are placed at the back of the reviews;
2. in some law reviews, note titles are in lower case, while titles of articles written by scholars and practitioners are in all capital letters;
3. the name of a note author, if provided at all, is often placed at the end of the note rather than on the first page; and
4. most reviews do not provide biographical data for students, but do so for scholars and practitioners.[14]

4. Textbooks Textbooks are most commonly used in pedagogic settings. Like other disciplines, textbooks of law have an instructional communicative orientation. However, each discipline has some distinct characteristics. As J.M. Swales indicates, "a commonly identified communicative act such as defining can have different discoursal functions in different academic subjects as Science and Law."[15] V.K. Bhatia, commenting on legal textbooks, points out that special methodological and conceptual features of law require a different treatment of various commonly used communicative devices.[16]

Another interesting work on legal textbooks is that of D.U.W. Wickrama.[17] His work indicates that within a legal textbook there are significant variations in the rhetorical structuring. In fact, different parts of a case have different rhetorical structuring. A project titled "Improving Legal English: Quality Measures for Programme Development and Evaluation" was carried out at the City University of Hong Kong. That study concluded:

> Although in recent years we have seen a significant increase in the development of resources for legal writing, very few of them are targeted at second language learners … although certain aspects of the available books can be useful, most are generally unsuitable for use in such contexts. Three approaches are then offered for developing legal writing materials that will meet the criteria of suitability. First, the materials can be customized in various ways to meet the

14 *Id.* at 206.

15 John M. Swales, *Definitions in Science and Law-evidence for subject-specific course component*, 3(4) FACHSPRACHE 106, 11 (1981).

16 Bhatia, *supra* note 8, at 5.

17 O.U.W. Wickrama, Linguistic features of commercial law texts and their pedagogical implications (1982) (M.Sc. thesis, LSU, University of Aston in Birmingham).

> needs of second language users studying law in the medium of English. Second, the materials can adopt a more language and discourse-based approach. Third, rather than packaging materials exclusively in book form, they can be made available as a computer-mediated resource bank.[18]

C. Spoken Legal Language

Spoken legal language has always been of great significance and

> it is worth remembering that all legal systems have oral origins—the Roman legal system, the source of the most continental and Asian legal systems, was an oral system for most of the existence of the Roman empire; the common law system used in the English-speaking world has its origins in Germanic tribal law; Shariah, the Islamic legal system, developed in part from the orate system of desert Arabs—indeed the Prophet Mohammed (PBUH) was probably illiterate.[19]

W.M. O'Barr has found four varieties of spoken legal English in the courtroom.[20] These varieties include: (i) formal legal language, (ii) standard English, (iii) colloquial English, and (iv) subcultural varieties. The speaker, in fact, shifts from one variety to the other during his talk in professional legal settings in accordance with the requirement of the social context. Similarly, S.U. Philips has found that judges change their style of speech keeping in view the situation and different stages of courtroom proceedings.[21]

In fact, speakers in the courtroom manipulate their speech by using certain linguistic devices.

> [T]hrough a conscious or unconscious strategy, participants in courtroom proceedings try to phrase their questions and answers in such a way as to make themselves look better, and the opposing side worse. Thus, through a variety of verbal tactics, lawyers try to make their own witness look credible, sincere, and competent, while they attempt to make a witness for the opposing side appear dishonest, unreliable, and in general, incompetent. Witnesses and defendants, in contrast, try to use verbal strategies to enhance their image before the judge

---

18 Christopher N. Candlin et al., *Developing legal writing materials for English second language learners: problems and perspectives*, 22(1) English for Specific Purposes 229 (2002).

19 Gibbons, *supra* note 4, at 4.

20 William M. O'Barr, Linguistic Evidence: Language, Power and Strategy in the Courtroom (Academic Press 1982).

21 Susan U. Philips, *Contextual variation in courtroom language use: Noun phrases referring to crimes*, 49 International Journal of Sociology of Language 29, 50 (1984).

> or jury, and in a variety of subtle linguistic ways try to ward off the verbal demeaning of opposition in an effort to preserve a positive image.[22]

J. Gibbons points out that there is a growing debate concerning gender and language in the law, often showing an interaction between legal power and male–female power relations.[23] G. Matoesian produced research in this area related to language and disadvantage before the law.[24] To find out the differences between speeches of male and female witnesses, research has also been carried out by W.M. O'Barr and J.M. Conley.[25] They have found that traits of speech previously considered to be characteristic of women's style alone could be found in the speech of male and female witnesses alike. Further, they found that in the presence of these traits, the witness gave the impression of being less trustworthy than when his speech lacks these traits. W.M. O'Barr and his colleagues use the term "powerless" style for the speech having these traits.

According to S. Berk-Seligson, an additional discourse variable present in the speeches of witnesses or defendants who are testifying is "narrative versus fragmented" testimony style.[26] Persons testifying in narrative style will answer a question with a relatively long answer, whereas persons using fragmented style will answer in brief, non-elaborated responses.

> Whether a witness will answer a question in fragmented or narrative style is largely controlled by the interrogation attorney. Lawyers usually allow their own witnesses to answer in narrative style, but restrict witness for opposition from doing so. This practice is based on the implicit assumption of lawyers that jurors have a higher regard for witnesses answering in narrative style and have a poorer opinion of witnesses who testify in fragmented style.[27]

W.M. O'Barr found that witnesses who testified in narrative style were more competent and socially dynamic than witnesses who testified in fragmented style.[28]

Another stylistic variant in witness testimony is "hypercorrect" speech.[29] Hypercorrect style considers the frequent errors in grammar and vocabulary made

---

22 BERK-SELIGSON, *supra* note 2, at 3.

23 Gibbons, *supra* note 4, at 4.

24 Gregory M. Matoesian, *You were interested in him as a person? Rhythms of domination in the Kennedy Smith Rape trial*, 22(1) LAW AND SOCIAL INQUIRY 55, 91 (1997).

25 William M. O'Barr & John M. Conley, *When a juror watches a lawyer*, 3 BARRISTER 8, 11 (1976).

26 BERK-SELIGSON, *supra* note 2, at 3.

27 *Id.*

28 O'BARR, *supra* note 20, at 7.

29 BERK-SELIGSON, *supra* note 2, at 3.

by a witness in an attempt to speak formally.[30] This style, when contrasted with a formal testimony style devoid of such errors, was associated with mock jurors' negative perceptions of the witness's convincingness, competence, intelligence, and appearance of being qualified.

The coercive nature of courtroom questions has also received considerable attention from linguists.[31] Many researchers argue that questions in a courtroom vary according to the degree to which they coerce or constrain an answer.[32] They have given an order of coerciveness in different types of questions.

The impact of the interpreter on court talk is another area of research in spoken legal language. Many researchers have documented studies related to interpreting in the courtroom. Their research shows the extreme difficulty of providing accurate interpretation in courtroom contexts, where even minor inaccuracies may lower the standard of justice. In this context, "the role of the interpreter, as performed currently in American courthouses at every judicial level, often serves to alter the pragmatic intent of speakers in the course of on-the-road judicial proceedings."[33] In addition, Berk-Seligson states that "[c]learly adequate resourcing is a basic first step in resolving this issue, with more training for both lawyers and interpreters, but the very nature of interpreting and translation is that it is not an exact process—a consequence of the differences between human languages and cultures."[34]

III. Research Methodology

The purpose of this research was to recommend a legal English course for learners of law in Pakistan in response to their language problems. Therefore, the major research question under investigation was: What level of linguistic adequacy do the learners of law in Pakistan have for performing tasks related to their academic and occupational roles?

The subsidiary questions were:

1. What level of linguistic adequacy do the learners of law have in performing tasks related to reading skills in academic and occupational settings?
2. What level of linguistic adequacy do the learners of law have in performing tasks related to writing skills in academic and occupational settings?

---

30 O'Barr, *supra* note 20, at 7.

31 Gibbons, *supra* note 4, at 4.

32 Brenda Danet, *"Baby" or "fetus"? Language and the construction of reality in a manslaughter trial*, 32 Semiotica 187, 219 (1980b); Brenda Danet & Nicole Kermish, *Courtroom questioning: A sociolinguistic perspective*, *in* Louis N. Massery II ed., Psychology and Persuasion in Advocacy (Association of Trial Lawyers of America 1978).

33 Berk-Seligson, *supra* note 2, at 3.

34 *Id.*

3. What level of linguistic adequacy do the learners of law have in performing tasks related to speaking skills in academic and occupational settings?
4. What level of linguistic adequacy do the learners of law have in performing tasks related to listening skills in academic and occupational settings?
5. How important is it to have adequate command of English for academic and occupational purposes?

To answer the research questions, empirical research was conducted through a survey. I followed the method of purposive sampling. Four questionnaires were constructed for four population groups: teachers of law, recent law graduates, senior lawyers and judges. Data was collected from typical academic and professional legal settings in Pakistan. Piloting was done before the actual administration of questionnaires. For closed-ended items of the questionnaires, data was analyzed quantitatively by using SPSS (Statistical Package for Social Sciences), whereas open-ended questionnaires were analyzed qualitatively by reviewing responses, grouping related responses and identifying common themes. The respondents were provided different options for open-ended items of the questionnaires. These options provided the respondents a range of two extreme situations with an addition of an option for "no opinion." Three types of options were given in the questionnaires:

1. "extremely adequate," "adequate," "inadequate," "extremely inadequate" and "no opinion";
2. "extremely important," "important," "somewhat important," "not important and "no opinion";
3. "less than 25%," "25% to 50%," "50% to 75%," "more than 75%" and "no opinion."

IV. Findings of the Research

A. Overall Findings

The details of the findings have been presented in the dissertation that I completed during my stay at Pitt Law. In this article, I will provide the overall findings by taking into account the broader categories of the options: "adequate" or "inadequate," "important" or "not important" and "less than 50%" or "more than 50%"; and the summary of the qualitative findings of the study. The perceptions of the three population groups will be presented together in the form of combined group perceptions, whereas perceptions of the judges will be presented separately as the questionnaire that was meant for judges differed significantly from the rest of the questionnaires in terms of content and design.

The study introduced a major theme question, followed by subsidiary questions to expand upon the topic. The initial question was "[w]hat level of linguistic adequacy do the learners of law in Pakistan have for performing tasks related to their academic and occupational roles?"

The findings reveal that learners' command of English falls short of the mark: they lack the required linguistic skills and sub-skills to perform academic and occupational tasks in legal settings. The level of incompetence varies: the more complex the text/task, the higher the level of incompetence. The study expanded upon this major theme with subsidiary questions.

"What level of linguistic adequacy do the learners of law have in performing tasks related to reading skills in academic and occupational settings?" The members of the legal discourse community provided information related to the level of linguistic adequacy of learners of law in the skills of reading of cases, statutes, and textbooks/law journals. For the reading of cases, the findings related to the teachers, the recent graduates, and the senior lawyers revealed that a majority of learners have inadequacies in six sub-skills out of a total of eight. The most difficult sub-skill to judge is whether a particular case is analogous to or distinguishable from a pending case. The next most difficult sub-skill is finding the rule. In both of these sub-skills, more than 80 percent of the respondents were found to be inadequate.

Only two sub-skills, understanding procedural history and understanding citations, were perceived to be adequate by the majority of respondents, and the general impression was that learners of law have inadequate competence in reading comprehension for cases. The reason why learners have adequacy in only two sub-skills and inadequacy in the rest of the sub-skills is arguably simple: understanding procedural history and citation are much easier tasks, as the language used for procedural history and citation is not complex. The rest of the tasks included in the process of reading of cases are more difficult because of the complexity of language and thought.

According to the perceptions of judges, more than 50 percent of the lawyers that appeared in their courts had inadequate competence in reading cases. This was reported by 82 percent of the judges who provided information in this study. The qualitative analysis revealed that the task of reading cases was considered to be difficult and boring. Students were not provided with any guidance in this area and therefore tended to simply read summaries of the cases in spite of the fact that the data demonstrated the knowledge that reading cases is essential in a common law country.

According to educators, reading skills for statues, textbooks, and law review journals were insufficient. Of the respondents, 81.1 percent felt that learners have inadequate ability in understanding the complex structure of statutes, and 74.4 percent felt that learners have inadequate skill in applying statutes to cases. A majority of judges (63.4 percent) shared this sentiment and felt that lawyers who appear in their courts have inadequate ability to apply statutes to cases. According to 58.6 percent of respondents, learners possess inadequate skills at reading textbooks and law review journals. While lower than the findings related to case reading, this still represents a majority of respondents who felt that these skills are unacceptably low. The qualitative analysis revealed that reading textbooks and law review journals is comparatively easier because the language of textbooks and law review journals is not as complex as the language used in statutes. The respondents felt that special training is required to understand the complex language of statutes. I concluded that skills related to the reading of statutes, textbooks, and law review journals are not adequate.

"What level of linguistic adequacy do the learners of law have in performing tasks related to writing skills in academic and occupational settings?" The findings related to teachers, recent graduates, and senior lawyers revealed that learners have inadequate writing skills for academic and occupational legal settings. Out of the four sub-skills taken under consideration, the mechanics of writing is an area that is perceived to be the most difficult, as 85 percent of the respondents felt that learners have tremendous inadequacy in this area. The other three areas, organizing thoughts, appropriate formatting, and appropriate use of legal terminology, also were perceived as problems for learners as in all the cases more than 80 percent respondents felt that learners have inadequate ability in these areas. This means that in all the four areas of writing, more than 80 percent of the respondents felt that learners have inadequate competence.

The fourth population group, judges, also provided information about lawyers' linguistic adequacy in documents that lawyers submit to the courts. Like the other three groups, an overwhelming majority of judges (80 percent) felt that more than half of all lawyers have inadequate competence in writing mechanics. Of judges, 79.8 percent believed that more than half of all lawyers are inadequate in their use of legal terminology in writing; 72 percent of judges felt that more than half of all lawyers have inadequate ability in preparing legal documents to be presented to courts; and 62 percent of judges felt that more than half of all lawyers have inadequate competence in the appropriate formatting of legal documents that are presented to courts.

The qualitative data revealed that learners have inadequate competence in the mechanics of writing. According to the respondents, the main reason for this is an obsolete teaching methodology. The other main problem reported by the respondents was a lack of clarity. Extra effort is required on the part of the reader to comprehend unclear documents, which wastes already scarce time. Inadequacy in the use of subject-specific language was also reported.

"What level of linguistic adequacy do the learners of law have in performing tasks related to speaking skills in academic and occupational settings?" According to the perceptions of two groups, legal educators and recent graduates, learners have inadequate skill in spoken English in various academic situations, including asking questions of teachers, giving presentations, group or paired work, and mock oral arguments. Of the respondents, 67.6 percent felt that learners have inadequate ability in asking questions of teachers; 76 percent identified presentation skills as inadequate; and 78.3 percent were of the opinion that learners have inadequate

speaking skills for group or paired work. A larger majority (83.5 percent) felt that learners lack good speaking skills in mock oral situations. Overall, a vast majority perceived that learners are inadequate in speaking English in academic legal settings.

A majority of judges (75.6 percent) believed that more than half of all lawyers are inadequate in the use of spoken English in the courtroom. Analysis of the qualitative data revealed that students have inadequate ability in this skill, as it is not taught in law schools—despite the fact that spoken English creates a good impression and is a practical skill in everyday life. One of the reasons for inadequacy in this skill is lack of confidence. Qualitative and quantitative findings correlate with each other on this issue.

"What level of linguistic adequacy do the learners of law have in performing tasks related to listening skills in academic and occupational settings?" Five areas of listening skills were examined: listening to lectures in the class, listening to presentations, listening to fellow students in group/pair work, listening in mock oral arguments, and listening in occupational settings. The analysis revealed that the majority of respondents believed that learners had inadequate abilities in three areas of listening: listening to lectures in the class (61.7 percent), listening to presentations (52.3 percent), and listening in mock oral arguments (71.1 percent). However, listening skills were considered to be adequate for listening in group/pair work (64.4 percent) and listening in occupational situations (73.6 percent). Listening in the courtroom was analyzed separately in the specialized questionnaire for judges. The analysis revealed that 75.8 percent of judges felt that most lawyers were at least adequate in their ability to listen in the courtroom. The qualitative analysis revealed that difficulty in listening is dependent on the background knowledge of the topic under discussion and that learners face difficulty in listening with concentration.

"How important is it to have adequate command of English for academic and occupational purposes?" Perceptions of all the four population groups (teachers of law, recent graduates, senior lawyers, and judges) were examined in this question. According to the findings, all the population groups believed that English plays an important role in academic and professional legal settings in Pakistan. However, according to the qualitative findings with reference to general comments of the respondents, learners' command of English falls short of the mark. To overcome this problem, as the qualitative findings suggest, legal English courses should be conducted at various levels.

B. Summary of the Findings

From the findings of the study, the following main points can be deduced:

1. English plays an important role in almost all academic and professional legal settings;
2. learners' competence in English falls short of the mark: they lack the required linguistic skills and sub-skills for performing different academic and occupational roles in legal settings;
3. the level of incompetence varies: the more complex the text/tasks, the higher the level of inadequacy; and
4. a specific course for English is required to address the problem.

V. Responses to the Research

A. Rationale for Recommending a Legal English Course

To recommend an outline for the proposed course, I followed certain steps to provide a rationale for my syllabus design. First, in the light of the findings of the needs analysis, objectives for the course were set. Next, keeping in view the strengths and weaknesses of different approaches toward syllabus design, an eclectic approach to the proposed course was selected. Finally, taking insights from the studies in the language of law (as reviewed in Part II, above), and taking into account the findings of the needs analysis, I made decisions with regard to the specification, sequencing, and grading of course contents.

B. Recommended Course Outline

The outline designates 13 specific units within the entire course structure. For each unit there is a description of the unit objective(s) followed by information related to the topics to be addressed. The recommended course outline is as follows:

Unit 1: Structures

(a) Objective: After the completion of this unit, learners will be able to write correct English in terms of grammar, punctuation, spelling, and other mechanics of standard writing in academic and professional legal settings.
(b) Topics: All the major topics related to Standard English writing like parts of speech, voice (active and passive), narration (direct and indirect), spelling techniques, punctuation, etc.

Unit 2: Vocabulary

(a) Objective: After the completion of this unit, learners will be able to understand the meaning of difficult words used in legal settings.
(b) Topics: Judging the meaning from the context, prefixes, suffixes, technical terms, common terms with an uncommon meaning, words having Latin, French, or Old English origins, polysyllabic words, unusual

prepositional phrases, combination of words having different sources or levels of formality, such as *will, shall*, etc.

Unit 3: Reading

(a) Objective: After the completion of this unit, learners will be able to read the following adequately: law-related information in newspapers, legal textbooks, law review journals, cases, and statutes.

(b) Topics: Skimming, scanning, reading for main idea and inferences, techniques related to reading of cases and statutes.

Unit 4: Case Briefs

(a) Objective: After the completion of this unit, learners will acquire the skill to synthesizing cases.

(b) Topics: Purpose and format of a case brief. Synthesizing cases.

Unit 5: Organization in Writing

(a) Objectives: After the completion of this unit, learners will be able to (1) produce written texts in a coherent manner; (2) edit their written texts adequately.

(b) Topics: (1) Brainstorming; (2) How to write a good paragraph; (3) Editing.

Unit 6: Speaking

(a) Objective: After the completion of this unit, learners will be able to speak adequately in academic settings.

(b) Topics: Major steps in preparing talks effectively: judging the audience, researching the topic, strategies for confidence building, voice quality, pronunciation, English stress and intonation system, etc.

Unit 7: Listening

(a) Objective: After the completion of this unit, learners will be able to become good listeners in academic and professional legal settings.

(b) Topics: (1) Be prepared to listen; (2) Listen with a positive attitude; (3) Listen to understand; (4) Focus your attention; (5) Concentrate on context; (6) Take notes; (7) Curb the impulse to interrupt; (8) Summarize and evaluate.

Unit 8: Mock Trial/Oral Advocacy

(a) Objective: After the completion of this unit, learners will be able to perform adequately in mock trials and actual courtroom.

(b) Topics: (1) Responsibilities in oral argument; (2) Purpose of oral argument; (3) Mechanics of oral argument; (4) Preparation of oral argument; (5) Techniques of oral advocacy.

Unit 9: Advanced Legal Writing Skills

(a) Objective: After the completion of this unit, learners will be able to write in an effective style (integrated with reading).

(b) Topics: (1) Omit surplus words; (2) Use base verbs, not nominalizations; (3) Prefer active voice; (4) Use short sentences; (5) Arrange your words with care; (6) Avoid language quirks.

Unit 10: Office Memorandum

(a) Objective: After the completion of this unit, learners will be able to write an office memorandum adequately.

(b) Topics: (1) Purpose of an office memorandum; (2) Audience for an office memorandum; (3) Steps before writing an office memorandum; (4) Form and content of an office memorandum.

Unit 11: Plaints

(a) Objective: After the completion of this unit, learners will be able to write plaints adequately.

(b) Topics: (1) Purpose of a plaint; (2) Steps in wiring a plaint; (3) Editing a plaint.

Unit 12: Written Statement

(a) Objective: After the completion of this unit, learners will be able to write written statements adequately.

(b) Topics: (1) Purpose of a written statement; (2) Steps in writing a written statement; (3) Editing a written statement.

Unit 13: Miscellaneous Genres

(a) Objective: After the completion of this unit, learners will be able to write miscellaneous legal documents adequately.

(b) Topics: (1) Complaints; (2) Bail application; (3) Acquittal application; (4) Application for a medical examination; (5) Application for an expert opinion; (6) Application for the summoning of records.

C. Guidelines for Implementation

The legal English course outline presented above is recommended for learners of law in Pakistan. The course is based on the potential linguistic needs of the learners, which have been investigated in this research project. The course is comprehensive for law students and law graduates who have recently entered the legal profession. Public and private universities in Pakistan can implement this course to improve the standard of legal education of their institutions. The course could be conducted in various other venues like bar councils, judicial academies, provincial and federal law departments, and High Courts and the Supreme Court. Private law firms can also conduct legal English courses for their employees.

For LL.B. students, the recommended course should be started in the first year of their legal studies and can go until the third year of their program. As the LL.B. program is offered at a great number of places in Pakistan, and different types of legal institutions have different academic calendars, different examination systems and different resources, each institution/university can make decisions about the number of units to be offered in a year. It is better to follow the order of the units in the proposed course as the units are arranged with an eye towards specific educational goals. However, teachers can rearrange the order of the units if they desire to do so for certain preferences and priorities and the availability of resources. Teachers can also start more than one unit simultaneously depending upon the choices they have in setting their timetables for the classes. For example, unit 1, which relates to structures, and unit 3, which is concerned with reading, can be taught side by side.

Keeping in view the level of linguistic adequacy of particular groups of learners and the availability of resources, certain units could be omitted from the teaching agenda. For example, unit 1, which relates to structures, can be omitted in some cases where learners' linguistic background is very good and they do not need practice in basics related to the structure of English. Similarly, institutions that have limited resources can choose to address the learners' present academic needs by omitting the units that deal with future occupational needs. For example, the unit that provides practice in writing an office memorandum could be omitted from a university setting, as it is required in a law firm where lawyers perform occupational tasks but is less relevant to academic needs of current students.

For each unit, communicative teaching methodology is recommended; therefore, teachers who have training in ELT can teach the proposed course. However, ELT teachers will have to work hard to prepare their lessons, as they need to be clear in their understanding of legal genres that are complex in nature. Moreover, teachers will have to design and adapt authentic materials from different sources such as available books on legal English, legal textbooks, the CCP (Civil Procedure Code), newspapers, cases, and statutes, as no specific textbook is available that fully caters to specific needs of law students in Pakistan.

VI. Implementation and the Enforcement of Rule of Law: An Evaluation

Right after the completion of the project, the recommendations were sent to the decision-making bodies in Pakistan: public universities, private law colleges, the Higher Education Commission of Pakistan, judicial academies and bar councils. Presently, this course is offered at a number of institutions of legal education in Pakistan. Some other institutions are in the process of getting approval from different decision making bodies to make the course a part of the curriculum. During the process of implementation, the legal community has raised some issues regarding the implementation of the course. Being a member of some of these decision-making bodies, such as the Legal Education Reforms Committee of Bahauddin Zakariya University and the Board of Studies of the University Law College, I have attempted to convey the perceptions of the stakeholders of these organization with regard to the implementation of the recommended course.

As far as the views of judges are concerned, there is strong support for the implementation of this course. Judges believe that the standard of legal education needs to be improved to enforce the rule of law. According to their observations, recent law graduates appearing in their courts do not have adequate command of the English language. A very senior judge of the Pakistan Supreme Court, Mr. Justice Tassadaq Hussain Jilani, who has been a member of the Legal Education Reforms Committee of the Bahauddin Zakariya University, very strongly argued in favor of English as the medium of instruction for legal education and compulsory legal English courses for law students. The Bahauddin Zakariya University implemented this course beginning in the fall semester of 2006.

As far as the perceptions of senior lawyers are concerned, there has always been a strong support for the implementation of this type of course at various levels. Some very senior lawyers are members of the Legal Education Reforms Committee of Bahauddin Zakariya University. We have the full support of these lawyers who believe that to enforce the rule of law, it is mandatory that Pakistan improve its legal education system. Improvements in legal English education are a part of these societal reforms.

Government officials in different decision-making bodies strongly support the implementation of the recommended course to improve the standard of legal English education. As the government officials represent the government's point of view, the government is very keen to bring about a healthy transformation of society in the post 9/11 world. The government is aware that Pakistan is at risk and that establishing the rule of law is a key to success in the fight against terrorism. In this context, the government of Pakistan has taken steps to improve the standard of legal education. For quality assurance in legal education, the government of Pakistan has decided to open up a number of law universities where English will be the compulsory medium of instruction and legal English courses will be offered to all law students.

The perceptions of the owners of private institutions of legal education are worth mentioning. There is a difference of opinion between private educational institutions, as some private owners are in favor of the recommended course, but most oppose its creation. Those who favor it argue that quality assurance in legal education is a must. As the language of law in Pakistan is English, English should be the only medium of instruction for legal education. Thus, legal English courses should be implemented to equip the students with the skills they require in their academic and professional settings. On the other hand, some representatives of private law colleges and decision-making bodies oppose the implementation of the recommended course. They argue that law should not be taught in English. Rather Urdu should be the medium of legal education as Urdu is our national language. Another argument they forward is that everyone should be able to study the law, regardless of whether they know English. The reason why the private owners of law colleges are against English as a medium of instruction is very clear: studying law in Urdu is easier for the majority of students. To sustain and further expand their businesses, they attempt to admit the maximum number of students in their institutions even at the cost of a quality education.

Overall, the course has received significant appreciation as it aims at improving the standard of legal education which is a must to bring a healthy change in a society, and to enforce the rule of law.

Chapter 11

The Impact of the U.S. Legal System on Peruvian Administrative Law

Adolfo Céspedes Zavaleta[1]

I. Introduction

After having studied many courses related to the ways in which American reasoning and philosophy has influenced the law during my LL.M. degree at Pitt Law in 2000–2001, I considered how this training would be useful for my work as a Peruvian attorney and a prospective law teacher. I did not recognize at that moment the different consequences it would have in my profession and the changes it would provoke at my places of work. Even more, I remember that my friends used to frequently question why I had decided to come back from the United States in 2002, when almost every young professional who comes from an underdeveloped country like Perú would happily remain in the United States to live and work.[2]

A few months after I had returned from my U.S. experiences, I had the chance to enter the Peruvian administrative bureaucracy, specifically at the Peruvian Federal Emergency Management Agency (FEMA)[3] in September of 2002, and then the National Fund for the Financing of State Owned Enterprises (FONAFE)[4] in July of 2005. At both places I worked as a legal consultant, and therefore, as a public officer.[5] In the past few years, I have also been given the opportunity to start teaching courses related to administrative law at two Peruvian universities, the University of Lima and the University of Piura. In both activities, I have applied

1 B.A. in philosophy 1999 (Universidad de Piura); LL.M. 2001 (University of Pittsburgh School of Law).

2 Perú currently has a population of 26 million people, with nearly 50 percent earning less than two dollars per day. Nevertheless, its gross domestic product grew almost 6 percent during the three years ending in 2007. See www.inei.gob.pe.

3 Originally known as "Instituto Nacional de Defensa Civil (INDECI)."

4 Originally known as "Fondo Nacional de Financiamiento de la Actividad Empresarial del Estado." *See* http://www.fonafe.gob.pe and http://www.ifc.org/ifcext/economics.nsf/AttachmentsByTitle/peru_assessment_english/$FILE/PERU+assessment+in+english.pdf.

5 *See Ley Marco del Empleo Público, Ley No. 28715* at www.congreso.gob.pe.

what I learned at Pitt Law in ways that have changed the usual procedures of Peruvian administrative law.

II. Analysis

When I received Professor Brand's invitation to prepare a chapter about the relationship between my U.S. and Peruvian legal experiences, I began to consider the huge impact of the time I spend at Pitt Law on two different but somehow connected fields: teaching and practicing administrative law as a public official. In the discussion that follows, I have tried to summarize this impact, in what I consider to be its three main aspects: from deductive to inductive reasoning, legal pragmatism, and case law and its usefulness.

A. From Deductive to Inductive Reasoning

Teaching experiences in civil law countries are specifically geared towards a deductive reasoning methodology. Students start learning the basic principles of law, its sources, the Constitution, statutes, and regulations. Students are then trained to apply what they have learned in resolving practical situations or specific cases.

Based on this teaching method, exams at Peruvian universities usually consist of a series of questions evaluating a student's ability to memorize legal principles or rules of law. In other instances, students are asked to describe and comment on the legal definition of a term contained within a statute. Examples of the type of questions often found in a law school exam at a Peruvian university, specifically in the administrative law area, include:

1. Describe the main sources of Peruvian administrative law.
2. Why is a public contract different from a private one?
3. Name at least five general principles of administrative law procedures.
4. Discuss public utilities and their relationship with the state.
5. Name the main components of regional and local governments.

The tests I have designed for my students are clearly different from these examples, reflecting the difference in my teaching methods. In the classroom, I have presented the students with practical legal experiences; fictional and non-fictional situations that require them to start from a particular point of view and reach towards a universal one.

My education at Pitt Law gave me a sense that inductive reasoning is one of the main features of American legal teaching methods. One could clearly see this teaching method when professors conducted their classes by discussing particular situations or judicial decisions related with the topic of the day and then asking the classroom about their opinions concerning that situation, in order to reach a common conclusion. This method has proven to be a real challenge for lawyers who come from legal systems that use a different style of reasoning, such as the Peruvian one. It has been interesting for both my students and for me to experience this different and new approach to legal education and the way in which we can examine legal problems. This method has had an impact on the students at the two universities where I teach and upon me, and can be seen in the different paths and approaches to legal education I have taken as a law professor.

One significant impact can be found in the tests I have designed for my students. These have consisted mainly of two or three practical cases that students must solve using the tools learned throughout the course. There is never a unique or perfect answer, as is normal in deductive reasoning tests, and so inductive reasoning proved to be an interesting experience for these "soon to be" lawyers. The training will benefit them greatly, however, as most of the time they will not find perfect or unique answers for the issues they will have to deal with in their professional lives. The following are examples of questions that could appear on one of my exams.

1. In the Peruvian regional government of "Saturn" there is an authority, called the regional president, who has the power to execute some legal powers related to the economy and the region's cultural development. One day, he decided to start executing them through the use of a legal instrument called "ordenanza" which has, in the region of Saturn, the same hierarchy as a statute given by the congress. But, in this "ordenanza" he regulates not only Saturn's territory but also one who is closest to it. At the same time this legal tool directly conflicts with a Peruvian statute, and some parts of the Peruvian Constitution. As his legal counsel, what advice would you offer to Saturn's regional president?
2. A citizen wants to start a business in the city of "Andromeda" and he needs a license in order to operate it, which can only be obtained by asking for it at Andromeda's city council. This institution has to publish the requirements you need to fulfill in order to get the license in a document called TUPA ("Texto Único de Procedimientos Administrativos"). When a citizen approaches the city council, he is obliged to pay one hundred dollars for the license, notwithstanding that no publication was ever made concerning the requirements or costs to obtain that license. Citing legal cases that were decided by the Peruvian Constitutional Tribunal, explain what you would to do if you were that citizen.

Students at both universities developed a new way to resolve problems in an exam setting and began to think with a combination of deductive and inductive reasoning. They also seemed happier with this method than the traditional one. Moreover, inductive reasoning helped them to use their intelligence in ways that later were useful to them when they were practicing at a law firm or working for a public agency.

I also used inductive reasoning methods as the author of "Regional Law: Essential Regulations of Peruvian Decentralization Process" (title translated to English), in order to determine a new classification for countries based upon the ways in which they are decentralized. Thus, I started looking at practical experiences, such as the case of the United Kingdom or Chile—countries that do not seem to fit in any of the traditional classifications used in legal decentralization theories. From there, I tried to discern what elements make these countries different from others, and so I continued researching many other countries and, in that way, reached a possible new classification system for this topic.

In the end, I would say that a mixture of both inductive and deductive reasoning is the closest one can get to creating a perfect legal education experience in Peru, as in some situations one finds it more useful to guide students through a deductive reasoning method (for the specific construction of Peruvian legal foundations), but in other cases, inductive reasoning can make students think from a different perspective, discovering that, in law, the most important skill is to be able to apprehend the concrete aspects of the case and the specifics of the situation to be a good lawyer,[6] and not just to learn the statutes, legal terms, and regulations by memory.

B. Legal Pragmatism

I would define legal pragmatism as a way of thinking and acting that allows us to overcome difficulties in order to reach a concrete legal, political, or economic goal in a very short period of time. Pragmatism is defined as a practice that fully resembles the phenomenon of indeterminacy.[7] Attention to empirical evidence is a necessary condition of legal pragmatism. In that sense, "there is an emphasis upon post-hoc evaluation of the validity of an idea or principle in terms of the consequences it produces, and ethical judgments derive from an objective, problematic situation that indicates an objective need to the observer."[8] As Rorty has stated, clarifying this concept, "we should cease trying to ground our web of beliefs and values in anything other than pragmatic corrigibility. All disciplines have equal value, contributing to different aspects of human life."[9]

A pragmatic approach to public administration issues will try to resolve, in the fastest possible way, the peculiarities of the specific situation presented without serious questioning about the rigid methods used or about the values that must be applied. This method arguably has material advantages over other techniques used

---

6 *See* Agustin Gordillo, An Introduction to Law 31–38 (Esperia Publication 2003).

7 *See* William James, Pragmatism 26–38 (Longman, Green & Co. 1907).

8 Gary J. Jacobson, Pragmatism, Statesmanship, and the Supreme Court 102–03 (Cornell University Press 1977).

9 Richard Rorty, Contingency, Irony and Solidarity 51–93 (Cambridge University Press 1988).

in daily public law conflicts. This attitude is very important when we deal with bureaucracy issues. It is common in civil law countries for almost every officer in the public administration field to work very slowly and with a complex and extremely careful way of acting. This is due to the many controls and rules that the executive power has in civil law countries for the management of public resources, which can cause delays and frustrate the public officer's intentions of putting into practice many good ideas.

Since I began to work as a public officer, I have tried to apply a "legal pragmatism" point of view, searching for good results instead of only complying with formal procedures, and acting as fast as the regulations allow me, trying to fill the gaps found in the statutes with clever strategies. I think this legal pragmatism has helped me to deal with very difficult situations when most of my colleagues did not know what to do.

I want to emphasize that mechanisms of control for public administration activities in Latin American countries are very strict. They have a great impact on the conduct of public officers in most situations since any departure from the literal text of the statutes or the exact reading of the regulations will likely result in accusations of administrative fault. Thus, any ideas for reforming public administration in Peru—and most Latin American countries—and any attempts to apply these ideas to try to change the formalistic procedures of our public law, carries the risk of being accused of administrative fault and possibly contractual and criminal violations as well. Therefore, pragmatism in public administration is a very difficult thing to practice in civil law countries, as the regulations are very rigid, and "administration by results" is a difficult concept to accept by public officers.

Administration by results is defined as a system that allows one to perform his/her duties and responsibilities according to the positive results that decisions lead to, and not only according to procedures or extreme complexities. From my particular point of view, in the specific case of state-owned enterprises, legal pragmatism must be used in many different situations because of the nature of these institutions, created to operate as enterprises, with commercial goals to fulfill and, at the same time, controlled by public regulations. In my daily duties as an attorney for FONAFE, I try to show the many different legal roads that can be taken by my bosses to reach their policies' fulfillment in ways other than the traditional ones and in less time. A lot of compromise and a practical way of thinking are required to understand these actions, but in the end they prove to be more effective than the rigid and extremely ordered traditional methods.

As a specific result of this legal pragmatism learned in the United States, I co-designed and promoted a new statute for the state owned enterprises in Perú, which builds on concepts of legal pragmatism oriented towards the economical benefits these companies can obtain by rewarding the ones who have the best corporate governance practices and ethical behavior with less regulation and more freedom to operate, and punishing the bad ones with more regulations and more strict control of their activities.

C. Case Law and its Usefulness

Case law helps to interpret civil law statutes in modern and fascinating ways. Every text needs to be interpreted, because of the weakness and, at the same time, complexity of common words.[10] Interpretations are judged by their ability to make people understand the meaning of their object, and so "they should be supported by constitutive reasons, which show how they do so."[11] According to Habermas, a correct interpretation "fits, suits, or explicates the meaning of the interpretandum, that which the interpreter is to understand."[12]

If we translate these general ideas about interpretation to the legal arena, a good start could be the expression of Thomas Hobbes, who, in 1651, maintained that: "all laws, written, and unwritten have need of interpretation."[13] Indeed, interpretation is essential to our legal practices.[14] The necessity of interpretation in the legal field is strongly connected with administrative law, because of the need for acceptable reasons to justify the administrative decisions rendered.

From the comparative perspective, there is a slight difference between the civil law and common law systems concerning the necessity of interpretation. Because of the certainly more *a priori* nature and systematic thoroughness of the codified system of law, legal interpretations based upon it tend to have some continuity and predictability. On the other hand, "what strongly commends the common law approach to legal interpretation is its ability to arrive at just and principled decisions in a manner that—unlike the more abstract and deductive system of codified law—does not force the human subject or the problems requiring litigation

---

10 The interpreter is not free to assign any meaning he wishes to the text. He is disciplined by a set of rules that specify the relevance and weight to be assigned to the material as well as by those that define basic concepts and that established the procedural circumstances under which the interpretation must occur.

Owen M. Fiss, *Objectivity and Interpretation*, 34 Stan. L. Rev. 739, 744 (1982).

11 *See* Joseph Raz, *Why Interpret?*, 9 Ratio Juris 351–55 (1996).

12 Jürgen Habermas, Moral Consciousness and Communicative Action 27 (Christian Lenhardt & Shierry Weber Nicholsen trans., 1996). The German philosopher affirms that understanding what is said requires participation and not merely observation. In this sense, "the interpreter does not have to give meaning to the thing he observes; rather, he has to explicate the given meaning of objectivations that can be understood only from within the context of communication processes."

13 Thomas Hobbes, Leviathan 205 (Michael Oakeshott ed., Touchstone Books 1962).

14 The concept of "translation" is also recurrent to the legal activity, especially when we deal with written texts. In this way, law becomes a discourse that interacts among virtually all the discourses of our world, being the ultimate translation into the ordinary language of the citizen. The law in this particular concept constitutes "a method of cultural criticism and cultural transformation, as well as cultural preservation." See James Boyd White, Justice as Translation. An Essay in Cultural and Legal Criticism 269 (University of Chicago Press 1990).

into a rigid and pre-established mold of disembodied and sometimes doctrinaire logical and legal categories."[15]

It is an undisputed fact that civil law thinking about the legal system assigns to the courts a restricted role in lawmaking. In fact, in contrast to common law systems, limitations upon the scope of judicial activity are essential to the validity of the lawmaking process in civil law systems.[16] There are many historical and philosophical factors related to this issue, which may not all be covered here, but I can summarize them in terms of a system's thinking about the judicial process.

The more mechanical a system's conception of the judicial function, the more restricted is its idea of this function and of the propriety of judicial lawmaking.[17] This is particularly true in the civil law system where the essentially dogmatic and positivist legal education, the abstract and extremely formal judicial opinions, and the fact that the judiciary belongs to the general bureaucracy of the state encourage judges to conceive of their function as a restricted and limited one. In contrast, an American judge is usually encouraged and stimulated to leave his mark on the law, because of, among other reasons, the doctrine of *stare decisis*, the power of judicial review, the independence of the judicial branch, and the long and detailed form of American judicial opinions.

Additionally, in opposition to the common law system, civil law does not usually work with precedents;[18] previous decisions of a court do not have binding authority. Thus, administrative law in civil law countries is not connected with the use of the *stare decisis* doctrine, as is the case in the United States.[19] The principle of *stare decisis* plays an undeniably binding role in American administrative law interpretation, as part of its common law approach. Because of this, while applying

---

15 Walter B. Mead, The United States Constitution, Personalities, Principles, and Issues 172–73 (University of South Carolina Press 1987).

16 *See* Arthur Taylor von Mehren & James Russell Gordley, The Civil Law System 1142 (Little Brown Publishing 1977).

17 There are many reasons which explain this "anti-judiciary" tradition. If we take the case of France, logical explanations of this idea will be found in the unlimited trust in Rousseau's doctrine of the general will, the works of Montesquieu and his poor conception of the judicial branch, the necessity to control executive acts more than the acts of Congress, and the existence of the *referé legislátif* (a special legal institution which consisted in the remanding to the legislative power the last decision in cases concerning the interpretation of "dark parts" of a statute).

18 There are some exceptions to this general rule, like the concept of *doctrina jurisprudencial* in Latin American countries, an idea borrowed from the Italian legal system, which means that two or more consistent decisions of the Supreme Court in special constitutional cases must be applied in the same way by the lower courts. However, the doctrine of *stare decisis* does not represent what the civil law courts usually do in their daily activity.

19 However, as MacCormick says, "the authority ascribed to precedents is a reason to decide a case, but it is not a definitive reason, not even a good reason." Neil MacCormick, *Legal Reasoning and Practical Reason*, 8 Midwest Studies in Philosophy 276 (1982).

case law to my daily duties, one of the very first things I did when I began to work for the National Fund for the Financing of State Owned Enterprises was to make a summary of all the cases that were researched by various law firms' briefs. I called this paper "FONAFE Legal Issues" and it was extremely helpful for my performance at that job. The document consisted of a list of all the main issues that well-known attorneys have treated and researched in the briefs made during the previous three years for FONAFE, and specific questions related with concrete cases. I knew I could relate the cases that were handed to me in the present time to these previous ones, using the "legal issues" to solve them in very similar ways, applying a "*stare decisis*" kind of approach. This document is now used by every new employee who enters FONAFE's legal division.

In the same way, as a professor, I try to teach my classes using a lot of practical examples, cases, and decisions, most from the Peruvian Constitutional Tribunal. This court has had an impact on the traditional way in which administrative law is studied in civil law countries, because with its decisions it has changed many old concepts and regulations, and so it is extremely important for the students to be informed about it, as would be the case with an American law student and the U.S. Supreme Court's decisions. Thus, case law proved to be a fast and handy tool for public administration in both my working and teaching experiences. This is clearly a contribution from the American legal system to Peruvian Administrative Law; one can trace back to the time I spent researching hundreds of cases during the months I was an LL.M. student at Pitt Law.

Now, as a co-founder of the Development and Decentralization Institute,[20] a company which deals with decentralization issues, and provides legal and financial counseling to the regional and local governments in Perú, I can firmly say that inductive reasoning, legal pragmatism, and case law are three main features of the services we provided as a group of people who think that public administration could be developed in better and faster ways.

As a general conclusion, I might add that it would be very helpful if the three aspects I have identified and described in this chapter could be researched in deeper ways. Perhaps we can try to explore how other countries similar to mine can use them, and in that regard we might begin changing the traditional Latin American style of administrative law for the betterment of their societies and the public interest in general.

20 *See* www.grupoidd.org.

Chapter 12

Working with Precedents to Develop the Rule of Brazilian Commercial Law in a Global Scenario

Daniela Ballão Ernlund[1]

I. Introduction

The Brazilian legal system was developed based on Roman law. As a Roman legal system, the rule of law in Brazil focuses on the ordinary person and the private relations between individuals. The philosophy behind the system is the sense of justice and morality present in all civil code legal systems.[2] While Brazil was colonized by the Portuguese, who introduced civil law to the country, the American legal system was shaped in accordance with the common law applied by English settlers. The common law system was originally developed in the United States as a direct result of the power of the British Empire. The common law was developed to organize life in society so that a judge only had power to intervene in a conflict between people when public order was threatened. The sense of justice and morality so present in the civil law was superseded by the sense of societal organization under public control in the common law legal system.[3]

In the modern age, the world seems to be one. The technology of information and the increase of commercial transactions between different countries and cultures has been the main reason for the deep transformation experienced by the international community. Consequently, the essence of both systems has been changed and it is more common to see characteristics of one legal system present in the other.[4] The Brazilian legal system is no longer considered a pure Roman system and the rules encoded are no longer considered the only source of law. Modern Brazilian legal scholars have given more importance to the study of court precedents as a method of legal development. Some court decisions have been so important to Brazilian law that they have actually had the power to change the law.

1 LL.M. 1997 (University of Pittsburgh School of Law); LL.B. 1995 (Faculdade de Direito de Curitiba).

2 René David, Os Grandes Sistemas do Direito Contemporâneo 23 (Martins Fontes ed., 4th ed. 2002).

3 *Id.* at 25.

4 *Id.* at 26.

In the same sense, over the past several years, American common law has been developing under a legal concept different from the original system introduced by Britain. We can find several rules encoded by the American legislature and applied in court decisions. For example, the Commercial and Debtor-Creditor Statute, the Bankruptcy Code, and the Consumer Credit Protection Act are studied in American law schools as sources of American law. According to the scholar Richard Newmann,

> a common law country has two types of sources of law: judicial precedent, on one hand, and, on the other, statutes and statutes-like material, such as constitutions, administrative regulations, and court rules. … [I]n English common law, courts were the original lawmakers, and legislatures arose afterward, acquiring the power to make new law and to change law already made by courts. Courts, of course, retained the ultimate power to enforce all law. And, because interpretation is essential to enforcement, courts used their power to limit the effect of intrusive statutes, which judges treated with suspicion and even condescension until well into this century.[5]

Under this new legal reality, there is no longer a material difference between the civil code and the common law legal system. Similar cases have received similar final decisions when comparing democratic jurisdictions with different legal systems. The sense of justice has been considered equal in countries with democratic principles.[6] Thus, this chapter will discuss the importance of judicial precedents in the development of Brazilian law in a global context. After demonstrating the importance of judicial precedents, I will provide support for the conclusion that the study of court decisions is a valuable method of teaching law in universities. American legal reasoning might be a good method of studying and developing law even in Brazil, a civil law country.

The discussion below will mainly focus on Brazilian commercial law. It will demonstrate that judicial precedents have had a significant influence on the development of Brazil commercial law. In a civil law system, commercial law is the body of law concerned with all legal entities created to conduct business in the country[7] and may be also be called corporate law.[8] For this reason, commercial law is considered a legal tool for the economic development of a capitalist country.[9]

---

5 Richard K. Newmann, Jr., Legal Reasoning and Legal Writing 137 (Little, Brown and Company 2d ed. 1994).

6 David, *supra* note 2, at 26. Both Brazil and United States are constitutionally democratic countries following the theory of Montesquieu.

7 1 Rubens Requião, Curso de Direito Comercial 14 (Saraiva eds., 25th ed. 2003).

8 The study of commercial law in Brazil includes the study of the law of corporations and all institutions related to them, such as bankruptcy law, antitrust law, letter of credit law, contracts law, and industrial property law.

9 Requião, *supra* note 7, at 6–7.

As a tool for increasing capital, commercial law requires less strict rules and much more flexibility for the courts to decide any conflict arising inside or outside of corporations.

II. The Commercial Law

A. The Origin of Commercial Law

Most scholars say that the first rules of commercial law for western civilization originally appeared in the Roman Empire, around the 1st century B.C. The terms *mercatura* (market) and *commercium* (business) first appeared during this period.[10] At that time, Rome was the center of commerce and received goods from all over the world, especially grain that had been shipped from Asia to Rome.[11]

Even though the commerce of goods was present in the Roman Empire, it was only during the Middle Ages that commercial law appeared as an independent body of law. During the Roman Empire the legal compilations by Justinian, the Corpus Juris Civilis, had been considered effective enough to regulate the business relations between private parties. However, during the Middle Ages, society felt the need to organize the life of businessman, and the *consuetudini*[12] had a great impact on the development of the law of merchants.[13] The commercial law rose out of usages and customs of Italian merchants. At that time, Italian merchant courts[14] had the authority to recognize usages and customs as principles and rules of actions so that the decisions provided by the courts were the real origin of the commercial law and are still applied by western civil law systems.[15]

B. The Commercial Code in Brazil

As Brazil became independent of Portugal in 1823, the country adopted the Commercial Code of Napoleon[16] as its body of commercial law.[17] The Commercial Code of Napoleon was edited in 1808 and was adopted as law by other European

10 Alfredo Rocco, Princípios de Direito Comercial [Principles of Commercial Law] 9 (Ricardo Rodrigues Gama trans., LZN ed., 2003).

11 *Id.*

12 "*Consuetudini*" is a Latin word that means a personal in the market who is able to provide professional advice.

13 Rocco, *supra* note 10, at 14–15.

14 The Court of Merchants is now known as the Board of Trade, which is "an organization of merchants, manufactures, etc., for furthering its commercial interests, advancing its prosperity, etc." Black's Law Dictionary 119 (5th ed. 1991).

15 Rocco, *supra* note 10, at 17.

16 The Napoleonic Commercial Code was the code applied in some countries of continental Europe.

17 Requião, *supra* note 7, at 16.

countries, such as Belgium, Greece, Holland, Italy, Spain, Portugal, and some South America countries, due to Napoleon's imperialism.[18] Decisions of merchant courts and famous scholars' opinions were both used as legal authority by the French legislature during the Napoleonic Empire. The Napoleonic Code's purpose was to compile all the rules of most European courts in order to make them easily enforced throughout the whole of continental Europe.[19]

The first Brazilian commercial code was adopted in 1850. According to Brazilian scholars, it was the first commercial code adopted in all of the Americas, drawing from the French Code of 1808, the Spanish Code of 1829, and the Portuguese Code of 1833.[20] The Brazilian Code of 1850 was only revoked by the Brazilian Civil Code of 2002, which joined the civil and commercial law into one code. This Brazilian law unification followed the European civil law system's tendency to have only one code for all private law.[21] However, this unification does not mean that commercial law disappeared in favor of civil law. The Civil Code of 2002 has one section dedicated to corporate law. It means that the Civil Code keeps in its body the commercial law of Brazil, providing rules that relate to legal entities (corporations and partnerships) with social and economical scope to develop Brazilian capitalism.[22]

C. The Brazilian Commercial Law Legal Sources

One of the most legendary Brazilian commercial law scholars is a professor of commercial law at the Law School of the Federal University of Paraná State, Professor Rubens Requião. In his book *Course of Commercial Law* he argues that the first source of commercial law is the law stated in the form of a code or statute. According to Requião, the commercial law of Brazil must first follow the legislative law and can rely on national usages and customs only as a secondary source. Requião taught that

> [b]y the reason of having been a customary law, founded in the style of medieval merchants, the commercial law keeps traditional usages and customs as a subsidiary rule. The codes rising in the 19th century had complied usages and customs incorporated by the original Boards of Trade in Italy. The legislators of the Boards of Trade knew and recognized the technical capacity of the merchants to create their own rules for development of their business.[23]

18 Cesare Vivante. Instituições de Direito Comercial 16 (LZN eds., 3d ed. 2003).

19 Rocco, *supra* note 10, at 30–34.

20 Requião, *supra* note 7, at 16–17.

21 All countries that have a civil law legal system have the law divided into two kinds of law: public and private. Black's Law Dictionary, *supra* note 14, at 830.

22 The capitalism principle is provided by BRAZ CF §§ 1 and 175.

23 Requião, *supra* note 7, at 29 (translation by the author).

Some articles of the former commercial code provided usages and customs as sources of commercial legal transactions.[24] Furthermore, the Supreme Court of Brazil has ruled that usages and customs contribute to the law of merchants. In a case before the Supreme Court addressing imputed liability for damages, the Court held in accordance with the usage of trade and thus considered the beginning of a requested performance a reasonable mode of acceptance to the law.[25]

Since the scope of this chapter is to demonstrate the enlarged effect of the decisions of Brazilian courts, it is worth noting that judicial precedents have developed the commercial law even in a civil law system such as Brazil. The technical capacity or technical knowledge of merchants must be recognized to develop commercial law, and Brazilian courts have begun doing so. Some recent Brazilian scholars have said that "[l]aw is a word that means (i) rule; (ii) decisions and (iii) legal structure … Studying law only as rule is, however, partial and incomplete."[26]

Thus the law, even in a civil code legal system, is not just the law stated by the legislature in the body of statutes or codes. It also includes the precedents of courts which are considered law for historical reasoning by the major scholars and an important source of legal reasoning to the legislature, lawyers, and students of law.

D. German Law and the Science of the Positive Law Scholar

The idea that law is only rules stated by the legislature in a body of statutes or codes came from the positive law philosophy mainly derived from German and Austrian scholars. According to positive law, the law is only that which is "actually and specifically enacted or adopted by proper authority for the government of an organized society."[27] Even though the influence of this concept of law in the western world is considerable, the history and the practice of law have not accepted positivist legal theory completely enough to explain the "Science of Law."

Historically, the influence of Roman law on the law of Germany was also very significant. In 1495, during the imperialism of Maximiliano, German jurisprudence reached some importance in the whole region. The same philosophy appeared in Germany in the eighteenth and nineteenth centuries, with the study of law being isolated to the morality and customs applied during several centuries in other

24 There were some articles in the former Commercial Code that clearly provided usages and customs as legal sources of Brazilian Commercial Law. Braz. C. Co. § 154, 168, 179, 186, 201, 207, and 291.

25 Maria Elvira Siciliano Villares, Fernando C. de S. Barros & others v. Corretora S.B. Câmbio e Títulos S.A Superior Tribunal de Justiça [STJ] (Highest court of appeals on all non-constitutional matters) Agravo Regimental no Agravo de Instrumento nr. 6.418-SP (1990).

26 Eros Roberto Grau, O Direito Posto e o Direito Pressuposto [The Placed Law and the Presumed Law] 18 (Malheiros eds., 5th ed. 2003).

27 Black's Law Dictionary, *supra* note 14, at 806.

countries of continental Europe.[28] One famous and classic German jurist, Rudolf von Jhering, introduced the concept of jurisprudence as "a science to be utilized for the further advancement of the moral and social interest of mankind."[29] Jhering defined the law as a "complex of legal effected rules of a specific State."[30] Under this concept, Jhering isolated rules stated by the legislature from rules issued by courts. For Jhering, only encoded rules are a part of the "Science of Law."[31] Judicial decisions, in accordance with Jhering's theory, are the application and/or interpretation of the law in an individual case drawn from society.

Jhering's legal philosophy influenced Hans Kelsen, an Austrian-American legal philosopher, who influenced all new constitutions of western countries. According to Kelsen, legal theory should both validate and give order to law. In his theory of pure law, Kelsen defended the science of jurisprudence, reasoning that

> [t]he courts of justice rule on individual law; however, under a judicial order which institutes the legislative power or recognized customs as fact of law, courts of justice should apply the general law previously enacted by Legislative act or by customs. Judicial decisions are the continuation of the creation of law process, not the start.[32]

Kelsen's legal methodology was very important in consolidating democracy and legality in most civil law countries. This was a positive aspect of the Kelsen's Pure Theory of Law. Notwithstanding Kelsen's approach, in the middle of the last century, German jurists acknowledged Roman law as always having been present in German's legal institutions. This has been repeated in France, Austria, and other countries that have experienced the deep influence of Roman law in their legal systems.[33]

Such acceptance was very important to the study of law (including the meaning of legal precedent) in civil law legal systems. According to scholars of the nineteenth century, the law is a product of popular interest.[34] In this aspect, David states that "customs carry out an important function; they are the structure upon the creation of law and provide instructions for legislators, judges, and scholars to apply them in accordance with the law."[35] This is the currently accepted legal opinion in Brazil. During the last century, customs have influenced decision

---

28 DAVID, *supra* note 2, at 59 and 60.

29 Rudolf von Jhering, at http://encyclopedia.jrank.org/JEE_JUN/JHERING_RUDOLF_VON_1818_1892_.html.

30 1 RUDOLF VON JHERING, A FINALIDADE DO DIREITO 218–19 (Bookseller ed., 2002).

31 *Id.* at 230.

32 HANS KELSEN, TEORIA PURA DO DIREITO [PURE OF LAW THEORY] 272 (Martins Fontes eds., 2d ed. 1987).

33 DAVID, *supra* note 2, at 60–61.

34 *Id.* at 144.

35 *Id.*

makers and even the legislature. In addition, judicial decisions have begun to provide legal rules, mainly in the commercial sphere, as we can see in the two precedents discussed below.

III. Some Relevant Cases that Ruled the Commercial Law

A. The Disregard Legal Entity Theory

In an Appeal to the Supreme Court of Justice,[36] the Minister of the Supreme Court of Justice, Ruy Rosado de Aduiar, applied the theory of "disregard of legal entity" in order to impute liability to the shareholders of a share company for whose acts they were responsible. In the opinion of the judge that decided the case, the legal entity in fact did not exist. The shareholders had used the legal entity to perform acts against the law and to benefit themselves. The judge reasoned that the theory of disregard of legal entity was based on Kant's theory and accepted by the American legal system. Since there was not a law stated by the legislature which allowed the application of this theory, the Supreme Court of Justice held that the Brazilian Courts of Justice had the power to disregard the existence of any legal entity whose acts had been in fact performed by shareholders or directors of the company against the law.[37]

Later, the Brazilian Civil Code of 2002 was amended to include Article 50 with the purpose of giving legal authority to several judicial decisions that had been based on the theory of disregard of legal entity throughout the country. Article 50 of the Brazilian Code states that a judge, in case of a party or prosecutor's claim, may consider a legal entity as if it does not exist for liability purposes. In such an event, the shareholders or the administrators of the legal entity might be personally liable for the legal entity's liability if the fraud was committed in fact by them, and not by the legal entity. The theory of disregarding legal entity has been discussed by many scholars.[38] The judicial decision mentioned above was also a case discussed by jurists and used as precedent for several subsequent decisions.

---

36 Case nr. Resp 86506-SP.

37 Teleparker Ltda Serviços Gerais v. Alarbank Industria e Segurança Ltda. Superior Tribunal de Justiça [STJ] (Highest court of appeals on all non-constitutional matters) Resp nr. 96.47596-SP (1996).

38 *See, e.g.*, Fabio Ulhoa Coelho, Lineamentos da teoria da desconsideração da pessoa jurídica 39; 528 João Casillo, Desconsideração da pessoa jurídica (Revista dos Tribunais), at 25–37, *quoted in Teleparker Ltda Serviços Gerais v. Alarbank Industria e Segurança Ltda. Superior Tribunal de Justiça [STJ]* (highest court of appeals on all non-constitutional matters), Resp nr. 96.47596-SP (1996).

B. The Law of Corporate Reorganization—the Parmalat Case

Another recent judicial decision that provided a rule of commercial law in Brazil was the decision of the Justice of São Paulo State, dated February 11, 2004, in the case of Parmalat Brasil S/A. Parmalat Brasil S/A is a corporation organized in Brazil in accordance with Brazilian Commercial Law. It has been for many years a well-known dairy brand in Brazil. The main and controlling stockholder of Parmalat Brasil was Parmalat Finanziaria S.p.A, a corporation organized in Italy under the Commercial Law of Italy.[39]

In December of 2003, Parmalat Finanziaria S.p.A initiated legal proceedings requiring reorganization of the company and the president and financial director of the company were arrested in Italy, accused of fraud against international and national financial systems. The news about Parmalat Finanziaria, published in newspapers and magazines around the world, brought economic instability to the business of Parmalat in Brazil. Before this, the company in Brazil had been doing well and all internal business procedures had been followed for the warranty of investors. As a result of the fraud in Italy, the share price of Parmalat Brasil plummeted and the creditors of Parmalat Brasil began to call for guarantees that the company would not enter into bankruptcy.[40]

The main problem was the national bankruptcy law current at that time in Brazil. This law was thoroughly discredited by attorneys and scholars and did not provide legal support for a multinational company that might have difficulty due to a temporary economic problem. It did not help the company either to continue its business or to keep its workers employed. Because of this, the judge for the case of *Banco Sumitomo v. Parmalat Brasil S/A*, in February of 2004, decided to apply a new bankruptcy law that had not yet been enacted by the legislature and approved by the president of Brazil. In his reasoning, a

> judge is not an employer who must live closed, out of the world, and out of current reality, merely watching facts happening around him, as a shadow of the principal actors of social life. ... Following the French Government opinion about the company crises, it is not sufficient to be a jurist, it is important to be a realist, with the purpose of thinking about life conditions in the modern world where very important economic activities have developed.

In this way, the judge of the São Paulo jurisdiction ordered the application of the draft of Law 4376/93 in order to give Parmalat Brasil the right to reorganize under the new concept of bankruptcy law.[41] Because of this judicial order, Parmalat was

---

39 *See* Afonso Champi Jr. and Djalma Gonçalves Barbosa, Diário de uma Crise—Lições do Caso Parmalat. [Crises Diary—Lessons of Parmalat Case] (Qualitymark eds., 2004).

40 *Id.* at 98–99.

41 *Id.* at 99–100.

able to reorganize itself and remain active in world business. This controversial decision created much discussion in the Court of Appeal and is a good example of the new function of justice in Brazil. In fact, this decision provided reasons for enactment of the new bankruptcy law in February 9, 2005, and became a good case for discussion by professors.

IV. Legal Methods of Argumentation

Working with judicial precedents in a law school has been a challenge for a law professor in Brazil. Even though the courts of justice have been using precedents in their decisions, law schools in Brazil are used to working with objective and empirical methods of study. In law schools, Brazilian professors traditionally provide lectures on theories in their fields under an empirical philosophy. However, the practice of law in the judiciary and the legislature has demonstrated a deep and quick transformation of practical law that legal theories in the classroom might not be able to keep up with. Law professors have an obligation to teach this transformation and change the method of their teaching in order to have much better results to their lectures.

Some European scholars have defended the legal reasoning applied in the common law legal system. According to Atienza, "[w]orking with cases is a necessary legal method to the law, even though it is considered unperfected in other circumstances. The jurist uses the law with open rules that might change case to case. The law shall be opened to permit further legal opinions that might be different from the previous one."[42] Thinking this way, the objective and empirical method of studying law is not as effective since students do not learn to critique whether a legal rule is correct and can be applied in further cases. They do not have the legal reasoning skills to truly practice law because they have been trained to answer tests according to the opinions of the lecturers, not according to what they think is actually fair. In this method, they spend hours memorizing theories but not learning both sides of an argument.

In American law schools, students spend hours reading casebooks that, unlike textbooks, have neither instructions nor explanations that will serve to answer the questions posed. They then engage in a Socratic discussion with their teacher and classmates and ultimately discover on their own that a proposition is self-evident only if it must be true because its opposite is unthinkable.[43]

42 Manuel Atienza, As Razões do Direito. Teorias da Argumentação Jurídica 78 (Landy eds., 2d, 202).

43 Thomas R. Orr, Educational Method on Trial: The Case of *Socrates v. Dewey*, http://www.angelicum.net/html/educational_method_on_trial.html (visited on Nov. 29, 2006).

V. Conclusion

This chapter has stressed the similarities between the common law and the civil law systems. Special emphasis has been given to the important function assumed by the judicial precedents in both systems. Civil law is no longer based only on the statutory rules enacted by the legislature. Judges dealing with commercial issues have handed down more flexible decisions. The purpose of such flexible decisions has been to provide judicial support more adequate for the current reality of the world than simple statutes alone can provide. It is also true that the common law is also not pure case-based law. Some statutes, acts, and codes have been organized in order to provide more objectivity to circumstances of life in society.

These considerations call for the introduction of more flexibility and less dogmatism in Brazilian law schools. Even in a civil law system, the Socratic method of teaching can be useful for the student to understand the meaning of the law. Working with precedent can be difficult in the beginning for a professor not prepared to provide legal support for an unthinkable discussion. But it will be much more useful for the student to learn how to analyze and think in the relative safety of a classroom under the watchful eye of a professor, even if the only goal is to awaken that student's understanding. Using a judge's methodology from the start of law school seems more effective than trying to learn the skill later.

Nevertheless, law professors should not abandon the empirical logic adopted by the legislature when working with statutes. The lecturer should follow the more relevant legal theories in order to stimulate student understanding of the meaning of the law or the interest of the legislature in a specific area of law. Since there are two sources to develop the law in both systems, a professor of law should have the sensibility to apply a mixture of both reasoning methods in his or her lectures. According to Atienza, the law should be on one hand a system of rules, and on the other hand a system of procedures that allow for different analysis and reasoning.[44] However, to create an authentic general theory of law that reaches both systems and that arrives at a "theory of society," it is necessary to develop the dynamism of legal reasoning as demonstrated in this chapter.[45] It is important to expand the limits of domestic law to permit comparative law, which has shown itself to be very constructive in the development of the "science of law," in accordance with the current life of a global society.

44 Atienza, *supra* note 42, at 232.
45 *Id.*

Chapter 13

Western Education and Eastern Development: Ensuring Effective Development Assistance in East Asia Through Capacity Building

Jose Luis C. Syquia[1]

I. Introduction

The level of corruption in a country is a direct consequence of a weak rule of law and poor governance; the latter, in turn, impedes the ability of foreign aid to achieve the desired impact of creating sustainable development due to leakages in the government's financial and budgeting systems, and a resilient bureaucratic substructure. In the Philippines, for example, it has been observed that poor long-term economic performance reflects flaws in public sector governance and that these failings are rooted in weaknesses in the structure of public administration and in features of the broader political economy within which such structures function.[2]

Some points are obvious: development in the East Asian context will almost always involve external aid, whether in the form of technical or financial assistance; and this assistance is normally conditioned upon adopting principles, policies, and systems that are commonly perceived to be western in origin, i.e., trade liberalization, privatization, and market economies. A primary issue that is often underestimated is whether these conditions are acceptable to the local population, and a more serious concern lies in the fact that the recipient country may have the tendency to become dependent on foreign aid and thus run the risk of failing to establish within its own economic and political structures the necessary elements of self-sustainable development. In this scenario, the end result that it is

---

1 Associate Professorial Lecturer (University of Santo Tomas); Adjunct Professor (Asian Institute of Management), Partner, Syquia Pascual-Lopez & Santos Law Offices; LL.M. 1998 *cum laude* (University of Pittsburgh School of Law); LL.B. 1997 (University of Santo Tomas); B.A. in philosophy 1992 (University of Santo Tomas).

2 THE WORLD BANK GROUP, PHILIPPINES: FROM SHORT-TERM GROWTH TO SUSTAINED DEVELOPMENT 11 (2005).

hoped will be achieved through foreign aid is not realized, and the need for more assistance is created—thus starting a vicious cycle.

This chapter will deal with the problem of aid ineffectiveness as a direct consequence of a failure to achieve support—at both national and local community levels—for critical legal and institutional reforms that are meant to address loopholes and plug leakages in the system. In so doing, it will discuss the most basic ingredient of effectiveness: that of gathering support through capacity building. I will trace hindrances to popular acceptance of a reform agenda all the way back to their roots in the classroom, where the mindsets of both the decision maker and the general public have been formed, and will present a practical approach to forging a harmonious link between a generally western reform principle and the eastern context in which it is sought to be applied. As it turns out, the formula for such a feat is not at all beyond the reach of East Asian decision makers and executives—most of whom, by the way, hold advanced educational degrees from the west (or from developed countries, for that matter).

The approach presented in this chapter will be based on actual experiences—failures and successes—specifically showing how legal and institutional reforms aimed at fighting corruption and improving aid effectiveness in the Philippines were either ineffectively or successfully launched through various initiatives. As these initiatives were intended to introduce "western" principles, it will become apparent that the ultimate impact upon the country hinged on how well these initiatives have been acclimatized to local communities. I will discuss how capacity building efforts could be utilized to engage the various stakeholders, not only at the national level, but also—and more importantly—at the regional and local government levels. I will also discuss the value of the U.S. application of the Socratic method whereby individuals are encouraged to participate in the development of a professor's conclusions, and how it can be applied to gather stakeholder participation and galvanize their ideas so that these stakeholders not only are considered contributors to the thought process, but indeed become owners of the entire reform agenda. This approach is not without problems, and so I will also point out areas of difficulty and continuing concern, most especially in approaching decentralized local government units enjoying the constitutional right of local autonomy.

In discussing the topic of corruption—due to the fact that this subject matter takes different forms and can cover diverse activities, depending on where it occurs, its scale and intensity, and the behavior involved[3]—I will focus on the public sector, specifically considering grand-scale corruption on the expenditure/procurement side (as opposed to the revenue-generating side). I do this not only because these examples involve large amounts and tend to have a greater impact upon the lives of a country's constituents and its economic standing in the

3 *See* Philippine Center for Investigative Journalism, Investigating Corruption: A Do-It-Yourself Guide (Sheila S. Coronel and Lorna Kalaw-Tirol eds, 2002), for a more detailed discussion on the various types of corruption.

international community, but most especially because this type of corruption has a direct and negative consequence on aid effectiveness. Even so, this chapter is not intended to be an exhaustive treatise on corruption, and so any discussion of this subject will be limited to those aspects that are relevant to the coverage suggested above.

II. Corruption in East Asia: Focus on the Philippines

Some economists have observed that informal institutions still manage to bring in impressive economic performance among East Asian countries, as in the cases of China, Indonesia, Korea, the Philippines and Thailand. These countries have attracted large inflows of private investment over a long period, despite being featured prominently in the "world's list" of most corrupt countries.[4] This observation has since been challenged by the occurrence of the East Asian financial crisis. In fact, it is now recognized that the East Asian financial crisis was rooted, at least in part, in the absence of adequate formal and institutional systems that, in effect, created an atmosphere of favoritism and non-transparency in government and financial transactions. Indeed, this absence led to the proliferation of informal and non-legal arrangements to fill the void, and while these have attracted private investments, the profile of these investments were either short term or took the nature of "sweetheart deals" between government and favored firms.

According to the Philippine Center for Investigative Journalism (PCIJ), while these "sweetheart deals" resulted in spectacular economic growth, over the long term the sustainability of such a growth has been put in doubt, especially after the East Asian economic crisis in 1997.[5] Jose Edgardo Campos reports that "the East Asian financial crisis has heightened the concern not only over good governance but also over the relationship between governance and corruption. Many critics of the Asian miracle have argued that the governance structures underpinning the East Asian economies have been largely responsible for the crisis."[6]

While the East Asian financial crisis was the result of an amalgamation of various financial, political and economic factors, systemic corruption played an important role in the outflow of short-term investments from such countries as Vietnam, Indonesia, Thailand, and the Philippines, and thus contributed as well to the collapse of the financial markets in these countries. Views on the root causes of the crisis range from those that blame the prevalence of close government ties with business elites that gave rise to regulations based on relations and "crony capitalism," to those that see the crisis as a result of premature liberalization of capital markets and the activities of speculators rather than too excessive investment

---

4 The Boom and Bust of East Asia: Corruption 2 (Jose Edgardo Campos ed., Ateneo de Manila University Press 2001).

5 Coronel and Kalaw-Tirol, *supra* note 3, at 17.

6 Campos, *supra* note 4, at 1.

encouraged by moral hazard.[7] I tend to take the former position, because of the inherent uncertainty that a corrupt administration fosters, both on the side of the investor and on that of the government.

With respect to the investors' side, the absence of legal and institutional frameworks that adequately protect private property rights and ensure open and transparent competition in access to government projects has created an atmosphere of uncertainty because public officials lack the backing of credible institutions that serve to convince legitimate business firms that investing in the country would not be a risky venture. And even if firms were willing to commit funds—whether through legitimate means or "sweetheart deals"—the type of investments a corrupt bureaucracy tends to attract are those with a get-rich-quick attitude. In other words, corruption inhibits a government's ability to garner secure, long-term investments, and favors public contractors propped up by sovereign guarantees. As observed by Susan Rose-Ackerman:

> The corrupt nature of the deal may give the firm a short-run orientation. There are two reasons for this. First, the concessionaire (or contractor) may fear that those in power are vulnerable to overthrow because of their corruption. A new regime may not honor the old one's commitments. Second, even if the current regime remains in power, the winner may fear the imposition of arbitrary rules and financial demands once investments are sunk. It may be concerned that the ruler will permit competitors to enter the market or worry that its contract will be voided for reasons of politics or greed. Having paid a bribe in the past, the firm is vulnerable to extortionary demands in the future.[8]

Corruption not only generates uncertainty on the part of the contractor or investor, but also on the part of the public officer in power. For example, when I was in Thailand in May 2005 to speak before public officers on the benefits of assessing public procurement systems, national newspaper headlines were then focused on a controversy over the procurement of the baggage handling system for the new Suvarnabhumi Airport. Allegations of bribery of government officials rose all the way up to the Prime Minister, Thaksin Shinawatra, and eventually led to calls for his resignation.[9] A year later, swelling demands for Thaksin's resignation on allegations of corruption reached their climax with a coup d'état that ousted him from power on September 20, 2006—Thailand's first in fifteen years, but only one among many military takeovers in the nation's modern history.[10] Thaksin's ousting

---

7 *See* Gregory W. Noble and John Ravenhill, *Causes and Consequences of the Asian Financial Crisis*, *in* THE ASIAN FINANCIAL CRISIS AND THE ARCHITECTURE OF GLOBAL FINANCE 8–9 (Cambridge University Press 2000).

8 SUSAN ROSE-ACKERMAN, CORRUPTION AND GOVERNMENT: CAUSES, CONSEQUENCES AND REFORM 34 (Cambridge University Press 1999).

9 *See* THE NATION (May 24–25, 2005), www.nationmultimedia.com.

10 *Thaksin Ousted in Coup (AP)*, THE PHILIPPINE STAR (Sept. 21, 2006), at 1.

and the allegations of corruption against him are quite intriguing, as they came in spite of his noted achievements on pro-market reforms in the Thai economy, and, more so, because the coup reportedly created even more uncertainty over the future of Thailand, initially raising concerns among business leaders and investors on the country's democracy and a slowdown in its economy.[11]

Needless to say, the type of corruption that normally generates this type of uncertainty would have to be grand scale. PCIJ reports another example involving former President Joseph Estrada of the Philippines, where, in 1999, the government paid the development corporation of a well-known religious leader P1.22 billion (US$23.5 million) for land that was going to be affected by the construction of a highway. The developer paid over P15,000 (US$288) per square meter, when zonal values were less than a third of that amount and market values of land in nearby areas were much less.[12] According to the same report, Estrada had a direct hand in the transaction, because the amount reached the threshold for government contracts that required the president's prior approval. He directed the Toll Regulatory Board to acquire the property from the "favored" corporation, and signed the final approval of the deed of sale and the contracts for land acquisition.[13] Estrada was eventually ousted from power on January 20, 2001, through a popular uprising labeled "People Power II," under allegations of graft and corruption, and faced criminal charges before the Philippines' anti-graft court, the Sandiganbayan.

The story of corruption and the uncertainty it fosters do not necessarily end with the ousting of the chief executive. For example, even with Estrada facing graft charges, and much to the dismay of the general public, the succeeding administration also encountered its share of allegations and scams, including the Supreme Court's January 2004 nullification of a P1.2 billion (US$23 million) purchase contract by the Commission on Elections (COMELEC) of nearly 200 ballot counting machines that would have modernized the Philippines' antiquated electoral system—known to be riddled with opportunities for poll fraud.[14] Among the grounds and irregularities cited by the Court was the provision of an unrealistic technical compliance requirement (99.9995 percent accuracy rating) in the bidding documents, and the award of the contract to the winning bidder despite its failure to meet these requirements. The Court stressed in *Information Technology* that:

> [T]he essence of public bidding is violated by the practice of requiring very high standards or unrealistic specifications that cannot be met—like the 99.9995 percent accuracy rating in this case—only to water them down *after* the bid has been awarded. Such scheme, which discourages the entry of prospective *bona*

---

11 *Thai Economy Faces Slowdown Over Coup (AFP)*, The Philippine Star (Sept. 26, 2006), at B-12. *See also* Alex Magno, *Coup*, The Philippine Star (Sept. 21, 2006), at 12.

12 Coronel and Kalaw-Tirol, *supra* note 3, at 13.

13 *Id.*

14 *See Information Technology Foundation of the Philippines v. Commission on Elections*, 419 S.C.R.A. 141 (Jan. 13, 2004).

> *fide* bidders, is in fact a sure indication of fraud in the bidding, designed to eliminate fair competition.[15]

The Ombudsman subsequently recommended that graft charges be filed against COMELEC officials and commissioners, and that those officials be dismissed and the commissioner be impeached.[16]

At the same time that corruption breeds illicit interests and contracts, it also effectively wards off legitimate investments due to the increased costs of doing business and measures that either limit competition or utterly prohibit outsiders from participating in public contracts. The latter of these effects is exemplified in local government procurement contracts where bidding is limited to favored suppliers or contractors. At times, the favoritism is brazenly "legitimized" through requirements from local mayors that suppliers and contractors set-up offices within the locality and secure local permits as a pre-condition to being able to participate in bidding. The reason for this type of restriction in some localities is obvious. When I reviewed the procurement contracts of a particular provincial government in the Philippines, covering the period from 2003 to 2005, I found that when outside firms were allowed to bid on its public contracts, the bids came in around 20 percent lower than when competition was limited to such "local" firms.

Moreover, when competition is limited, the direct effect is overpriced projects and products of inferior quality. In a report I was tasked to draft for the European Union Commission in 2005 through 2006, I found that provincial governments in the Philippines are generally unable to achieve satisfactory levels of competition on their public contracts, that local governments generally lack adequate accountability measures to ensure that collusive and fraudulent practices are properly addressed, and that there exists a common weakness in establishing accurate contract cost estimates.[17] Taken together, these findings lead to an overall negative impact on the level of economic development local governments in the Philippines are able to achieve.[18] This conclusion complements a 2003 PCIJ report that exposed how local governments were wasting public funds, mostly based on reports from the Philippines' Commission on Audit (COA). Some of the salient examples in the PCIJ report include:[19]

---

15 *Id.* at 188.

16 *See Borra, Five Other Comelec Execs Liable in "Mega" Deal*, The Philippine Star (July 1, 2006).

17 *See* European Union Commission, *Improving Efficiency of Provincial Procurement in Ten Provinces* (May 2006).

18 *Id.*

19 *See* Philippine Center for Investigative Journalism (PCIJ), *While Congress Hounds the Supreme Court, Local Governments are Off the Hook* (Nov. 3–4, 2003), *available at* http://www.pcij.org/stories/2003/localprocurement.html.

1. A municipal government lost more than P135 million (US$2.6 million) in 13 irregular deals and projects it undertook in 2000 and 2001.
2. A city government purchased furniture in 2000 and 2001 that was found to be excessive in quantity and overpriced by more than P110 million (US$2.1 million). It also had an allotment of P152,910.00 (US$2,940) for 1,699 standard pencils—which is roughly P90 (US$1.7) for each one, where the normal price is just P4.50 (US$.09) per pencil.
3. In 2001, a city government paid P850,000.00 (US$16,346) for dental chairs that were never delivered.
4. A scanner worth around P500,000.00 (US$9,615) was purchased by a municipal government in 2001 for P1.4 million (US$26,923), and it had yet to be used when the COA team visited it in late 2002. This same municipality also bought real estate for P25 million (US$480,769), which the COA said was P8.6 million (US$165,384) more than the land's real value. Although the site was intended to be a multilevel housing project, the multimillion-peso lot has since been turned into a garbage dump.

These examples clearly show that if a public officer were suffering from weak moral fiber, it would be easy for him to accept bribes in an environment that shows no sincere effort at fighting corruption. Similarly, a private firm has several reasons to pay off officials for procurement contracts. As Rose-Ackerman describes:

> First, a firm may pay to be included in the list of pre-qualified bidders and to restrict the length of the list. Second, it may pay for inside information. Third, bribes may induce officials to structure the bidding specifications so that the corrupt firm is the only qualified supplier. Fourth, a firm may pay to be selected as the winning contractor. And fifth, once a firm wins the contract, it may pay to get inflated prices or to skimp on quality.[20]

In the case of the procurement of Thailand's baggage-handling system, it was reported that the CTX machines purchased were far more expensive than the rival 6500 machines, made by L3 Communications, and that the Airports of Thailand Plc. (AOT) could not explain how the former were better than the latter.[21]

The immediate result of corruption in public procurement is that the public receives overpriced projects with either inferior quality or, at most, questionable technical advantage. On a larger scale, systemic corruption on the expenditure side eventually distorts the allocation of economic benefits from the state, as decisions on the choice of projects are then based on the ability to offer a higher return to the public officer involved, rather than on the needs of his constituency. In the end, the biggest losers are the poor who need these services the most, as money is taken

---

20 Rose-Ackerman, *supra* note 8, at 27–28.

21 *Scanner Scandal: Contractor Says it won't Pay Big Fines*, The Nation (May 25, 2005), at 4A.

away from education, health care and public services, and spent for useless "white elephants" and infrastructure projects.[22]

To place this discussion in perspective, PCIJ tells the story of a mother whose daughter was about to give birth prematurely at a city-owned hospital but had to wait in line for an available incubator. Given the shortage of the machines, the mother had to sign a waiver freeing the doctors from liability in case anything happened to the infant while waiting for an available incubator.[23] According to the same report, there would have been no shortage of incubators had the city government been more careful with its expenses and procurement planning, considering that the city lost nearly P62 million (US$1,192,307) on overpriced equipment and hospital beds—including the purchase of 188 beds for P36.4 million (US$700,000), despite the fact that importation documents obtained from the Bureau of Customs showed that the real cost should have only been P2.4 million (US$46,153).[24]

Grand scale corruption usually involves major government projects and programs, because corrupt actors frequently transfer large financial benefits to private firms through procurement contracts and awards of concessions. Of course, a share is always allotted to the corrupt official, so that, in total, these cases have a staggering impact upon the government's budget and the country's growth prospects.[25]

In the Philippines, a 1998 study of projects funded from congressional initiatives, such as the Countrywide Development Fund (CDF), Congressional Initiative Allocations (CIAs), the Public Works Fund (PWF) and the School Building Fund (SBF)—otherwise known as "pork-barrel"-funded projects—provide a clear picture of how the pie is cut among the numerous actors, and how much remains. It was reported that for public works, 12 percent to 20 percent of the budget for the project goes to the lawmaker, 1 percent to 2 percent can go to the Department of Budget and Management (DBM) personnel responsible for releasing the budget, 10 percent goes to the head of the implementing agency, 7 percent goes to the mayor, and 3 percent goes to the local community leader—leaving roughly 63 percent for project implementation.[26] For medical supplies and educational materials, 40 percent to 50 percent of the budget for the project can go to the lawmaker, 1 percent to 2 percent can go to the DBM personnel, and 10 percent goes to the head of the implementing agency—leaving around 40 percent to the supplier. It is thus clear that, for pork-barrel-funded projects, corruption systemically cuts across several agencies and branches of governments, as legislators have to depend upon budgeting and implementing agencies to get the pork through—but not without first slicing and sharing it among all those involved.

---

22 Coronel and Kalaw-Tirol, *supra* note 2, at 18–19.

23 PCIJ, *supra* note 19.

24 *Id.*

25 *See* Rose-Ackerman, *supra* note 8, at 27.

26 Pork and Other Perks: Corruption and Governance in the Philippines 38–43 (Sheila S. Coronel ed., PCIJ 1998).

Given all this, it is not surprising that in a survey conducted by the Social Weather Stations (SWS) in June 2000, more than three-quarters of the respondents said that from 30 percent to 50 percent of Philippine government funds were being wasted due to corrupt practices involved in public projects and procurement. Assuming a conservative estimate of 20 percent, what this means is that in 2001, when the Philippine Government's public procurement budget amounted to P82 billion (US$1.6 billion) for the national government and P22 billion (US$423 million) for local governments, an estimated P21 billion (US$403 million) was leakage due to corruption.[27]

Five years later, not much had changed in the Philippines. In a 2006 SWS survey, it was reported that public sector contracts usually allow 15 percent to 20 percent for bribes, and that 18 percent of the enterprises surveyed admitted to having been asked by government officials for a bribe in the supply of goods and services. On a regional scale, a 2005 World Bank report shows the Philippines and Indonesia ranking very poorly, in comparison with their East Asian neighbors, with respect to corruption.[28] To sum up, one major cause of aid ineffectiveness in East Asia is the fact that bureaucratic corruption creates leakages within the system, so that only a diminished percentage of the original budget reaches the intended recipients and beneficiaries, and projects are not identified on the basis of necessity, but rather on the amount of return they might provide to the corrupt actors.

One may be tempted to think that it would be best for donor countries and institutions to consider withdrawing assistance to developing nations that exhibit the propensity for leakages and waste; but this approach obviously fails to take into account the value of economic assistance, and the impact an economic crisis within a country may have upon an entire region and across the globe. One need only look back at the 1997 East Asian financial crisis. As noted by Gregory Noble and John Ravenhill, "the contagious effects of the crisis spread to financial systems beyond East Asia—first Russia and then Brazil suffered massive capital outflows."[29]

Indeed, East Asian countries are well aware of the barriers to development created by weak governance structures, and the effects these bring upon the economy. In Vietnam, for example, substantial and earnest efforts have been undertaken to push forward in the country's transition from a closed to a market economy. These include its endeavor to join the World Trade Organization (WTO)

---

27 Jose Luis C. Syquia, *The Legislative History of Republic Act No. 9184, and the Policies and Principles Behind Procurement Reform in the Philippines*, 11 Law. Rev. 5 (Nov. 30, 2003), citing the Sponsorship Speech delivered by Senator Edgardo J. Angara for the Procurement Reform Bill, entitled "Building Honest Roads to Progress" (Oct. 24, 2002).

28 The World Bank Group, *supra* note 2, at 12, *citing* Transparency International and Credit Lyonnais Securities Asia.

29 Noble and Ravenhill, *supra* note 7, at 1–2.

and the recent passage of various laws by the National Assembly to fight corruption and increase foreign investments. These laws include the new Procurement Law, the new Investment Law, and the new State Auditing Law. Vietnam has also been receiving more Official Development Assistance (ODA) through the years, where disbursements increased from around US$400 million in 1993 to more than US$1.6 billion in 2000.[30] However, the issue in Vietnam is the same as in other countries—impact. Just recently, for example, a Vietnamese newspaper report cited the ineffective use of ODA as a continuing problem in the country.[31] The State Auditing Agency of Vietnam had itself released a more telling account on the issue where, in a 2005 audit report, it stated that the government's state budget lost VND4.5 Trillion (US$281,250,000) in that year due to inappropriate spending decisions, particularly in basic construction projects, and misconduct at all stages from the planning stage to the delivery stage.[32]

These developments have contributed to a heightened interest in governance and the rule of law among international financial institutions (IFIs) with large investments in East Asia. It was widely believed that institutionalized corruption was made possible by a dysfunctional, politically malleable legal system.[33] In 2005, the World Bank reported the following observation for the Philippines:

> An explanation that is influential among researchers and policy circles in the Philippines is that poor long-term economic performance reflects flaws in public sector governance. These failings are rooted in weaknesses in the structures of public administration and in features of the broader political economy within which such structures function. The instability and disappointing development outcomes of the "weak state" have undermined the effectiveness of public institutions to work for the common good and weakened the sense of a meaningful social compact. More specifically, they have constrained policy implementation, contributed to the fiscal problem, undermined the investment climate and, by reducing the effectiveness of service delivery, diluted the benefits of the growth that has occurred.[34]

III. Hitting the Spot that Matters

More than ever after the 1997 crisis institutions such as the World Bank, the Asian Development Bank (ADB), and the United States Agency for International

---

30 The World Bank, *Country Procurement Assessment Report: Vietnam, Transforming Public Procurement* 1 (Oct. 2002).

31 *Awareness Needed to Curb Ineffective Use of ODA*, Vietnam News (Oct. 20, 2006), at 2.

32 *Shocking Losses!*, Vietnam Financial Times (Sept. –Oct. 2006), at 17.

33 *See* Campos, *supra* note 4, at 2.

34 The World Bank Group, *supra* note 2, at 11.

Development (USAID) were not only interested in offering assistance for the construction of roads, school buildings, and the purchase of textbooks and medicines but were also providing technical assistance and grants for the improvement of public sector management and governance. This included public procurement and financial management reforms, improvement of service deliveries through improved local government performance, professionalization of the civil service, improving the performance of the internal revenue agency, and strengthening regulatory capacity. In the words of the World Bank, "[S]trengthening governance in public institutions and reducing opportunities for corruption will be important to boost investor confidence and to deliver services more effectively."[35]

There is indeed a compelling reason for concern on the part of both development partners and the developing countries. In 2006 alone, it was reported that the Philippines received commitments for US$10.08 billion of Official Development Assistance (ODA) loans, with a majority of these having a blended grant element comprising more than half (54.84 percent) of the total overall value.[36] In Mindanao, Southern Philippines, financial assistance for roads and infrastructure projects from development partners, such as the World Bank and the ADB, have been substantial, but as reported by Marites Danguilan Vitug, these projects have been slowed by delays and misbehaving contractors, corruption, political patronage, and the inability of the Department of Public Works and Highways (DPWH) to discipline erring firms—regardless of whether these projects are locally or internationally bid out.[37] Vitug's reports further show that large contracts from World Bank funded projects in Mindanao,

> won through international bidding and supposedly under the strict guidelines of the World Bank, can still be bogged down by problems caused by incompetent management.
>
> More importantly, these cases reinforce strong doubts about the integrity of the prequalification and bidding process in particular, and the DPWH in general.[38]

While the report generally covers projects funded from 1993 to 1998, it appears that the problem still persists. For example, I recently assessed a foreign-assisted project for the construction of a farm-to-market road in which the beneficiary was a municipality in Mindanao. During the assessment, the team discovered that there were no documents to confirm that the contractor had a valid contractor's license and that a recently approved change order had deleted major items and effectively

35 *Id.* at 5.

36 Asian Development Bank, *Asia Aid Effectiveness Forum Preparatory Materials—Philippines Procurement Reform* 3 (Draft Report dated July 26, 2006), citing National Economic Development Authority, 14th ODA Portfolio Review (2006).

37 *See* Coronel, *supra* note 26, at 186–212.

38 *Id.* at 191.

reduced the contractor's scope of work to mere clearing and grubbing. Upon site inspection, we discovered that, although a written report had shown that the project was 80 percent accomplished, the road was not passable, major excavations had not been done, and the contractor had concentrated on extending the road from its original length of 4.5 km to 5.5 km, instead of fulfilling its obligations under the original program of works. To top it all off, we began to question the need for the entire project, considering that it was located deep within a mountain and that, in order to reach it, the team had to travel via a rough road that was more than twice the length of the project and almost impossible for a four-wheeler to traverse.

It is apparent that while ensuring aid effectiveness requires the improvement of public sector management and governance, special attention has to be given to public procurement. Not only is this area especially prone to grand-scale corruption, but the skimming of funds from local and ODA projects have the effect of lessening the desired impact upon the intended beneficiaries and end users. More importantly, this negative impact cannot simply be viewed on a one-to-one correspondence. The effects of corruption can cost much more than the amount stolen from the public, especially when it involves the social sector—such as ghost deliveries of vaccines to a particular rural community that will suffer higher mortality rates as a consequence, or the under-delivery of desks and armchairs to provincial elementary schools whose students would have to continue to bear sitting on the floor.

It is also evident that fighting corruption, whether in public procurement or in other areas of governance, requires not only reforming legal and institutional frameworks, but also—and more importantly—addressing the human element. Surely, no matter how perfect a law may be, and no matter how well an institution utilizes information technology, there will always be another person on the other side of the counter. Conversely, no matter how faulty a government's processes may be, if government officials have incorruptible values, graft and corruption would not be as problematic as it is now.[39]

IV. Laying the Groundwork for Reforms in Public Procurement

Given the common goals of fighting corruption, plugging the leakages in public expenditure and improving governance, the Philippine Government and its development partners mapped out various strategies to move forward. One major achievement is the Government Procurement Reform Act, Republic Act (R.A.) No. 9184, which was signed by the president on January 10, 2003, and took effect on January 26, 2003. The law itself was part of a broader public procurement reform program, for which the Philippine Government took full ownership. This program

39 *See* Jose Luis C. Syquia, *Reforming Government Procurement and Going Electronic*, 10 Law. Rev. 11, 12 (Oct. 31, 2001).

primarily focused on and achieved equally substantial results in addressing the following objectives:

1. addressing calls for good governance by reducing the opportunities and level of corruption in public procurement;
2. streamlining the procurement process and developing a single omnibus law that would eliminate the numerous procurement laws, rules and regulations in existence;
3. providing for effective policy guidance on public procurement through the creation of a top-level inter-agency Government Procurement Policy Board (GPPB), with a Technical Support Office (TSO) that would perform the needed groundwork and undertake the actual tasks of monitoring the implementation of procurement reforms;
4. developing a cadre of procurement professionals in all national agencies and local governments, through capacity building and training programs, including a professionalization program;
5. increasing transparency in public procurement through increased civil society participation in both monitoring activities and policy formulation;
6. providing specific criminal, civil, and administrative sanctions for corrupt, collusive, and fraudulent practices in public procurement; and
7. incorporating information technology into the procurement process through the development and operation of the Government Electronic Procurement System (G-EPS).[40]

In recognition of the Philippines' initial achievements on the public procurement front, World Bank country director to the Philippines Joachim von Amsberg acknowledged that "the Philippines has one of the best procurement laws of any country and if it was implemented for all public procurement there will be huge savings … and it has brought down the cost of textbooks, brought down the cost of roads, of infrastructure."[41] Clearly, the passage of the procurement reform law has been a landmark achievement in the Philippines—effectively linking both administration and opposition politicians to focus on a common goal. However, while the observation of von Amsberg gives due recognition to the efforts of all the reformers within and outside the government who have been feverishly and unceasingly fighting corruption on public procurement on all fronts, it brings to the fore an equally important challenge: implementing the reforms effectively.

Initial reports and assessments have shown that a number of corruption and criminal cases relying upon the provisions of the new procurement law have

---

40 *See* Jose Luis C. Syquia, *Institutionalizing Public Procurement Reforms Through the Government Procurement Policy Board and the Technical Support Office*, 8 Law. Rev. 4 (Aug. 31, 2003).

41 *WB Urges "Quality Spending" for RP*, The Philippine Star (Aug. 11, 2006), at 1 and 8.

already been initiated or filed. For example, in early September 2006 the Office of the Ombudsman ordered the preventive suspension of a city mayor in Metro Manila, his vice-mayor and ten city councilors, for approving several contracts for garbage collection and disposal without the benefit of public bidding. The laws that were reportedly used as the bases for the criminal investigation and the eventual suspension were the Philippines' Anti-Graft and Corrupt Practices Act and the Government Procurement Reform Act.[42] However, the ultimate test of success of the procurement law is not the number of cases filed under it, but whether it has effectively lessened corruption in public expenditures, and lowered the costs of contracts. Undoubtedly, this requires the full cooperation of critical players in both national and local government units; and thus requires reaching out to the human element of the reforms.

Having established the legal and institutional frameworks, the next logical step is selling the reforms to the various political units and implementers in the field, and cascading these to all levels of government, down to the smallest local communities—clearly a step in which capacity building will prove to be especially relevant.

V. The Socratic Method Applied

There are several reasons for aid ineffectiveness, but one major cause is that policy makers in developing countries adopt western policies they have learned about from developed countries, but fail to sell the idea to the public at large. In effect, while policy makers take the first step towards policy development by pushing aside the "old ways," no certainty exists as to whether the "new ways" will appropriately fill the void. Thus, expectations that arise among the different dissatisfied groups will often be in conflict.[43] Poor people in developing countries see very few foreign aid dollars that donor countries spend on their behalf. One major reason for this is that these dollars have to go through recipient governments that use the aid for their own set of purposes, which can be (and often are) at variance with the welfare of the general populace.[44]

Distrust from the general public may even arise, so that foreign aid is regarded as a way by which western powers influence policy making within a developing country. Indeed, foreign aid is now commonly viewed as a way through which a donor government's wealth is recycled back to it with interest, through conditions that require the recipient government to purchase equipment manufactured within

42 *Peewee Won't Give Up City Hall*, The Philippine Star (Sept. 3, 2006), at 16–17.

43 *See* David Cushman Coyle, National Development and How it Works 12 (New American Library 1963).

44 *See* Melvyn Krauss, How Nations Grow Rich: The Case for Free Trade 62 (Oxford University Press 1997).

the donor country or to hire its consulting firms.[45] The Philippines is no exception to this inclination, as exemplified in 2003 when a Senate inquiry looked into suspicions that the United States was meddling in Philippine economic policies through a USAID (United States Agency for International Development) project called "Accelerating Growth Investment and Liberalization with Equity" (AGILE), which had at that time satellite offices within key executive departments, including the Departments of Finance, Budget and Management, and the Central Bank. The contract of the U.S. consulting firm that took the lead for the project was not extended, and a new project was introduced in its stead.

There is a clear need to address the problem of aid effectiveness, not only so that roads, bridges, and school buildings are built, but also so that the principles of effective democratic institution are fully integrated within a developing nation's society—not in the context of merely photocopying western principles and systems, but through localized concepts that have seamlessly developed within indigenous environments. This is a challenge for donor governments and organizations that have adopted what has been referred to as an "in-out" approach, whereby initiatives are introduced in a developing country by the donor through the creation of parallel institutions that are not necessarily representative of the people.

Some donors have supported the establishment and initial operation of non-governmental organizations (NGOs), so that money is channeled through these NGOs instead of through existing public institutions. While these NGOs may be successful in advocating for some reform measures, this approach will not necessarily have the impact of reforming government institutions and behaviors, because the reform initiative will be regarded as external and will not develop the trust, confidence, and ownership of critical players from within the government. Moreover, once the donor funds have been exhausted, it is not uncommon to see several of these NGOs deviate from their original altruistic visions and missions and turn into high charging consulting firms—particularly in the case of those that have failed to come up with sustainability plans.

Of course, working through government institutions has its own challenges. While it may be more effective in garnering local ownership, it requires a sense of "letting go" on the part of the donor, so that the views of the recipient agency are expressed to some extent. In the Philippines, the position of procurement reformers has been that it would be better to have a less-than-ideal reform with strong government ownership, than a "state-of the-the-art" reform with little or no ownership, as the latter has very little chance of succeeding.[46] This means that aid

45 Interview with Mr. Miomir Serbinson, former Director of International Public Sector Development, European Branch, Price Waterhouse Coopers (Sept. 15, 2006).

46 Asian Development Bank, *supra* note 36, at 10, citing JOSE EDGARDO CAMPOS AND JOSE LUIS SYQUIA, MANAGING THE POLITICS OF REFORM: OVERHAULING THE LEGAL INFRASTRUCTURE OF PUBLIC PROCUREMENT IN THE PHILIPPINES 10 (The World Bank 2006).

effectiveness should not only factor in the problem of corruption, but also the issue of authentic participation from all the stakeholders.

One cannot expect to successfully cascade public reforms by simply creating parallel institutions. Rather, there must be buy-in on the part of everyone involved in the reform process—from those working within the government to the simple folk living in far-flung localities—a task that requires addressing certain nuances that are normally overlooked by an executive living within the confines of his office. Thus, attaining effective development assistance takes the form of a hard sell, and a reform-minded policy maker may have to remove his bureaucrat's cap in favor of that of a street-smart salesman.

In the trenches of institutional reforms, development is first and foremost an educational matter, and effective reform presupposes an educated public that not only understands the reform, but also believes in it wholeheartedly. This leads us back to the classroom because, in both instances, the mindset of all the actors, including the policy maker, becomes critical.

VI. In the Classroom

Children learn what they live and tend to follow actions more than words. In East Asia, when a reform initiative is perceived to be western in origin, support cannot be won by simply requiring compliance with legislation, especially when the law reflects a foreign approach. This is very much similar to a student who is simply spoon-fed textbook materials versus one who feels part of the thought process that led to the professor's conclusions. This analogy is more realistic than academic because an eastern policy maker who may have been educated in the west (but who has only digested the learning materials without absorbing the approach by which he was educated) runs the risk of failure. A common source of frustration is the discovery that the knowledge he brought back with him has found little or no market in his own country.[47] The problem here is that the policy maker has merely adopted western principles without adapting these to his environment and, as experience would bear out, the road towards successful reform is a long and arduous one, requiring considerable patience and a carefully thought-out strategy for managing the politics of the process.[48] This is especially true in an environment rife with a culture of corruption, because mere words will not be sufficient to cut through an established mindset.

Strong morals capable of countering temptation are best taught during a child's formative years and then constantly nourished through good examples. However, this does not mean that one has to throw in the towel when confronted with a bureaucracy of contrary tendencies. Provided that the necessary legal and institutional frameworks exist to break the layers of moss so that the sunlight of

47 *See also* Coyle, *supra* note 43.

48 *See* Campos and Syquia, *supra* note 46, at 30.

transparency shines on an otherwise murky environment, I believe that public officers, regardless of their age, may also be "taught" how to behave appropriately, or at least work within a system that is perceived to be functioning effectively—whether through a revived motivation to do the right thing, or pressure to follow a proper lead. Unlike a child in class, however, a public officer is not expected to have a *tabula rasa*, and may be expected to have a frame of mind that is formed in accordance with existing customs and "standard operating procedures" within his particular agency. This means that while instruction would still have to be maintained as a primary method of learning, it would have to give in to more participatory and ownership-building approaches, so that even opposing factions are regarded as partners in the entire process.

As a product of the Philippine education system, I have been fully immersed in the concept of "recitation"—a process whereby a student is asked, or ordered as it were, to stand up in class and answer questions thrown at him by the teacher. I was introduced to this system as early as my preparatory year at age four, where an answer of "I don't know because I played over the weekend and forgot to study" would merit a smack on my palm with the teacher's ruler. This process would continue on through my elementary years (six years at the time), and on to high school (which would normally take four more years). During all these years, we were trained to speak when called upon and—although we were allowed to raise our hands and volunteer—there was the constant fear of giving the wrong answer. Of course, as we grew older, the fear of smacking turned into the fear of humiliation and a failing mark.

By the time I took undergraduate studies at university, the recitation system had taken root in us. We were taught during the first year of college that this approach found its basis and justification in the so-called "Socratic method." This was the first time I had heard the term, and I remember wondering why this was never explained to me earlier, since it had been an integral part of the system that formed my mind. I merely dismissed my question by telling myself that I was probably too young to understand such a complex principle, and that it was effective in instilling discipline within the class. At any rate, by the time the Socratic method was explained to us, we were made to understand by experience that this method was intended to show how little a student knew about a subject matter through the process of squeezing and testing his knowledge until a mistake is exposed, so that—having accepted the need for knowledge—the student is now open to learning more.

The Socratic method indeed involves seeking knowledge through questions and answers, and is a process whereby a teacher refutes narrow definitions given by a student through counter-examples designed to show the uninformed or restrictive nature of the given definition.[49] However, the Socratic method is not supposed to end with the teacher telling the student "you are wrong, sit down, this is the right answer." It was not supposed to be used for purposes of determining

49 *See* T.Z. Lavine, From Socrates to Sartre 22 (Bantam Books 1984).

whether or not a student has properly memorized his book. On the contrary, it uses the technique of the counter-example to mount a series of questions meant to expand the number of examples, cases, and particulars to be included in a given definition so that at the end of the process the student acknowledges the limitations of his original definition but is involved in the process of crafting a more accurate and encompassing one.[50]

In college, I decided to major in philosophy, knowing full well that this would mean having to face more recitations than students majoring in other studies. Despite this risk, I believed I would finally be able to argue my thoughts and beliefs in class and challenge ideas thrown upon me by my professors. With some disappointment, but with more resignation than ever, I found out that this would not be the case in most instances. For sure, I was made to stand in the middle of the classroom, but this was not so much to debate a philosophical issue with another student or with the professor as to once again be asked to recite passages from books, based on memory. Looking back, I should have taken my cue from the fact that the term "recitation" has its root from the word "recite," and not "debate," "argue," or "expound." The fact that it was not called "Socratization" should have been a dead giveaway.

I entered law school right after college, and the fact that the same approach was taken by my law professors did not surprise me at all. More than ever, I was made to stand in class and recite, verbatim, sections of various laws. In some cases, a group of us would be required to remain standing during an entire class for several days in a row with our books closed. During all my years at law school in the Philippines, I cannot remember a time when I actually had the opportunity to argue a case with my professor in class, and when I was asked about my opinion regarding a particular decision so that this could be laid open for discussion and debate. Instead, I was either required to recite case facts and decisions or to provide answers to questions asked by the professor. An answer not found in the books would automatically bring an embarrassing remark from the professor and an invitation to someone else to speak. It goes without saying that my memory seemed to have worked more than my understanding during these years. But at times guesswork would sometimes be resorted to, as it was not uncommon for a professor to ask questions with answers that could not be found in the assigned readings.

Having exclusively gone through an educational system that was supported by the practice of recitations, I expected to find the same approach when I decided to pursue my Master of Laws (LL.M.) in the United States. In fact, for me, the entire thought of reciting in a U.S. classroom was almost a *parti pris* that I did not even have to dwell on. So, during my first day in class at the University of Pittsburgh School of Law, imagine my surprise when I was not required to stand in order to "recite," and when the professor did not bother grading each of my "recitations." To top it off, when I decided to ask around about the style of "recitations" in U.S.

50 *See id.* at 23.

institutions of higher learning, I was shocked to find out that people had not heard of such a term in relation to the context I had given it in the classroom, as they referred to it more as "class participation." Slowly, I realized that the reason behind this was that a student's views were sought not only to determine whether he had read or memorized a particular case, but more importantly so that a professor could gather and galvanize various opinions that he could use to expound on a particular subject matter within the classroom.

This meant a world of difference for me, because I was now able to share with the class my opinions on various assigned cases, more than merely letting the professor know whether or not I had read and memorized them. I felt that I was part of the thought process that flowed through everyone in the classroom. It seemed that the role of the professor was to toss a pebble of a subject matter to the class and guide it as it rolls into a snowball of ideas. I felt capacitated within the classroom, because I no longer had the feeling of being spoon-fed definitions, but was now rather part of the process of developing concepts and approaches.

At first, I felt that recitations were much more difficult than class participation and that I was at an advantage over my American counterparts, as I had been trained to memorize and recite with my books closed. I soon realized, however, that class participation had its own challenges, because it required understanding cases and situations on top of memorizing facts and decisions. Although the system I had been accustomed to had its strengths in building my courage to stand up and answer questions under pressure, it had not taught me to understand the environment and situations surrounding a particular case or to appreciate the various approaches that could be taken in resolving a conflict. I was trained to present and argue a given principle, but I had not been trained to think outside the box. Equally important was the realization that, although I was accustomed to pointed remarks from my professors, I was not trained to accept criticism from peers within the classroom in a way that allowed me to distinguish the negative from the positive. Conversely, I also had to learn how to disagree without being disagreeable, how to attack an issue without focusing on the person propounding it.

VII. In Practice—Initial Efforts at Selling Procurement Reforms in the Philippines

While in the safe confines of academic institutions, I was told that the classroom was supposed to be a training ground for real life; that, to an extent, a class was supposed to reflect the realities of life in a microcosm. However, I have always thought that these statements pertained to the various interactions among students and between students and professors and that the lessons of life could exclusively be found within the pages of my textbooks. It was only after several years into my practice that I realized the actual level of impact that a classroom experience could have upon the developmental psyche of a country.

Certainly, during my first years in the Philippine academy as a teacher, force of habit led me to treat my class in the same manner as my Philippine law professors had treated me: education through recitation with established solutions and approaches. As I was further immersed in development and policy reform, however, I realized that, while such an approach was successful in fostering discipline within the class, it had the tendency of creating unhelpful apprehensions in the field—both on the side of the policy reformer and on the side of the audience.

The first set of apprehensions lies with the policy reformer who focuses too much on a fixed formula. It has been implied earlier that an effective policy maker is also a good communicator, because he has to successfully sell the reform to his constituents and develop a network of entrenched champions who can further push and cascade the initiatives to the various national and local units of the government. He should be a credible advocate of the reform and should recognize the fact that policy advocacy and implementation is rarely a linear process.

As communicating reforms deals with persons rather than institutions, one has to accept the possibility that an effective approach to any situation can easily vary depending on the personalities involved. Derick Brinkerhoff and Benjamin Crosby believe that, while policy statutes set goals and objectives, the extent to which those are clearly stated in terms of a sequence of cause and effect can vary and, as a result, policy implementation can often be multidirectional, fragmented, frequently interrupted, unpredictable, and very long term.[51] This is exemplified by the public procurement reform efforts in the Philippines where, despite the completion of the legislative process and the enactment of the new procurement reform law, the members of the reform coalition knew that "a long and precipitous road remained to be trudged" as they faced the daunting challenge of getting the new law implemented effectively.[52] With this realization, an effective reformer knows that in order to keep up he should avoid acting like a traditional and legalistic bureaucrat and should instead be a creative manager who is able to think outside the box.

While modern management courses train students to "think outside the box," this concept is not common in traditional legal educational institutions, particularly in the Philippine setting, where students are trained to study long established legal principles and provisions, and to adopt jurisprudential interpretations and applications thereof. The graduate of a traditional law school may thus know the answers to a problem, but would not be expected to know how to manage an issue—at least as far as policy advocacy and reform are concerned. Clearly then, one has to distinguish between approaches meant to ensure compliance with statutory provisions and those aimed at advocating for a policy and implementing it. While a traditional legal expert would comfortably navigate through issues

---

51 Derick W. Brinkerhoff and Benjamin L. Crosby, Managing Policy Reform: Concepts and Tools for Decision-Makers in Developing and Transitioning Countries 23 (Kumarian Press, Inc. 2002).

52 Campos and Syquia, *supra* note 46, at 30–32.

arising under the former, his natural tendency to focus on established interpretations as foundations upon which to build legal arguments may hamper his ability to compromise, adapt, and innovate. On the other hand, while a progressive policy manager may not be equipped with the tools to interpret and argue specific provisions of a law, the absence of a fixed and singular approach allows him more flexibility to view a policy from the standpoint of all the stakeholders. In other words, while a traditionally trained legal expert would comfortably argue a case or an issue involving infractions of a given law, he may encounter difficulties and apprehensions when asked to find a solution to the ineffectiveness of the same law to curb violations—because then he would be stepping beyond his comfort zone.

In the Philippines, the effectiveness of training programs for public procurement practitioners recently faced criticisms due to their failure to capture the concerns of local governments. The complaint was that the case studies and examples provided were based on high profile national projects, and were naturally more complex than regular local government requirements—thus making it difficult for the participants to apply these in actual cases. Although donor institutions readily offered grants to address this gap, I remember that the initial reaction of a particular government executive was to question the need for the grants and the relevance of the training as in her view all that had to be done was to require stricter compliance with the law on the part of the local governments. This executive provides a good example of the dichotomy mentioned earlier because there was an apparent failure on her part to dig deeper into the cause of the problem and appreciate it from the point of view of the local governments as stakeholders. Her initial reaction reflected a traditional classroom mentality whereby the audience was expected to automatically comply with legislated reform measures and work out its own difficulties in comprehending, and thus applying, the concepts that it has been lectured on throughout the training programs.

Although there was a need to simplify the training materials, it was again initially felt that this meant merely deleting portions that were not applicable to local governments and small communities without realizing that simplification actually meant having to adapt the materials to the situation of local communities that did not have to implement large and complex infrastructure projects but were still faced with a different set of issues and difficulties. More importantly, a major consideration that was missed during the discussions was the lack of strong support for the law from the local governments, which arose from a general view that they were not consulted during the policy development stage. Had this historical aspect been considered, it would have immediately been apparent that the initial approach would not have addressed the root cause of the problem—the point of conflict which had then be allowed to fester. As such, a policy manager should have seen this as an opportunity to garner the support of the local governments. If the training programs could be properly been reconfigured to capture and reflect their situation, they may been effective communication tools to demonstrate the position of local governments as important stakeholders in the entire reform process.

The second set of apprehensions lies with the audience, where apprehensions may arise due to a lack of consultation. As mentioned above, in the case of public procurement reforms in the Philippines, despite the importance of the local government units as primary stakeholders, there was a failure to establish appropriate consultations with them during policy formulation. Admittedly, while effective policy reform requires taking time to involve all the appropriate stakeholders in government, critical time elements and deadlines in the advocacy and legislation of the law limited the extent of technical consultations with the local governments. For this reason, while the law had successfully passed Congress, the effect of this lack of consultation was immediately felt in the form of apprehensiveness from the local governments against the new requirements and procedures. It was no surprise that within the same year the law was passed (2003) some leagues of local governments issued a statement requesting that the president suspend the application of the law. Although the call for suspension was legally untenable, it exposed an anxiety that had to be addressed if the reforms were to be effectively cascaded to the local governments and *barangays*.[53]

Even before the enactment of the law, there already existed a realization that one principal method for communicating the procurement reforms to the local governments was through orientation and training programs. For this reason, a year before the procurement law was passed, as an initial step to garner support from the local governments and the regional offices of national agencies, a small group of technical experts from within the government was formed for the purpose of running a nationwide orientation/training program on procurement reforms. There were five in the team, including myself, and most of us held director-level positions within our respective agencies: the Department of Budget and Management, the Department of Public Works and Highways, and the National Economic and Development Authority. Despite the small size of our team, we faced the daunting challenge of orienting the procurement, budget, and finance officers of 79 provinces, 117 cities, 1,493 municipalities, and 41,939 *barangays* nationwide. Needless to say, given the sheer size of the coverage area, despite all the orientation programs we undertook, there simply were not enough of us to even cause a dent on the local governments, even as successes were well underway with respect to the line agencies of the national government.

After the passage of the procurement law, the purpose of our training programs shifted from orientation and selling to actual technical instruction. Having failed to sell the reforms to the local governments, the five of us directly felt the brunt of the resistance from these stakeholders because we had in effect given the procurement reforms a face in the provinces outside Metro Manila. Given this strong resistance, most training sessions turned into day-long policy and technical debates where

53 In the Philippines, a *barangay* is the basic political unit which serves as the primary planning and implementing unit of government policies, plans, programs, projects, and activities in the community, and as a forum wherein the collective views of the people may be expressed, crystallized, and considered, and where disputes may be amicably settled.

each of us had no choice but to patiently engage and address all issues thrown at us, all the while leveraging our technical knowledge and experience. Each session was nowhere close to the typical atmosphere of a classroom that we were all used to and any approach that appeared to thrust the law unto the audience obviously had the risk of further aggravating an already tense and anxious crowd that could range from 100 to 1,200 participants per "class." Clearly, the Socratic method, where the teacher, or speaker/lecturer as it were, called upon participants to speak up for the purpose of exposing weaknesses in an argument, had no place in such a situation. What seemed to work, however, was a consultative approach where instead of trying to limit and avoid the influx of comments, we managed the gathering of views and complaints, thus allowing the participants to consider our training sessions as opportunities to be heard. We engaged their issues with answers backed by experience and technical analysis, and, with their ideas in hand, reached a conclusion that either addressed the issue or assured them that their concerns were valid and had reached the proper ears.

Since the law had already been passed, we had to assure the audience that for issues that could not be resolved we had the authority to present their concerns to the GPPB, the central regulatory and policy-formulating agency. Otherwise the entire process would have appeared to be simply farcical. As Brinkerhoff and Crosby note, "it is important that public agencies employing consultation convey the message that they are sincerely interested in stakeholder views, not simply looking for 'rubber stamp' approval of decisions already made."[54] Indeed, while this approach would not strictly coincide with that of the Socratic method, both are intended to reach the common goal whereby, at the end of the process, the student or audience is involved in the process of crafting a more accurate and encompassing concept, in our case, a policy developed through empowered participation.

By 2004, despite our regular sorties, there was still much ground to cover, and, as the new law gained ground, the need for more in-depth trainings multiplied. To address this, the newly formed GPPB created several composite training teams comprised of regional directors of the DBM, budget officers, auditors, and procurement practitioners within the various regions of the Philippines to continue the training program in their respective jurisdictions. The GPPB also tapped the state-owned universities and colleges (SUCs). With this set-up, all that the GPPB had to do was to train and monitor these trainers so that the latter could effectively train both national agencies and local government units in the provinces on its behalf.

To implement this plan, our original team of lecturers was asked by the GPPB to conduct a series of "training-of-trainers" on the new procurement law for the composite team members from February to March 2004. This activity was made possible through funding from a World Bank Institutional Development Fund grant. This was followed by another training program from October to November 2004 on the newly issued standard bidding documents as harmonized with the

54 Brinkerhoff and Crosby, *supra* note 51, at 66.

procurement rules of the World Bank, Asian Development Bank (ADB), and the Japan Bank for International Cooperation (JBIC), three of the largest development partners in the Philippines. In August 2005, with funding from a grant managed by the World Bank under the Second Asia Europe Meeting, the GPPB conducted refresher workshops for the composite teams and SUC trainers for purposes of ensuring that the trainers remained knowledgeable about the procurement law and were updated on recent developments.

Armed with continuous training programs and certificates to prove that they were authorized by the GPPB, the composite teams and SUC trainers were expected to be a major factor in rolling out the procurement reforms to the various regions of the country, especially those outside Metro Manila. Two years later, however, it seemed that the training programs had fallen short of expectations. Feedback from the local governments revealed that:

1. the training programs were too theoretical and the lecturers did not appear to be very knowledgeable about actual scenarios;
2. the quality of the training programs and the lecturers was unsatisfactory, with several incidents where the lecturers were unable to answer the questions asked;
3. the training programs were insufficient with respect to depth of substance;
4. the training programs were not being properly managed, the number of participants per session was too large, and the costs were too high, thus creating the impression that the regional trainers were more interested in getting compensated rather than effectively conducting the trainings;
5. there were numerous unsynchronized training programs where the lecturers not only contradicted each other but even made statements that did not seem to be in line with the policy and technical opinions of the GPPB;
6. the training modules were not customized to fit the local government situations; and
7. the training programs were not being cascaded to the *barangays*.

These problems may have initially come as a surprise to the GPPB, especially as it had just recently conducted revalidation workshops for the composite teams and SUC trainers in April, May and July 2006. It should have been apparent, however, that some lapses existed with respect to the selection of the trainers, the format of the training program, the monitoring and evaluation of the training programs, and the content of the modules. These lapses were too serious to ignore. Given the crucial role that capacity building had in the government's procurement reform program as a central communication tool, a failure in this aspect would erode the little support the reformers had generated so far in the provinces, particularly in the local governments.

VIII. Follow Through: How to Bring the Classroom to the Trenches

Although the new legal framework had an appropriate institution to implement it, i.e., the GPPB, and although the idea of running regional training programs for public procurement officials was generally considered to be an appropriate implementation initiative, it seems that the approach and methodology were flawed from the beginning so that the implementation of the program did not produce the results that had originally been intended. While the training program was supposed to be only a preliminary step leading to a full-blown professionalization program for procurement officials in government, its importance could not be underestimated for the following reasons:

1. A professionalization program would involve substantive certificate courses composed of in-depth modules on procurement and related topics and so it is naturally more wieldy to implement than short courses in the smaller communities over a shorter time.
2. The objectives of a training program as a capacity building initiative are different from when training programs are utilized as communication tools and each would thus be governed by a different set of indicators to measure effectiveness. For this reason, although a professionalization program would definitely be more effective in terms of creating a cadre of professionals in government agencies, it may not necessarily be as effective as shorter training courses in gathering support from the local communities and regional offices, especially during the birthing stages of the reform.

In the case of procurement reforms in the Philippines, several factors may have contributed to the overall ineffectiveness of the regional training program. First of all, while the pool of lecturers should have been composed of individuals whose profile exhibited both technical knowledge of public procurement procedures and experience as teachers, in actuality those recruited were either technical personnel in their respective government agencies or academicians, not both. The former were the members of the regional composite teams, while the latter were the professors tapped from the SUCs. This meant that the discussions were either too technical and esoteric or too theoretical and non-situational. To make matters worse, there were several reports that the lecturers' discussions conflicted with the opinions of the GPPB. This may have involved lecturers who were also procurement practitioners in their own agencies and who were using their own practices as examples, regardless of whether or not these were actually in compliance with the new rules.

And then there were the complaints about conflicts between lectures given by the auditors of COA, the state auditing agency of the Philippines, and those of the GPPB. While the latter had the legal mandate to issue all policies and opinions pertaining to procurement, the former had the authority to allow or disallow public contracts. The danger was that a practical-minded procurement officer in an agency would tend to follow mistaken advice from a COA auditor so as not to risk a disallowance of his transaction. The end product of all these factors was confusion among the targeted audience and a concomitant lack of any support from the provinces and local governments.

In addition, the materials used for training the pool of lecturers were generally the same materials used by the original group of lecturers for the information campaigns. What this meant was that, although the training program for the composite teams and the SUC trainers were labeled as a "training of trainers," it was more of a technical training with practically no provision for the development of trainers' skills. As a result, when these "trainers" were finally sent back into the field, most of them ended up either leveraging excessively on their own personal experiences on procurement or "parroting" the original lecturers. On one hand, the trainers who based their lectures on their own practices eventually encountered difficulty in discussing the principles behind the materials, and could not reconcile the materials with their personal views. While these trainers may have been able to relate to the problems and technical issues of the implementing agencies, their failure to relate to the principles behind the reforms, and their tentativeness, made them ineffective channels of communication. On the other hand, those who merely copied the manner by which the original materials were presented could not engage and address technical issues and were therefore not regarded as credible authorities by the audience.

Finally, there was practically no monitoring and evaluation conducted by any central authority because the GPPB had not yet established a practice by which selective field visits would be conducted or a system by which the trainers would be rated by both the participants and the GPPB. It was not until June 2006 that the GPPB conducted random field interviews to assess the effectiveness of the training program and thus realized firsthand the problems that had by then festered for some time. As mentioned earlier, revalidation workshops were undertaken in April, May, and July 2006, with the objective of gauging the knowledge and effectiveness of the trainers. Once again, however, it seemed that these failed to achieve the purpose and were in fact negatively received by several trainers. There were a couple of reasons for this, namely:

1. that the process was conducted in a manner that was reminiscent of undergraduate years, whereby the trainers were required to go through graded written examinations and mock presentations before the class, and had to answer questions posed by several junior staff of the GPPB, thus failing to consider the fact that the participants were themselves professors and senior government officials some of whom were even deans of colleges and directors of government agencies;
2. that the ratings were based solely on the answers and presentations given during the workshops, and not on actual ratings of the trainers' participants, thus failing to capture an accurate picture of how these trainers actually performed in the field;

3. that the question-and-answer portion after each presentation was conducted more like a classroom recitation that only involved the presenter and the GPPB panelists, thus preventing any form of interaction between the presenter and his peers and a sharing of ideas within the entire class; and
4. that, although the workshops were originally intended to screen off the ineffective trainers, GPPB management eventually decided not to pursue this approach, thus making any grading system moot.

For these reasons, the revalidation workshops not only failed to generate any meaningful management decision based on accurate evaluation results, but even generated hesitation or outright resistance from several trainers, especially the senior public officials in the teams who felt that junior personnel with little or no field exposure on procurement and no experience as educators had no right to question them and critique their manner of teaching.

Those responsible for the revalidation workshops downplayed the impact of such a flawed approach but they failed to consider the fact that the trainers were our champions in the provinces and that, as such, any resistance on their part would have the effect of multiplying the resistance in the field by the number of their audience. In one instance, one trainer complained that the examinations should have been given to them before they were sent to the field instead of after they had already conducted several lectures. Since the decision was made not to remove any trainer garnering a failing mark during the revalidation workshops, this particular trainer felt all the more that grading them merely placed all the trainers in a tenuous position. According to her, although an assurance was made that the results would be kept secret, there was no certainty that the grades would not be leaked out or viewed accidentally by others. Thus, if one were to get a low mark, this would only have the effect of raising doubts in the minds of previous and future audience about the trainer's capability and her lectures in particular, as well as the entire program in general.

IX. Profiling and Capturing the Audience

Some lessons are worth considering from the Philippine government's initial attempts to garner the support of the agencies in the provinces and the local governments for procurement reforms through a capacity building program. In cascading the reforms to the local governments, one has to acknowledge the reality that policy changing decisions on both national and local levels remain political so there will be policy winners and well-entrenched losers that will in several cases involve the local chief executive. According to Brinkerhoff and Crosby, "the existence of powerful opposition helps explain why it is often so difficult to get policy change processes moving, or in some cases why it stalls before it can begin."[55] Indeed, this observation is exemplified in the case of procurement reforms that seek to topple established practices and cultures within local governments that have gotten accustomed to decentralized authority.

Given these concerns, it would be prudent to identify possible champions within the local government who could network with external and national level champions, support the reform from within, and push these further to their component units. In effect, under a well-oiled and fully functioning reform program, the national government would be able to rely on the provincial governments to implement the reforms and push these down to the component cities and municipalities. In turn, the city and municipal governments could be relied upon to reach out and promote effective reforms in their respective *barangays*. This latter portion is especially important because local townsfolk are apt to be suspicious of strangers who try to persuade them to experiment with something unfamiliar.[56] As such, securing their buy-in as the ultimate beneficiaries of a reform program may require the support of familiar faces, such as their *barangay* captains or their municipal mayors.

There were occasions when we were fortunate enough to receive the support of a governor or a mayor. In these instances, we experienced minimal problems in the implementation of internal reforms, and in cascading these to the *barangays*. By its very nature, this situation is ripe for consideration as a pilot case study to achieve early successes for confidence building. Unfortunately, it continues to be an exception rather than the general rule in the Philippines, as local chief executives and their families tend to be well entrenched within their jurisdictions and thus stand to lose so much more by faithfully implementing an anti-corruption program such as the procurement reform law. As PCIJ reports: "The devolution of powers and resources since the enactment of the Local Government Code in 1991 means that local governments have much more clout and much more money now than in the past. The potential for abuse is therefore also greater."[57]

There are also instances where a newcomer manages to unseat a ruling family in a local government, whether through a miraculous victory in a legitimate electoral process or through more radical measures, such as the criminal conviction of the local chief executive and his family or a popular uprising. This ushers in a new breed of politicians in that particular locality. In this situation, the politician and his technical team are generally new to the game of politics and are backed up by a platform that promises sweeping reforms. This situation opens a rare opportunity to push for anti-corruption reforms within that local government. Once again, it also opens a window of opportunity for a pilot case that would record early successes to build confidence and may be communicated to other stakeholders during the training program. To succeed, however, one must bear in mind that, while reform-minded newcomers are neither burdened with entrenched political and financial

---

55 Brinkerhoff and Crosby, *supra* note 51, at 19.

56 Coyle, *supra* note 43, at 30.

57 Betrayals of the Public Trust: Investigative Reports on Corruption 276 (Sheila S. Coronel ed., PCIJ 2000).

interests nor dictated to by existing cultures of red tape, they are also very likely to be unfamiliar with the local government's administrative structures, unaware of the time and energy required to overcome bureaucratic inertia and resistance, and unschooled in using the levers of power to accomplish change.[58]

For these reasons, one has to target primarily those most actively involved in policy formulation within the local governments, whose decisions are based on maximizing scarce resources rather than on political trade-offs, and those who are expected to stay long after a politician vacates his office and would thus make decisions beyond a term of office. In other words, one has to be able to connect with the technocrats within a region, province, or local government unit. An approach that has proven to be effective is to identify a group of highly motivated individuals from among the participants of regularly conducted training courses so that they may be formed into a well-bonded network of champions through specialized workshops, such as training-of-trainers workshops, with a fully functioning support system.

This is exemplified by our experience with the Integrated Multi-Sectoral Capacity Building Program for the Autonomous Region in Muslim Mindanao (ARMM) undertaken by the Asian Institute of Management (AIM) with assistance from USAID and the Japan International Cooperation Agency (JICA). This course was developed to address the ARMM's need for management and management-related capabilities to be able to think through, develop, design, implement, and nurture a wide range of related social, political, and economic, growth and development projects, programs, and advocacies.[59] The training programs were not only targeted at the governance hierarchy of ARMM but at other stakeholders as well, including civil society organizations and local governments, and was undertaken in partnership with Mindanao-based training institutions in order to sustain the intervention.[60] To achieve the objective of strengthening the leadership and strategic management capability of the ARMM executives and enhancing their managerial competencies in managing development, the design, approach, and learning materials used for the training courses reflected AIM's belief that the professional development manager should have basic functional, personal, organizational, and environmental management skills, as well as the ability to analyze and systematically process information in an integrative manner for decision-making purposes. Thus, three types of customized training interventions were designed under the project:

1. leadership and strategic management briefings for top executives of the ARMM in Mindanao;
2. a middle management course for development managers of the ARMM in AIM's Manila campus; and

58 Brinkerhoff and Crosby, *supra* note 51, at 20.

59 Asian Institute of Management, Integrated Multi-Sectoral Capacity Building Program Overview (2005).

60 *Id.*

3. basic management courses for development managers of the ARMM in Cotabato City, Mindanao.[61]

Some modules of the AIM training courses included modules on development and governance perspectives, decision making, human resource management, local experiences on management, and an action plan for collaboration and development in the ARMM. The courses focused substantially on developing personal management skills that were sensitive to the prevailing sentiments of the Muslim communities in the Southern Philippines, which generally exhibited the indicia of minority groups, including feelings of neglect and isolation. The courses were also structured to overcome internal weaknesses and address external threats to the success of development programs, such as negative traits that normally characterize communities suffering from protracted armed conflicts. To top it all off, during the courses the facilitators kept tabs on those participants who exhibited a high level of interest in the subject matter, were able share relevant experiences during class, actively participated during the discussions, challenged issues with an open mind, and generally showed good potential to be trainers themselves. This handful of individuals was then invited to a special training-of-trainers workshop some months later, with the clear intent that they would be tapped to echo the knowledge gained during the basic management courses to their Muslim community.

The workshop was intended to provide these future trainers with the proper tools to cascade the basic management training programs to their communities, and thus included more intensive management modules, complemented by modules intended to develop the trainers' skills on handling class presentations and participation. To ensure continuity and effectiveness, the trainers were then provided with a support system by AIM, whereby they could seek guidance from its roster of professors and take advantage of its network of alumni, until they gained sufficient confidence to roll out the training programs and undertake development programs on their own.

X. Building Support

The intended overall end result of any policy reform initiative that seeks to impact the implementation of development programs and projects such as procurement reform should be not only to attain the buy-in of the central agencies, but also to secure the meaningful participation of the communities. This requires not only the ultimate end users or beneficiaries of the program or project, but also as the bedrock of authentic democratic institutions. From experience, we learned that cascading reforms require capacity building where all stakeholders believe that they have been truly involved in the process; and such belief has to translate into

61 *Id.*

full-fledged ownership by the community, in particular, and by the nation, in general. As Coyle observes: "The community improvement programs in many underdeveloped countries are not only of considerable economic value; they are even more valuable as exercises in 'basic democracy,' the town-meeting type of natural democratic action that under favorable circumstances can serve as the foundation for national democratic institutions."[62]

The problem is that resistance from local governments to a particular national policy that appears to intrude into their decentralized powers is not unusual. This explains why there exists a need to identify and coalesce the champions from within and among them. This is not a simple task, however, because most of those in the audience will either be lukewarm to the reform or opposed to it. This was our experience in pushing for procurement reforms in the Philippines because, although it was easy to identify, motivate, and mobilize champions in the legislative and executive branches of government, we found practically no strong and consistent support from among the local governments.

With this scenario, it appears that resistance would not be dissipated by a lecturer who is viewed to be a hardliner, as he would provide no appealing option to an obstinate official and would only induce the lukewarm local officials to take a side which, given the imposing character of the lecturer, would most probably be in support of his own unit and peers. The effect discussed here is reminiscent of the resistance encountered from the trainers themselves during the re-validation workshops and I believe that both types of reactions can be traced back to the problem of using the typical teacher–student mindset of the classroom in a scenario that calls for persuasion and participation rather than compulsion or dictation.

In other words, it should be clear to the trainers that while they have a responsibility to instruct their local government participants on the rigors of the law, this is not their sole task, and their ultimate objective should to painstakingly build support and eventual ownership, rather than to impose compliance. This objective cannot be achieved by lifeless lectures and one-way discussions to a crowd of 100 or more disconnected spectators. It can, however, be achieved through stimulating discussions managed by a lecturer with fewer than 50 participants, where issues and views are properly raised, debated, and considered in light of the current local environment.

In some instances, to secure the buy-in of some critical stakeholders, certain compromises will have to be made. But one should bear in mind that any such compromise does not automatically guarantee certainty of support. We learned this lesson quite early during the congressional debates for the procurement reform bill, as one such compromise currently appears in the body of the law in the form of provincial preference for contractors and suppliers for priority projects (a.k.a. pork-barrel-funded projects). The legal section that was the subject of the compromise provides that, within five years from the effectiveness of the procurement law, a contractor who participates in the bidding of a provincial priority program or

62 Coyle, *supra* note 43, at 30.

infrastructure project, whose principal office is within the province conducting the bidding, and who submits the lowest bid among the provincial bidders but whose bid is still higher than the lowest bid made by a contractor from outside the province, shall be given the right to match the lowest outside bid.[63] This effectively gave firms from within the province conducting the bidding the right to match bids from outside firms until January 26, 2008. We believed this would lessen resistance from the regions and provinces, as it was their congressmen who asked for it. Despite this, the local governments still exhibited strong resistance to the law when it was passed and some city governments even went to the extent of requiring a mayor's permit to do business in the city as a precondition for eligibility to participate in their biddings.

XI. Profiling the Trainer and Providing the Tools

It is probably obvious by now why a technical expert would not necessarily be a good trainer for a capacity building program that doubles as a communications tool; why an experienced teacher would not be an effective mouthpiece to an audience composed of seasoned field officers and implementers; and why the regional training program for procurement reforms in the Philippines was flawed from the beginning. It is also becoming obvious that traditional teaching methodologies in Philippine classrooms do not work when the objective is to effectively communicate policy reforms to seasoned public officials and build their capacity to implement these reforms. Several reasons for this have surfaced.

First and foremost, while a traditional teacher generally instructs and educates students on a subject matter he presumably knows more about than his students in all aspects, a policy trainer should be able to both instruct his participants and accept ideas and approaches that may be unfamiliar to him. Simply stated, a policy trainer should realize that he does not have a monopoly on knowledge, even in a classroom setting.

Second, while a traditional teacher is used to managing class recitations, he may (unfortunately) not necessarily be adept in managing class participation. While the former is basically a one-way process of eliciting answers to test students' knowledge of a topic, the latter is a two-way process by which knowledge is shared and the student becomes involved in the thought process. Moreover, capacity building deals more with practical applications than with theoretical approaches and, if a trainer is to win over his participants, it is not sufficient to be well read on the latest resources without also being able to show in-depth experience in the subject matter.

During my first year as an adjunct professor at AIM in Manila, I was asked to discuss a couple of modules on public procurement before a class composed of seasoned implementing officers for World Bank projects. These modules were

63 Rep. Act No. 9184, Art. XIII, §§ 44–45.

part of a two-week program called Project and Procurement Management Course (PPMC), offered by AIM's Center for Development Management (CDM) globally, with participants normally coming from the Philippines, China, Indonesia, Vietnam, Lao PDR, Sri Lanka, Maldives, and other countries in East Asia, the Pacific Islands, and Africa. My initial hesitation came from the fact that, although I had substantial experience on public procurement policy formulation, monitoring, evaluation, and technical assistance, and although I was well versed on all the procurement guidelines of ADB and the World Bank (having been involved in efforts at harmonizing the Philippines' procurement rules with those of ADB, the World Bank and JBIC), I had practically no experience in operations at that time, particularly on World Bank projects. My fears turned into reality as the participants raised detailed technical and operational issues they had been encountering in the field, such as those involving community-based projects. Suffice it to say that the participants saw right through my lack of operational experience despite my substantial knowledge of policies. Since that time, I have made it a point of immersing myself in both aspects of public procurement, if only to be an effective trainer.

Third, even though a participatory system of education as adopted in the United States approaches a topic through a sharing of ideas rather than through simple recitation, and thus takes an extra step to involve a student and the entire class, it is still necessarily confined to the established principles and jurisprudence supporting the subject matter found in the assigned readings and texts. For this reason, while a participatory classroom discussion actively galvanizes various thoughts and ideas from the students, it is still basically linear in that the entire class is being guided through a particular doctrine by way of contextual examples and cases.

A capacity building program, on the other hand, will normally have as one of its objectives that a participant be able to understand a given set of principles and applications. Reaching this goal is rarely a linear and coherent process, especially when the process itself is utilized as a communication tool. This is reminiscent of the manner in which policy change is managed and is a clear example of the classroom reflecting reality because, in the same manner that policy reform and advocacy is generally described as unpredictable, fragmented, and composed of winners and losers, these same winners and losers will be the very persons sitting in the training courses.

As such, the term "class participation" is pushed up a notch further into the area of ownership and constituency building, which means that the trainer should be able to reach out to the participants and bring them into the policy process. This ability to reach out is both a technical concern and a management concern, so that a trainer should be well versed with the various participation options at his disposal for policy legitimization and ownership building. This includes information sharing, consultation, collaboration, and joint decision making. The trainer should be able to utilize these in varying degrees within and outside the classroom so that critical stakeholders feel empowered to take ownership for policies, thus making implementation easier and increasing the chances for sustainable policy change.[64]

Fourth, as mentioned earlier, the trainer should be prepared to be flexible in certain areas and approaches that he knows fall within the bounds of the law. Most importantly, his willingness to take in and consider the views of his participants as probable alternatives should be obvious to all, in a way that does not erode his authority and conviction in particular, and the policy's objective in general. An effective trainer is therefore both a teacher and manager.

Furthermore, pushing policy reforms to the provinces and cascading these to the local communities through capacity building programs requires trainers who have the mentality of strategic managers, rather than traditional managers. Traditional managers are internally focused, prioritize technicalities and administrative requirements over substance, are overly concerned with day-to-day bureaucratic routines, and generally suffer from tunnel vision. Strategic managers, on the other hand, are outwardly focused, able to adapt to external environments even when circumstances are unpredictable and processes are nonlinear, and are able to step out of the box to obtain a broader perspective. One important difference between the two types of managers is the fact that, while traditional managers are basically unwavering hardliners, strategic managers do not find it difficult to accept other points of view and tend to see opportunities for improvements in what may otherwise be seen as mistakes.

In policy reform, it is much harder to gather support and promote implementation once lines are drawn. Once again, Brinkerhoff and Crosby deal with the distinction between the strategic and the technical in provide four excellent guiding principles of strategic management which may be applied in developing the profile of an effective policy-reform trainer:

1. The strategic approach is oriented toward the future. It recognizes that the environment will change. It has a long-range orientation, one that tries to anticipate events rather than simply reacting as they occur. The approach leads managers to ask where their organizations and their collaborators are at the present, where they want to be after a certain period, what they need to get there, how to develop strategies and the means, and how to manage those strategies to achieve their stated goals and objectives. It recognizes that the future cannot be controlled but argues that by remaining strategically focused and anticipating the future, organizations and their stakeholders can help to shape and modify the impact of environmental change.
2. The strategic approach has an external emphasis. It takes into account several components of external operating environments, including technology, politics, economics, and the social dimension. Strategic thinking recognizes that each of these can either constrain or facilitate the organizations involved in policy implementation.

64 *See* Brinkerhoff and Crosby, *supra* note 51, at 54–70.

3. The strategic approach concentrates on assuring a good fit between the environment and policy implementation organizations, and attempts to anticipate what will be required to assure continued fit. Under conditions of rapid political, economic, social, and technical change, strategies can quickly become outmoded. Resources traditionally available to implementing organizations may dwindle or evaporate suddenly.
4. The strategic approach is a process. It is continuous and recognizes the need to be open to changing goals and activities in light of shifting political, economic, and social circumstances. The process is not a one-shot approach—it is ongoing—and thus requires attention to emerging needs and changing circumstances as they arise, and to the development of strategies to respond to those needs.[65]

A good example on the difference between traditional reformers and strategic reformers, as well as the implications of their characters on building ownership, is the initial advocacy for procurement reforms in the Philippines, as reported by Campos and myself:

> USAID eventually provided the assistance needed to jumpstart and shepherd the procurement reforms. Two U.S.-based procurement experts were brought in to work with the DBM in conducting an analysis of the problems of the government's procurement system and in preparing a draft omnibus law that would address these. Working feverishly, the consultants completed the study within six months, interviewing many officials while scouring mountains of documents. They completed a draft law shortly thereafter which covered practically everything that had to do with government procurement. …
>
> By August 1999, the DBM had two hefty documents necessary to initiate reforms in public procurement. As a critical first step in the process, it had to get the support of the major procurers within the Executive branch. The history of legislation suggested that, unless the Executive presented a united front to the Congress, Congress would not act favorably on its proposals. However, within the DBM, there seemed to be little support for the initiative. As it turned out, a major problem with the consultants had emerged during the whole preparatory process.
>
> While they had done an excellent job analyzing the problems and preparing an all encompassing draft law, they had failed miserably to secure "buy-in" from key DBM staff, including the undersecretary to whom they had to report. They had alienated practically every government official they had interviewed and/or to whom they had presented earlier drafts of the study. The consultants were not entirely to blame. They were completely unfamiliar with the culture

65 *See id.* at 40.

> in the government: their experience was limited to countries where dealing exclusively with the Minister was the *modus operandi*—and through "command and control" the rest would follow. In the Philippines, however, a considerable amount of painstaking ownership-building within an agency is necessary, and, for a proposal of this magnitude, within the Executive. Given the political sensitivity of procurement, this was paramount. As a result, the study and the draft law were shelved.
>
> Among the first tasks of the Transparency and Accountability Team (TA team) was helping the budget reform task force (BRTF) rekindle the procurement reform project. In close coordination with the BRTF, the TA team had to formulate a strategy to bring officials from both DBM and other key agencies to the table once again and gain their support and assistance for a new encompassing procurement law. After talking to members of the task force and other officials within DBM, the TA team learned of the short, colorful history behind the shelved reform and the resulting deep hole out of which the BRTF would have to dig. Many hours of discussion and brainstorming among the team and task force members eventually led to an innovative approach. Because the procurement consultants drew the ire of most if not all the senior procurement experts within government, the team and BRTF concluded that they could entice these officials to revisit the procurement reforms by inviting these officials to a series of workshops to "shoot down" the consultants' study section by section, line by line, and then develop their own version of the procurement reform law.[66]

The "shoot down" workshop proved to be a great success because it once again brought the technocrats to the drawing table and involved them in the entire process. At the end of the workshop, the participants had completed a set of principles which they agreed should guide the formulation of an omnibus law and they prepared and committed to an action plan for taking the process forward. Those principles included: (i) the formation of a technical working group (TWG); (ii) the conduct of continuous workshops of that group; and (iii) participation of members of the TWG in congressional debates.[67]

More importantly, these technocrats eventually gained full ownership over the entire procurement reform program, became our strongest champions, and continued to be involved long after the enactment of the procurement law. In fact, a clear sense of camaraderie developed among the members of the group which had by now been institutionalized into the Technical Working Group (TWG) of the GPPB. Even public officials from other agencies that eventually became involved with the TWG through the expanded membership of the GPPB attested to the amity and solidarity they have been experiencing each time the GPPB TWG convened. It thus comes as no surprise that the TWG continues to meet regularly every month

66 Campos and Syquia, *supra* note 46, at 8–9.

67 *Id.*

to thrash out and address policy issues and implementation problems encountered in the procurement reform program, and to continue to push the program forward without the need of any form of compensation, monetary or otherwise.

Thus, an effective and self-sustaining reform coalition had been organized at the national level, able to deliver effective technical solutions and feed into policy improvements. All these evolved from a simple two-day "shoot down" workshop through which a once amorphous and antagonistic assembly of technocrats were transformed into a unified, well-coordinated and empowered team of dedicated reformers, with the assistance of focused facilitators who strategically managed the thought process.

The profile of an effective policy-reform trainer and the characteristics of a capacity building workshop may be summed up as follows:

1. the trainer should have the mind-set of a strategic manager;
2. he should be armed with sufficient technical knowledge and tools pertinent to the reform being implemented;
3. capacity building programs should be supported by workshops with defined outputs that not only deal with technical matters, but are also meant to foster the creation of teams of dedicated individuals bonded by shared aims; and
4. one of the outputs of the capacity building workshops should be an action plan for pushing the reforms forward.

The action plan may not be achieved without an adequate approach, and that approach will need room for flexibility as it may have to shift mid-stream to fit the environment. An example of this is the innovative "shoot down" workshop discussed above, which was not initially planned by the reform coalition but was nevertheless used as a remedial measure.

Finally, one more lesson could be learned from our experience with the "shoot down" workshop. As mentioned earlier, by the end of the workshop, the participants had agreed upon a set of principles that served as their guideposts in pushing the reforms forward. This set of principles is just as important for the trainers as it is for the policy advocates, and every person involved in the reform program will have to learn it by heart.

Indeed, while a trainer has to be flexible and willing to compromise, certain personal positions for the sake of establishing an authentic consultative atmosphere; he should also be careful not to go to the extreme and lose any vestige of a position—lest he lose his credibility. Moreover, it should be kept in mind that the ability to compromise is greatly hampered within the classroom (or training room, for that matter), and so a trainer involved in a capacity building program that also forms part of an overall communications strategy should be able to know the boundaries of his ability to compromise, drawn by a determination of when a particular approach would be a clear violation of policy "non-negotiables." He should remember that whenever he conducts training programs in the provinces and rural areas he represents both the policy initiative and the institution behind it and, in a very real sense, he puts a face to the reforms.

Having said this, any weakness on the trainer's part will easily be regarded as a weakness of the reforms in general, and once he stands in front of an unfriendly group of participants it may be very easy for the trainer to give in to the temptation of taking the path of least resistance. For this reason, ownership building requires both an open mind and the determination to defend a position during debates as well as the wisdom of knowing when a particular approach will have to be applied. This wisdom may only be had when the trainer is armed with non-negotiable principles to serve as guideposts.

XII. Conclusion

This chapter is not about being able to sell an idea, but rather about selling an able idea. It is not about the need for more reforms on legislative, regulatory, and institutional frameworks but the need for more implementers of reforms; the need for people who are not only willing to think outside the box, but willing to walk the walk.

All sectors of society in developing countries, whether public, private, civil society, or even religious, have constantly been encountering such concepts as good governance, sound economic policies, trade liberalization, globalization, and other similar terms. These are all too often "buzz" words, but are now an indispensable part of any development manager's toolkit of ideas. These concepts frequently appear in the form of loan conditions propped up by grants and varied types of technical assistance, all for the purpose of ensuring that good "principles" are adopted and practiced by implementing agencies. But what do these really mean to the end users and the actual recipients of the assistance? While the practice of these concepts have often been hailed as success stories in the urban cities and capitals, we must asked if they have caused any impact in the life of a typical poor family living the rural barrio? From what I have gathered in my visits, assessments, and interviews with local communities in the Philippines, it appears that improved economic figures and policies reported by our president have largely failed to better the lives of our farmers, fishermen, and townsfolk, most of whom still regard themselves as marginalized by "imperialist" Manila. There is indeed a disconnect between statistics and experience, and this is further amplified by constant complaints about the actual effectiveness of foreign aid, and statements that most development efforts have only managed to benefit a few local corporations, enrich international firms, proliferate NGOs with identity crises, and continue to line the pockets of a few third-world wealthy families. Until these perennial problems are addressed by fundamental reforms, and until the rationales and benefits of these reforms are effectively communicated to the local communities, foreign aid will remain ineffective both in actuality and in the minds of the general public.

As I completed this chapter, the headlines of the business section in the Philippines' major newspapers announced that our country had received a US$410 million loan from the World Bank for education, health, and local government development projects.[68] Based on the reports, World Bank country director to the Philippines, Joachim von Amsberg—apparently following up on his encouraging remarks about reforms in the Philippines—said that "the country's improved fiscal policies made the increase in World Bank investments in the Philippines possible," given that investments of multilateral institutions in the country are often dependent on implementation of fiscal and economic reforms, and the government's ability to fight corruption.[69] The program will also fund revenue improvement and enhancement programs of local government units, including fiscal and management improvements to ensure financial stability.[70] As I read on, I was impressed by the fact that these loans allowed the recipient institutions to directly finance high priority line items under the regular national budget and that these were veering away from the traditional project-based development assistance approach.[71] My optimism was further buoyed by reports that the Philippine peso had climbed the day before to a four-year high of P49.88 against the U.S. dollar, up from a low of about P56 to US$1 in early 2005.

On my way to the airport to catch a flight to Hanoi, Vietnam, I excitedly related the story about the World Bank loan to my driver, but all he had to say to me on the matter was simply: "another burden for our people." In my mind, I began to justify my driver's pessimism by thinking that he was probably uninformed about the true nature of this loan. I thought that he would not have made his comment had he been aware that this loan was aimed at supporting our national program for basic education, improving the quality and learning outcomes in primary education, and developing a more equitable access to health insurance and health care so that the needs of the poor are more efficiently addressed. I felt comforted by this justification for a few moments until I moved over to the front page of the newspapers in my hand and read the glaring headlines: "Ombudsman Reversed SC Decision: Salonga, Solons Shocked by Ruling Clearing Comelec Execs"[72] and "Ombudsman Decision a Case for Ripley's."[73] These stories were related to my earlier account about how, in June 2006, the Philippines' anti-graft agency (the ombudsman) recommended the filing of graft charges and the dismissal of COMELEC officials, as well as the impeachment and the filing of graft charges against one of the COMELEC's commissioners, for entering into a P1.3 billion poll automation deal that was nullified by the Supreme Court for certain anomalies and

---

68 *RP get $410M Loan from WB*, Malaya (Oct. 4, 2006), at B9. *See also RP gets $410M in Loans from World Bank*, Philippine Daily Inquirer (Oct. 4, 2006), at B1.

69 *Id.*

70 *Id.*

71 *Id.*

72 Philippine Daily Inquirer, at A1 (Oct. 4, 2006).

73 Malaya, at A1 (Oct. 4, 2006).

for failing to comply with the procurement law. Apparently, in a move considered by several officials as "outrageous and shocking," "an unthinkable reversal" of the Supreme Court's decision, and a "brazen somersault," the ombudsman reversed its original recommendation and absolved all officials of the COMELEC and the private company that won the bidding from any criminal or administrative liability whatsoever.

Right then, it hit me that maybe I was the one who was uninformed, that I, with all my energies focused on national policies and statistics, was the one who could not see the realities in the field and that my driver knew all too well that without any significant and sincere efforts on the part of our government to fight corruption and hold corrupt actors liable, any additional loan will only further enrich these actors while pulling the poor and their children deeper into debt. I also realized that the absence of such sincere efforts on the part of our government was what fueled the cynicism in a majority of our people, such as my taxi driver, because they see things for what they really are, undisguised by national policies, commitments, and economic statistics.

Indeed, there have been a few poignant success stories and experiences, such as when a strategically oriented high ranking official of the Department of Education (DepEd), former Undersecretary Miguel Luz, organized innovative partnerships with NGOs, media, the private sector, and church groups to ensure that textbooks were actually being delivered to the public schools. Before being unceremoniously relieved of his post (for reasons that were perceived to be political), Undersecretary Luz even managed to enter into an agreement with Coca Cola Co. on the use of its delivery trucks for the distribution of textbooks to public schools in the far-flung rural areas, because these trucks have the capability to reach even the remotest localities in the Philippines.

My good friend and mentor, Procurement Service Director Estanislao Granados, Jr., constantly reminds me of another incident involving an official trip we both made to an elementary school deep in the mountains of Southern Philippines, known to be infested by rebels. Despite the distance, the quality of the road, and his age (although he would never admit to this), Director Granados asked that we go check on the deliveries of about a half dozen computers to that particular school. When we finally reached the site and talked to the teachers and students, it struck me how grateful they were that—despite their remoteness—they finally had computers with access to the internet. But they also reported that one computer had appeared not to work for several months because the closest available technician was living in the lowlands and had no means of getting to them. As I scoured the connections of the computers to see if I could offer any assistance, imagine their surprise when I found out that the cause of their problem was only a disconnected network cable! Though I made little of this incident, as it involved such a small matter, Director Granados helped put things in perspective for me as he said: "Imagine how important a single computer is for these people and how they were deprived of its use for so long, then you would realize how important your role was that day … simply by connecting that cable."

I then saw the wisdom behind my mentor's words. As far as those students and teachers in that far-flung public school were concerned, my simple act of connecting a cable that day was probably more valuable than all that we have achieved with the passage of the procurement reform law. And, to a larger extent, foreign aid and national policy reforms will not amount to much if one does not get his hands dirty in the trenches where the impact of even the smallest act is multiplied beyond expectation on a personal level.

Chapter 14

Comparative Analysis in the Area of Development of Informational and Communicational Technologies: Contemporary U.S. and Uzbek Legislation

Timur Arifdjanov[1]

I. Introduction

The evolution and wide application of information and communication technologies (ICT) have been important developments throughout the international community in the past few decades. The global community can rightfully be termed an "information society," and eight leading nations agree enough to have adopted the "Okinawa Charter on Global Information Society" in the summer of 2000.[2] The information revolution demands that countries with lower indexes of information and technological development, including Uzbekistan, make strong and even critical efforts in overcoming their backwardness.[3] At the same time, an information revolution provides individuals, nations, and mankind as a whole with tremendous development opportunities.

The application of sophisticated information processing and transmission technologies has crucial significance for the increased competitiveness and enhanced integration of the economy and the substantial growth of national governance efficacy at all levels, including state and private sectors of the economy. The introduction of technological prerequisites for development of open and democratic society, based on the right of citizens to free and operative access to information through the internet, is another important consequence of ICT development and its infiltration into all spheres of public life.

---

1 Legal Counsel, Pertsch and Partner, GmbH; Sub-regional Coordinator for Internet Monitoring (Civil Initiative on Internet Policy); LL.M. 2000 *magna cum laude* (University of Pittsburgh School of Law); LL.B. 1995 (University of World Economy and Diplomacy).

2 G-8 Summit Declaration, "Okinawa Charter of Global Information Society" (2000).

3 *See* Antoine Blua, *Central Asia: Efforts Under Way to Bring Region Up to Speed With the Internet*, *available at* http://www.eurasianet.org/departments/insight/articles/pp041303.shtml.

Within the last decade, Uzbekistan has made progress in the creation and development of its information infrastructure. A number of technical and technological projects are being carried out in different areas, including those oriented to state institutions and organizations. Substantial work has been undertaken to develop corresponding legislation. There is now a pool of highly qualified ICT specialists, and cooperation with international institutions in this field is also successful.

Nonetheless, the current level and existing problems of ICT development give rise to the need for a new approach that focuses on the formation of a general strategy of entry into the global informational space instead of solely concentrating on the development of certain communication branches within the country. Based on the available technological capabilities, the focus can be on framing the uniform information space, development of information resources, and the creation of databases and infrastructure accessible to state institutions, as well as to the general public. All of this will in turn affect ICT-related legislation.

To implement this strategy, due regard must be given to the examples of leading nations in their attempts at drafting ICT legal regulations, as well as to an analysis of Uzbekistan's current policy and legislation in the field. This will give us an idea of what must be done to establish more favorable national, political, and legislative environments for the development of ICT and integration of the country into the global information community.

Attempts to inoculate foreign laws into the body of domestic legislation directly, as have been made in some Commonwealth of Independent States (CIS) countries, have proved to be ineffective if not futile. Such practices have often been discontinued. To properly analyze foreign and international legislation with the intent of implementing the ideas and legal principles they contain into domestic law, it is indispensable that the professionals involved have an educational background that permits a valid analysis of those foreign and international legal systems and mechanisms, and provides the ability to adjust those systems to the domestic situation. Because the need to enrich domestic legal systems with new ideas has proven to be highly beneficial abroad, the choice for Uzbekistan has been either to attract foreign experts to work within the groups developing new laws or to educate local experts abroad.

I, along with several of my compatriots, was given the chance to gain this educational background through the study of an LL.M. degree at the University of Pittsburgh School of Law. After returning to Uzbekistan upon the completion of my studies, I shared my experiences with my colleagues and realized how lucky I had been. Setting aside the excellent teaching faculty of internationally recognized quality at the University of Pittsburgh School of Law, the very structure of the work with foreign students was the best method for producing high educational results as well as providing social stability. The opportunity given to us as LL.M. students to study among American J.D. students proved to be a serious incentive to compete and grow from both educational and linguistic standpoints. At the same time, we were in continuous contact with our LL.M. colleagues and could always share our experiences and compare our accomplishments. Having kept in contact with other LL.M.s of my year, I definitely know that they feel similarly.

The training that we received as LL.M. students was valuable not just because it expanded our knowledge of specific subject areas but also because it taught us how to absorb material from a different legal system. Every course we took was effectively a comparative law course because we considered the subject matter in the context of our prior legal education in our home countries. My work upon returning to Uzbekistan has made use of the practical skills I obtained in these courses to identify the foreign and international legal systems that could contribute to advancing Uzbekistan's legal framework for ICT.

During the last several years I have been in charge of the legal work on two ICT-related projects co-sponsored by the government of Uzbekistan and foreign—mostly American—funds related to the development of ICT in Uzbekistan. Simultaneously, as a legal expert in ICT, I have been involved in the preparation of two laws (e-signature and e-commerce) by working groups under the Cabinet of Ministers of Uzbekistan. This chapter will be more a descriptive discussion than a deep exploration of the details of these laws. Although it could be interesting to add the analysis of, say, European, Russian, or Chinese laws on the subject, I did not want to take the risk of overspending the reader's attention. Therefore, the main focus will be on U.S. legislation as a global leader in the area with only a slight allusion to EU and international pieces of legislation.

II. General Notions and Main Principles of ICT Regulation

The internet as a means of mass communication has achieved a stage of development and influence in society that requires state involvement through the adoption of laws regulating its operation and further development. To identify the direction of such regulation, a number of countries have conducted special research, established public associations, adopted legislation, and developed codes of conduct for the internet. Almost all of these documents are accessible online and their analysis would require a book in its own right. However, a brief description lets us understand the main direction of the legislative framework's evolution as well as the experience of internet regulation. The global nature of the internet makes it possible to assert that the problems of legislative regulation have a generic character and are more or less similar for all nations of the world. When attempting to regulate the internet, it is worth keeping in mind its peculiar features compared to other media.

Certain properties help define the unique essence of the internet. The internet is first and foremost global. It is the first truly global medium allowing, for instance, transmission of a message to the other side of the world to be as inexpensive as the same transmission to the neighboring house. The internet is incredibly decentralized. It was originally meant to operate without control. It is not dependent on a set of broadcasting towers or satellites. The internet is easily accessible. Anyone can publish on the internet. The cost of reaching thousands is in essence the same for reaching a single person. Launching a webpage bears the same start up costs whether it is intended to be seen by millions or by a single individual (though bandwidth costs vary). The internet is controlled by the user. The primary control of the internet, compared to broadcast media or phone networks, is in the hands of a user. That user may choose to employ cryptography to protect his or her privacy; parents may obtain technologies to protect children from undesirable materials; and individuals can be highly selective in how they choose to use the internet.

Several aspects of the internet facilitate the development of general legal principles:

1. Transparency: Lawmaking and law enforcing processes are to be open and transparent. Citizens should have access in print or through the internet to all laws, decrees, bylaws, and court decisions, including legal drafts and other norms.
2. Privatization and competition: In countries where the internet service providers (ISPs) are prosperous, they experience fewer controls than other communication industries, such as phone networks. There is a perception that privatization and competition facilitate development of all telecommunication services, including the internet. EU directives make privatization highly desirable if not mandatory. They require that existing telecommunication networks be open to competition.
3. Nondiscrimination: ISPs should have access to networks equal to that provided by telecommunication companies to their subsidiaries. Goods and services should be accessible for foreign competition and trade barriers shall be minimal, benefitting customers.
4. Licensing: Licensing requirements should not impede competition. Licensing should not restrict access to markets. General and business laws in themselves should satisfy consumer protection needs.
5. Technical standards: Technical standards should not create obstacles to competition. There is no need for individual licensing or excessive and detailed equipment standardization. Open standards and functional compatibility facilitate innovation, growth, and wider access.
6. Price control and universal services: Pricing policy, especially per-minute rates for local connections, can slow internet growth. Uniform local calling rates, as well as uniform price policies for internet services, can better improve internet accessibility. The principle of universal services for basic telecommunication access is an internationally recognized norm. Competition-based price policy can reduce prices and facilitate growth. However, it has to be properly balanced among corporative and individual users and urban and rural populations.
7. Education: A state system of education is inevitable for professional growth of specialists in electronic communication, networks, and programming. Wider audiences perceive the internet as a tool of trade, state, and human

development. Access to the internet in libraries and other public places can help realize this perception as fact.

8. Content in local language: Industries and NGOs should support the creation of internet pages in local languages. Support should be rendered to the development of standards for browsers and other software products created in local languages.

If we consider this list to provide general standards for growth in the ICT field, then there are specific legal issues attributable to the internet which should be addressed. These include:

1. Intellectual property: Adequate protection of intellectual property rights of the author must be provided.
2. Taxation: Taxation in the area of internet should not slow down development of e-commerce or hamper rendering electronic services.
3. Electronic transactions: Laws recognizing credit cards, e-money, and e-signatures should be introduced and incorporated into the legal field.
4. Privacy protection: OECD instruments and EC[4] directives on protection of privacy establish basic principles of privacy protection. All participants in networking communications should adhere to these principles.
5. Computer crimes: Effective means of counteraction to computer crimes, online fraud, and hacking, along with protection of anonymity and curtailing of state control, should be established.
6. ISP liability: Authors and content providers should be liable for improper, fraudulent, or obscene content. Users, parents, and schools can opt to choose blocking and filtering software to protect minors from harmful content.

The principles stated above will not only direct internet policy towards stimulating its economic potential, but they will also facilitate development of an open, democratic internet, contributing to better observance of human rights throughout the world.

A. Information Society: State Policy

Information and communication technologies have drastically changed contemporary society. Nonetheless, even in the most developed countries and economies the information highway is still in the stages of formation. Current achievements in this field can be compared to bricks of future great constructions. Although in certain areas, such as finance, industry, and education, the effect of

4 Directive 2002/58/EC of the EU and of the Council of July 12, 2002; Directive 97/66/EC of the EU and of the Council of Dec. 15, 1997; Directive 95/46/EC of the EU and of the Council of Oct. 24, 1995, http://www.europa.eu.int/eur-lex/pri/en/oj/dat/2002.

new technologies is quite conspicuous, the entire body of our civilization is still far from "informationally ideal."

To move toward the information ideal, 80–90 countries have launched the process of state policy formation on ICT issues. This process was proposed to facilitate the construction of an information society. Some nations, such as the United States, Japan, and South Korea, plan to embody this idea autonomously. Developed European countries, also having national programs, are consolidating resources and coordinating programs. National perceptions coexist with programs and concepts adopted by international institutions and communities. It is apparent that the transition to an information society provides a wide space for exploration, with many areas of *terra incognita*. It is therefore useful to examine these areas in order to explore the new challenges they represent. In this respect, the experience of the United States deserves special mention and attention.

1. The U.S. ICT Policy and Legislation The United States indisputably is the country with the most open policy and liberal legislation in information and communication technology. As the internet's birthplace, the United States still remains as a beacon in ICT development. Its ICT legislation unequivocally constitutes the most developed and vast body of law when compared to that of other countries. Despite the tragic events of September 11, after which the United States introduced certain restrictions aimed at providing more effective safety measures, general U.S. policy and legislation is undoubtedly directed to further support of internet growth and development.

Unlike countries with transition economies, where governments are dealing with establishing legal frameworks stimulating ICT development, in the United States the newest kinds of information technology—and the internet in particular—were initially developed without strong governmental interference. Personal creativity and profit were the basic incentives and propelling forces of information technology progress. Then, after a substantial increase of internet mass meant that it could no longer be self-regulated, the government entered the game, creating legal and economic conditions for further ICT development. For example, the report of the U.S. Federal Communication Commission titled "Digital Tornado: Internet and Telecommunication Policy"[5] demonstrates that the FCC had knowingly refused to regulate online informational services in accordance with the rules applicable to phone companies. The FCC emphasized the need not to overburden the internet with unnecessary state regulation. This limited government approach to interference helps explain the internet's rapid growth in the United States.

For purposes here, it is not necessary to scrutinize particular legislative samples. However, it is important to introduce a general picture of U.S. legal development in this field as a mechanism of state policy. I will enlist only a few

5 See FCC OPP Working Paper Series 29 "Digital Tornado: The Internet and Telecommunication Policy," 1997, *available at* http://www.fcc.gov/Bureaus/OPP/working_papers/oppwp29.pdf.

important examples of statutes in this area in order to avoid information overload from the immense body of American case law on the subject. Appendix A, at the end of this chapter, lists some of the major statutes regulating ICT in the United States. That list demonstrates that ICT-related legislation in the United States is vast and relates to almost all spheres of public development. It reflects the U.S. strategy of establishing a favorable and harmonious, freely accessible, and competitive environment for information development. Unfortunately, due to the rapid development of information technologies, legislators are often late in reacting to newly emerging legal phenomena. Although fundamental approaches to formation and regulation of the ICT legal environment in the United States do not change drastically, law enforcement methods acquire new traits associated with specific ICT developments. It is therefore worth reflecting on the dynamic of ICT legislative development in the United States.

Current ICT legislative development in the United States is affected by the tragic events of September 11. Transparency and accessibility of state systems, principles of state safety, and procurement of citizens' personal information appear to be the most vulnerable targets of increased governmental control. As a consequence, the U.S. government has already introduced amendments to existing laws and adopted some new ones limiting the freedom of the internet. The most serious alterations were made in the Internet Privacy Protection Act of 1997.[6] In particular, U.S. intelligence has the ability to check e-mails and trace suspects online with the purpose of preventing terrorist activities. This also applies to the tracing of financial and banking operations.

As a whole, the government attempts to protect American society from the threat of international terrorism. In the meantime, ICT development, particularly in the scope of e-commerce, e-government, and e-financing, continues to receive full governmental support. As an example, the U.S. government continues to prolong a tax moratorium for e-transactions and is examining establishing cyber-courts.

2. Uniform International Legislation in the ICT Sphere By its very nature, contemporary ICT has a global character. This in turn gives rise to attempts to regulate ICT legal issues through international instruments. Although each country's domestic law has its special features, the main legal principles in regulating ICT are not irreconcilable. The future may well bring the possibility of application of uniform laws in this area. Even now one can observe certain inspiring accomplishments in this field.

On January 30, 1997, the U.N. General Assembly adopted the Model Law on Electronic Commerce.[7] This constituted the first step in the area of development

6 Federal Internet Privacy Protection Act, H.R. No. 1367, 105th Cong., 1st Sess, 1997, *available at* http://www.cdt.org/legislation/105th/privacy; http://www.epic.org/privacy/internet/hr_98html.

7 UNCITRAL Model Law on Electronic Commerce, UNGA Resolution, 51st Session, A/res/51/162, 30 Jan. 1997.

of international law regulating the sphere of electronic commerce. The Model Law is not mandatory and is meant to be used by nations as a basis for development of their own national laws. It has contributed to establishing the legal grounds for activities in e-commerce, has provided core definitions of key ICT terms, and has recognized the legal authority of electronic documents and defined the standards for e-signatures as proof of the integrity of an e-document. This last element was expanded upon in another attempt at uniform international legislation in the Model Law on Electronic Signatures adopted in 2001,[8] which defines the legal status of e-signatures and institutes rules and requirements for their application.

3. Legal Analysis of the State Policy and Legislation of the Republic of Uzbekistan in ICT When developing the concept of entry into the information society, each country should assess its domestic conditions and advantages. Legislation that carefully reflects the state policy and forms the rule of conduct for legal entities and individuals within the country's borders is the most important subject for such assessment. Legislation in the field of informational technologies is a body of legal norms that regulates the entire complexity of public relations associated with the development of information, its broadcast, use, and free accessibility. The general trend in the development of the global informational community compels the enactment of informational legislation as an independent branch of law. Here I will try to describe the existing Uzbek legislation in order to define its current state and give an assessment of its readiness for joining the international informational community.[9]

The Uzbekistan Government has approved a "Program of Development of Computerization and Information and Communication Technologies for the Period including 2002–2010."[10] Section 2.2 of the program is dedicated to developing a "national segment of the internet." Under this program, the following parameters for of development of the internet in Uzbekistan are established for the year 2010:

1. installing more that 45,000 ports for joint access to the internet;
2. providing speed of access for international information networks higher than 512 mps;
3. achieving a level of internet usage of up to 11 of 100 citizens;

8 UNCITRAL Model Law on Electronic Signature, UNGA Resolution, 56th Session, A/res/56/80, 24 Jan. 2002.

9 *See also* United Nations Economic Commission for Europe, *Towards a Knowledge Based Economy, Uzbekistan Country Readiness Assessment Report* (UN Press).

10 WSIS, "Statement of the Government Delegation of the Republic of Uzbekistan," 2003, http://www.itu.int/wsis/geneva/coverage/statements/uzbekistan/uz.html. Approved by Resolution of the Cabinet of Ministers of the Republic of Uzbekistan No. 200 of June 6, 2002.

4. connecting not less than 74 percent of all state bodies and 60 percent of rural administrations to the internet; and
5. covering all cities and settlements in Uzbekistan with ICT services by the end of 2010.

The plan is to develop national databases of laws and regulations, statistics, financial statements of open joint stock companies, patents, etc. The program also contains provisions about educating specialists in ICT fields. Currently Uzbekistan possesses legal and normative elements regulating ICT relationships. Along with these elements, there exist state programs determining the development of certain ICT fields. Current Uzbekistan laws applicable in whole or in part to ICT relationships exist in several different areas. These state programs and legal sources can be found in Appendix B following this chapter.

The largest part of the legislation listed in Appendix B consists of the enactments, decrees, and instructions that define regulating mechanisms and establish certain limitations in the area of information and communication technology. A general Uzbekistan strategy on ICT development was not yet finalized when this chapter was written. Similar to legislative systems of other nations, the legislation of Uzbekistan regulating the ICT area is in its earliest stages. At the same time, there is an absence of an effective legal structure for ICT development. The reasons for this include insufficient theoretical preparation of certain fundamental normative ICT principles, as well as subjectively negative perceptions of the internet by domestic law enforcement agencies.

The lack of an ICT legislative framework in Uzbekistan, along with ineffective application of existing laws, has negatively affected the development of public relationships (for instance, in the area of a citizen's right to receive information, prevention of dissipation of defamatory information, and the protection of intellectual property). Moreover, with the growing impact of ICT on economic life, the weakness of the legal framework not only slows down economic development but also compels Uzbek users to employ services located outside the country, which is technologically easier to do than finding domestic internet providers.

B. Information Security

The basic legal document regulating information security in Uzbekistan is the law "On Principles and Guarantees of Freedom of Information."[11] The law defines information security as a "statement of security of interests of a person, society, and the state in the sphere of information."[12] The law also designates types of information which cannot be considered confidential and requires that the state shall perform state policy in a sphere of information security, which shall be dedicated

11 Law of the Republic of Uzbekistan "On Principals and Guarantees of Freedom of Information," adopted December 12, 2002.

12 *Id.*

to regulation of relationships in the information sphere and shall stipulate tasks for state bodies in a sphere of information security procurement.[13] Under the law, information security is divided into the three categories of informational security of a person, informational security of the society, and informational security of the state.

Informational security of the person is to be provided for by establishing necessary conditions and guarantees for free access to information, protection of private correspondence, protection against informational and psychological influence, and protection of personal data.

Informational security of the society is to be achieved by procuring the development of democratic civil society and freedom of mass media; disallowing unlawful informational and psychological influence to the social mentality; preserving and developing a spiritual, cultural, and historical heritage of the society and the scientific and technical potential of the nation; and establishing a system to counteract information directed at the destruction of national mentality, historical customs and traditions, and the destabilization of social and political systems.

Informational security of the state is to be provided by the implementation of various actions of economic, political, or other character, directed to counteract threats in the sphere of information security; to protect state secrecy, and state information resources against unauthorized access; to integrate of the Republic of Uzbekistan into the world informational space and advance telecommunication systems; to protect the state from the distribution of information containing declarations for the violent change of state power or territorial integrity, weakening the sovereignty of the Republic of Uzbekistan, or other encroachments on state power; and to counteract the distribution of information containing propaganda of war, violence, cruelty, terrorism, or religious extremism.

C. Main Legal Problems of ICT Development

Uzbekistan faces a number of key problems in developing normative regulation to overcome a lack of ICT development in light of global trends. These include:

1. determining a liberal state policy of the republic with respect to the Uzbek segment of the internet;
2. procuring unobstructed access for Uzbek users to the internet and its informational resources as well as unlimited information exchange, including in the international sphere;
3. determining the order and conditions of state institutions and bodies' connection to the internet (with due attention paid to providing broad audiences with the information concerning the activity of these institutions), including the operations of public libraries, schools, and other social and cultural entities;

---

13 *Id.*

4. defining the legal status of the information uploaded to the internet or communicated through internet media;
5. preventing publicly harmful activity in the internet (in particular, dissemination of defamatory and obscene information) as well as the creation of normative conditions for the effective identification of wrongdoers;
6. creating effective copyright protection and protection of other exclusive intellectual property rights for works uploaded to internet;
7. protecting private data, including that accumulated during the process of users' communication interchange and their communication with ISPs;
8. creating normative conditions for electronic data interchange, adhering to principles and order of use of internet address space, and confirming integrity and authorship rights in information, visual data, and means of transferral;
9. providing a normative base for electronic commerce, recognizing the legal effect of transactions entered into through the internet, determining the order of electronic payments; and
10. ensuring informational safety, including the prevention of the dissemination of computer viruses and of unsanctioned access to private information.

D. The Main Principles of the Legal Regulation of the Relationships Connected with ICT Development in Uzbekistan

In the course of the development of ICT legislation in Uzbekistan, it will be expedient to uphold the general principles that flow specifically from the features of the construction and function of the internet. The internet constitutes neither the subject nor the object of legal regulation. The subject is formed by the relationships of ISPs and users amongst themselves as well as with other individuals and state institutions with respect to information transmission and rendering services through the internet. The object is not the regulation of the internet itself, but the promotion of the legal principles seeking to be enforced by the governmental authority. ICT legislation associated with legal relationships over the internet has a global character.

The application of domestic legal norms to such relationships without regard to and awareness of the norms of other countries can be ineffective. This requires significant attention to the development of legal norms addressing the internet on the international level, primarily by means of accession to international conventions on ICT law.

Certain normative problems associated with the internet, including those on the level of cooperation of internet community members in the broadest sense, may and should be solved without governmental interference. The social significance of the internet as a means of practically unlimited access to global information resources requires establishing a legal framework regulating primarily the aspects of the internet specifically addressing vital rights and lawful interests of the person, society, and the state (such as personal privacy protection, preservation of public morals, and protection of state interests in the area of informational security, and public order). The versatility and diversity of sources of public relationships on the internet does not allow, while developing a corresponding legal framework, a focus on a relatively isolated, "specific" body of a legal regulation. Simultaneously with the development of new legal norms associated with specificity of internet functioning, it is necessary to introduce corrections (sometimes significant) into existing laws.

While establishing a legal framework for ICT development in Uzbekistan, due regard should be given to foreign experiences in identifying and implementing similar laws in order to ensure uniformity of the legal principles and enhanced implementation. The active participation of Uzbekistan in the international legal creative process should be sought as inevitable. The framework of state support for ICT development in Uzbekistan should consist of the following principles:

1. statutory conditions of free access to the internet and inadmissibility of unreasonable ISP activity limitations (including incorporation, taxation and licensing);
2. implementation of state-sponsored programs of internet connection for Uzbek users, with free access to the internet for libraries, schools, and other public institutions by way of direct budget financing and attracting investments by ISPs;
3. establishment of a non-discriminatory order of use of informational resources within the country as well as the order of international data interchange; and
4. creation of normative conditions for the development of free internet service markets in Uzbekistan, prohibiting monopolization and unfair competition.

E. Other Directions for ICT-related Legal Development in Uzbekistan

1. Prevention of Computer Crimes The expansion of subjective regulation for objective instances of publicly harmful activity committed via the internet (including wrongs and crimes) requires the introduction of new criminal laws and administrative code regulations in Uzbekistan. Special attention should be paid to the legitimacy of electronic evidence (fixation of legal facts) as well as to orders for collecting information about individuals falsifying or misrepresenting their identity. The law should also affix the obligations of the persons participating in data interchange on the internet (ISPs, in the first place) during investigations conducted by domestic law enforcement bodies. Some of these legal provisions should be incorporated into the Mass Media Law and Advertisement Law. It is necessary to bear in mind that a majority of crimes perpetrated on the internet have analogues in the physical world. For instance, while analyzing internet crimes, there is no reason to ignore legal provisions making pornography sales illegal, establishing liability for defamation and insults, or regulating the impermissibility of unethical and improper advertisement.

2. Legal Protection of Intellectual Property As a whole, there exists a stable system of legislative acts addressing protection of the results of creative activity and means of individualization (intellectual property) in Uzbekistan. At the same time, it is necessary to introduce certain corrections and updates associated with internet specific activities in the civil code and the laws "On Authors and Contiguous Rights," "On Trademarks, Service Marks and Places of Goods' Origination," and others. If international organizations decide to refer to domain names as an isolated group of intellectual property rights,[14] a similar norm should be incorporated into Uzbek law. The protection of intellectual property in the internet is objectively hampered by the lack of effective means of control of exclusive copyrights. It is unreasonable to assert the impossibility of copyright law application to internet relationships. Only certain aspects of exclusive rights can be modified (for instance, alteration of terms of their protection or a mechanism requiring mandatory author's consent to use the product, which is unreal when product is uploaded with a hypertext application). However, the final decision on a legislative level can be made only upon coordination of this issue at the international level.

3. Internet Taxation When considering taxing the internet, it is necessary to distinguish operations associated with procurement of internet access (ISP services) from those designed to render services (access to information, sale of goods, etc.). There seems to be no reason to depart from the general tendency to avoid or at least to place a moratorium on the introduction of specific internet taxation. Internet access services are taxable on general conditions with other connection operators' activity, while other "networking" transactions in themselves are not subject to taxation. Corresponding provisions should be incorporated into the Taxation Code of Uzbekistan.

III. Conclusion

Development of ICT-related legislation is most effective when it is based upon reasonable and appropriate analysis of both the domestic nation's conditions and legal traditions and the best examples of international legal proposals and standards. International elements should only be incorporated after thorough scrutiny and adjustment, but the globalization of the world's economy does not leave a nation the luxury of focusing solely on the domestic environment while disregarding the actions of the international community. Such a course of action would only continue the backwardness that Uzbekistan's ICT legal framework currently creates.

---

14 See ICANN, "CCTLD Sponsorship Agreement (.uz)," Mar. 27, 2003, http://www.icann.org/cctlds/uz/sponsorship-agmt-27mar03.htm.

Appendix A

Major ICT Legislation in the United States

1. The Telecommunication Act (Pub. L. 104-104, 110 Stat. 56, 47 U.S.C. § 609, 1996), amending the Communication Act (Pub. L. 416, 48 Stat. 1064, 47 U.S.C. § 151, 1934), makes alterations related to the regulation of new kinds of communication with the purpose of creating a more favorable development environment.
2. The Uniform Computer Information Transactions Act (UCITA) amends Article 2 of the UCC. This law determines general conditions for electronic transactions.
3. The Uniform Electronic Transactions Act (UETA) (1999) was drafted by the National Conference of Commissioners on Uniform State Laws (NCCUSL). It describes relationships connected with electronic transactions specifically and in detail.
4. The Electronic Signature in Global and National Commerce Act (E-Sign) (Pub. L. No. 106-229, 114 Stat. 464, 15 U.S.C. § 7001, 2000) establishes legal conditions for user identification and application of e-signatures.
5. U.S. anti cyber-crime laws (contained in Criminal code,[15] Homeland Security Act of 2002,[16] PATRIOT Act,[17] etc.) define principles of criminal content as well as measures of administrative and criminal prosecution and punishment for computer crimes.
6. The "E-Government Act" (H.R. No. 2458, 107 Cong., 2d Sess., 2002) creates conditions for electronic government in state and public institutions with the purpose of simplification and better efficacy of mutual cooperation and cooperation with civil society.
7. The Children's Internet Protection Act (Pub. L. 106-554, 106 Cong., 1st Sess., 1998) supports more rapid technological and commercial development of the internet. The CIPA provides that U.S. policy in this field shall be based on private initiative and avoid as much as possible restrictions and limitations by the state. It states that regulation of internet information services does not properly serve public interests.
8. The Federal Internet Privacy Protection Act (H.R. No. 1367, 105th Cong., 1st Sess., 1997) prohibits federal institutions from providing access to confidential information and records of individuals through the internet.
9. The Security and Freedom Through Encryption Act (SAFE) (H.R. No. 850, 106 Cong., 1st Sess., 1999) defines the legal scope of freedom to use and sell encryption means and devices and prohibits mandatory access by state and other structures to encryption keys. It authorizes the use of encryption

15 U.S.C., tit. 18, ¶ 1, ch. 47, § 1030.

16 Homeland Security Act (H.R. No. 5002, 107th Cong., 1st Sess., 2002).

17 USA PATRIOT Act (H.R. No. 3162, 107th Cong., 1st Sess., 2001).

despite utilized algorithms, code length, technologies and encryption means. No one shall be compelled to convey encryption keys to another person unless it is necessary for investigation in accordance with legal procedure.

10. The Family-Friendly Internet Access Act (H.R. No. 1180, 105 Cong., 1st Sess., 1997) provides parents with the means to control content accessible to children through the internet. ISPs must provide software that allows exercising such control.
11. The Citizen's Right to Know Act (Pub. L. No. 104-231, 110 Stat. 3048, 5 U.S.C. § 552, 1996) amends the election law by requiring the federal elections commission to make available information about candidates for U.S. Congress on the internet.
12. The Internet Election Information Act (1997) describes the possibility of providing free computer services to candidates being elected to federal office and participating in public debates. Its purpose is to distribute such information to a broad audience.
13. The Internet Gambling Prohibition and Enforcement Act (H.R. No. 4411, 109 Cong., 2nd Sess., 2006) addresses gambling, betting, and lotteries.
14. The Promotion of Commerce On-Line in the Digital Era Act (S.1726, 105 Cong., 1st Sess., 1997) stresses that the internet and global information infrastructure transform the ways of doing contemporary business. However, that potential cannot be fully realized unless businesses can be assured of the safety of information transmissions. To ensure the necessary level of safety cryptography means shall be available. Obsolete legislative bars on export of American "strong" ciphering means hamper development of electronic commerce. The proposal by the Department of Commerce to allow sales of ciphering means abroad, provided that federal government possesses the keys, in fact, had turned into a form of prohibition on the export of cryptography technologies. The Act encourages development of ciphering products and programs while prohibiting the federal government from taking steps that could prevent use and sales of cryptographic products.
15. The Internet Tax Freedom Act (H.R. No. 1054, 105 Cong., 1st Sess., 1998) (Pub. L. No. 105-277) indicates that it is impossible to trace back the exact path of the message in the internet. This gives rise to a possibility of multiple taxation, which may limit internet development. For example, in the United States, consumers and businessmen can be subject to application of 30,000 taxation laws. Therefore, there shall exist a well-coordinated policy in the area of internet taxation. This law introduced a tax holiday for internet activity for a period through the end of 2006.

Appendix B

Uzbekistan State Programs and National Legislation on ICT issues

(All Laws of the Republic of Uzbekistan are available at http://www.pravo.uz)

State Programs

1. Enactment by the Cabinet of Ministers (CM) of the Republic of Uzbekistan (RU) #307 on August 1, 1995. "National Program of Reconstruction and Development of Telecommunication Networks of the Republic of Uzbekistan for the period through 2010."
2. Enactment by the CM of RU #193 on April 22, 1999. "Program of Modernization and Development of a National Data Transmission Network of Uzbekistan for the Period of 1999 through 2003."
3. Enactment by the CM of RU #230 on May 23, 2001. "Computer and Information Programs Development for the Period of 2001 through 2005 and Procurement of Wide Access to International Informational Systems by the Internet."
4. Current Uzbekistan laws applicable in whole or in part to ICT relationships exist in several different areas.

Information Networks and their State Regulation

Legislation

1. The Law of the Republic of Uzbekistan "On Principals and Guarantees of Freedom of Information," adopted December 12, 2002.
2. The Law of the Republic of Uzbekistan "On Licensing of Certain Types of Activity," adopted May 25, 2003.
3. The Law of the Republic of Uzbekistan "On Radio-frequency Spectrum," adopted December 25, 1998.
4. The Law of the Republic of Uzbekistan "On Communication," adopted January 13, 1992, as amended.
5. The Law of the Republic of Uzbekistan "On Telecommunications," adopted August 20, 1999.
6. The Law of the Republic of Uzbekistan "On Legal Protection of Programs for Electronic and Calculation Machines and Databases," adopted May 6, 1994.
7. The Law of the Republic of Uzbekistan "On Mass Media," adopted December 26, 1996.
8. The Law of the Republic of Uzbekistan "On Electronic Documents Flow," adopted April 29, 2004.
9. The Law of the Republic of Uzbekistan "On Electronic Commerce," adopted April 29, 2004.

10. The Law of the Republic of Uzbekistan "On Electronic Digital Signatures," adopted December 11, 2003.
11. The Law of the Republic of Uzbekistan "On Informatization," adopted December 11, 2003.
12. The Law of the Republic of Uzbekistan "On Standards," adopted December 28, 1993.
13. The Law of the Republic of Uzbekistan "On Protection of Consumers' Rights," adopted April 26, 1996.

Presidential Decrees

1. Decree of the President of the Republic of Uzbekistan "On Establishing Public Educational Information Networks for the Republic of Uzbekistan," No. PP-191 of September 28, 2005.
2. Decree of the President of the Republic of Uzbekistan "On Additional Incentives for Provision of Computer Security of National Information and Communication Systems," No. PP-167 of September 25, 2005.
3. Decree of the President of the Republic of Uzbekistan "On Additional Incentives for Further Development of Information and Communication Technologies," No. PP-117 of July 8, 2005.
4. Decree of the President of the Republic of Uzbekistan "On Further Development of Computerization and Implementation of Information and Communication Technologies," No. UP-3080 of May 30, 2002.

Protection of Exclusive Rights in Information and Communication Technologies

1. The Law of the Republic of Uzbekistan "On Copyright and Contiguous Rights," adopted August 30, 1996, as amended on May 12, 2002.
2. The Law of the Republic of Uzbekistan "On Legal Protection of Software and Databases," adopted May 6, 1994.[18]
3. The Law of the Republic of Uzbekistan "On Trademarks and Service Labels," adopted May 7, 1993.[19]
4. Criminal Code of the Republic of Uzbekistan, adopted April 1, 1995.[20]

18 http://www.gateway.uz/downloads/ICT/ICT2169.pdf.

19 http://www.patent.uz/doclw01.htm.

20 *See* http://www.pravo.uz/about/crime.php.

Index

academic integrity: 51, 59
Africa: 13, 25, 27, 36, 173
Albania: 78
alternative dispute resolution (ADR): 42
Asia: 13, 133
Asian Development Bank (ADB): 150–151, 164, 173

Belgium: 75, 134
Bologna Declaration: 38, 72
Bologna Process: 38, 45
Bosnia and Herzegovina: 16–17
Brazil: 10, 131–140, 149
Britain: 57, 132

Canada: 17
capacity building: 4–5, 7, 142–181
case analysis: 53, 59
case/casebook method: 20, 30, 35, 48
Chile: 126
clinical legal education/method: 24, 28–33, 41–42
commercial law: 10, 54, 75, 95, 100–102, 131–138
comparative analysis: 14, 17, 57, 60
comparative law: 14, 53, 69, 91, 140, 185
consensus-building: 18
Convention on the International Sale of Goods (CISG): 101–102
corporate governance: 17, 127
corruption: 10, 25, 77, 141–180
Council of Europe (CoE): 100–102
Croatia: 16–17, 79
curriculum, curricula:
  comparisons: 68
  descriptions of: 24–25, 33, 39, 62–63, 66–67
  development of: 26–28, 53–54, 68–76, 104–105, 119
  generally: 5–11

democracy: 2–7, 23, 26, 65, 80, 136, 145, 171
deductive logic: 9
developing countries: 13–16, 26, 34, 151–154, 178

enforcement: 18, 83, 103, 132
England: 13, 20, 58, 75, 92
Europe: 13, 38, 67, 71, 91, 133–134, 136
European Community (EC): 49, 56–57, 187
European Court of Human Rights (ECHR): 49, 53, 59
European Court of Justice (ECJ): 49
European Higher Education Area: 38, 72
European Union (EU): 38, 61, 77–78, 146, 185–187
ex cathedra: 39, 70

France: 13, 16, 51, 57, 129, 136

gender: 110
Georgia: 3, 17
Germany: 13, 17, 51, 57, 63, 135
Greece: 57, 134
Guinea-Bissau: 16
Guyana: 15

Holland: 134
Hungary: 54, 57, 75

information and communication technology (ICT): 183–199
intellectual property: 95–97, 187, 191–195
International Court of Justice (ICJ): 3, 26
international law: 53–54, 190
internship: 29, 42, 56
Ireland: 3
Italy: 3, 8, 13, 83–91, 134, 138

Japan: 188

Kenya: 7, 23–36
Kosovo: 9, 78, 99, 100–102

Latin America: 13, 127, 129
language:
  foreign skills/study: 5, 53, 58, 73, 103–121,
  legal terminology: 14–15, 103–121,
  translation: 101, 128, 187
legal aid: 28, 31, 41
legal reform: 13–18, 38
legal representation: 24–25, 31, 41
legal systems:
  access to: 25, 33–34
  American: 78, 105, 124–125, 131, 137
  Brazilian: 131
  civil law:
    in legal education: 1, 63, 75, 89–90, 124–130,
    as a legal system: 40, 83, 124–130, 131–140
  common law:
    in legal education: 1–2, 63, 89–94, 113, 131–140
    as a legal system: 131–140
  comparative: 79, 83, 95, 100, 128–129, 131, 184–185
  generally 1–6, 11, 13–16, 37, 109, 150
  Pakistani: 103–104
  Roman: 131, 136
  Serbian: 43, 61, 80
  tension between: 16–17, 65, 90–95, 100
  Ukrainian: 53
legislation: 5, 10, 17, 48, 78–79, 101, 156–175, 183–199

Macedonia: 16–17, 20, 79
mediation: 8, 37–44
Mexico: 9, 95–98
moot court:
  generally: 36, 57–59, 72–76, 102
  Jessup: 36, 58
  Vis: 36, 58, 74–75

Netherlands, the: 57–58, 75
Norway: 13

Organisation for Security and Co-operation in Europe (OSCE): 77

Pakistan: 103–120
pedagogy: 31–35, 37, 45, 95
Perú: 123–130
Philippines, the: 141–180
plagiarism: 51, 54–56
policy reform: 13, 17–21, 16–162, 170–181
Portugal: 16, 133–134
positive law: 49, 62, 135
privatization: 61, 77, 141, 186
public service: 24–27, 33–35

Roman law: 68, 81, 83–94, 131, 135–136
rule of law:
  Brazil: 131
  defined: 107, 141
  generally: 2, 6–7, 26, 40–41, 44, 150
  Kosovo: 99–100
  Pakistan: 103–104
  programs: 11, 37–38
  recommendations for: 5, 79, 102, 105, 119–121
  Serbia: 37–38, 61, 76–77

Saudi Arabia: 15
Serbia: 8, 17, 37–43, 61–79
social justice: 24–25
South Korea: 188
sustainable development: 14

Taiwan: 3
teaching methodology:
  generally: 7
  Kenyan: 32
  lecture/lecture method:
    as part of civil law education: 1, 90, 139–140
    as a teaching method: 29–35, 47–53, 66–71, 75, 171
  reform of: 52–53, 56, 72–74
  selection of: 40, 43, 46–47, 76
  Serbian: 39, 70

Socratic method: 8, 10, 37–40, 48, 53, 70–75, 102, 140–142, 154–163
transparency: 61, 77, 143–180, 186, 189

Ukraine: 45–60
United Kingdom, the: 126
United Nations Development Program (UNDP): 23, 77
U.N. General Assembly: 189
U.N. Security Council: 101
United States (US): 2, 4, 6, 8–10, 16, 20, 23, 27, 37–40, 43, 50–51, 57, 63–66, 90, 99–100, 102, 107, 123, 127, 129, 131–132, 150, 155, 158, 173, 188–189
U.S. Agency for International Development (USAID): 13, 77–78, 151, 155, 169, 175
Uzbekistan: 7, 183–195

World Bank: 15, 77–79, 141–180
World Trade Organization (WTO): 77–78, 149

Yugoslavia (former): 15, 72

For Product Safety Concerns and Information please contact our EU
representative GPSR@taylorandfrancis.com
Taylor & Francis Verlag GmbH, Kaufingerstraße 24, 80331 München, Germany

www.ingramcontent.com/pod-product-compliance
Ingram Content Group UK Ltd.
Pitfield, Milton Keynes, MK11 3LW, UK
UKHW022128190926
475702UK00013B/1692
* 9 7 8 1 1 3 8 2 6 9 2 2 4 *